27

Kentucky
Country

Kentucky Country

Folk and Country Music of Kentucky

CHARLES K. WOLFE

THE UNIVERSITY PRESS OF KENTUCKY

Frontispiece: Unidentified musician. *Courtesy University of Louisville Photographic Archives, from Jean Thomas, The Traipsin' Woman, Collection.*

Some of the research for this book was funded by grants from the Faculty Research Committee of Middle Tennessee State University.

Lines from the song "Kentucky" by Karl Davis © 1942 (renewed) Warner Bros., Inc. All rights reserved. Used by permission.

Quotations from Jesse Stuart, *Man with a Bull-Tongue Plow,* are reprinted by permission of the Jesse Stuart Foundation.

Library of Congress Cataloging in Publication Data
Wolfe, Charles K.
    Kentucky country.
    Bibliography: p.
    Discography: p.
    Includes index.
    1. Folk music—Kentucky—History and criticism   2. Country music—Kentucky—History and criticism   3. Bluegrass music—Kentucky—History and criticism   I. Title.
ML3551.W64 1982   781.7769   82-40183
ISBN 0-8131-1468-3   AACR2

Contents

Illustrations follow page 88.

To the memory of my parents,
Dilla and Orville Wolfe

Acknowledgments

The authors of printed sources I have used have been identified in "Sources and Further Reading." In preparation of this book I also profited from conversations and correspondence with a number of other historians, folklorists, collectors, and musicians, including Peggy Bulger, Robert Cogswell, Harlan S. Daniel, Burt Feintuch, David Freeman, Linnell Gentry, Archie Green, Doug Green, Bill Harrison, Kaw Hendricks, Doyle Jones, Pete Kuykendall, Bill Lightfoot, Gus Meade, Lynwood Montell, John Morris, Robert Nobley, Tony Russell, Mike Seeger, Ivan M. Tribe, Edd Ward, F.W. Woolsey, and David Wylie. Special thanks go to Norm Cohen and the staff of the John Edwards Memorial Foundation at UCLA; to Bob Pinson and the staff of the Country Music Foundation Library and Media Center; and to Loyal Jones and the staff of the Berea College Appalachian Center. Special thanks also to Carl Fleischhauer of the American Folklife Center, Library of Congress, for his advice on illustrations, and to the late Reuben Powell, the unofficial historian of Renfro Valley, who shared so much of his knowledge with me and other historians. Finally, a special note of thanks to my wife, Mary Dean, for her continued help and encouragement on this project and others over the years, and to my two special consultants, Stacey and Cindy.

Echoes from
a Lost World

One afternoon in 1975 a woman from Bowling Green, Kentucky, brought an unusual document into the office of Charles Guthrie, a folklorist at Western Kentucky University. It was an old piece of lined tablet paper, yellow and brittle with age, covered on one side with a beautiful, archaic handwriting, done in pencil and faded, hard to read even in the bright summer sunlight. The woman was a former student of Guthrie's, Faye Scott Anderson, and the piece of paper had belonged to a relative of her husband's, Ola Ashinhurst. Ola had been a lifelong resident of the hilly Pennyroyal region, near the Clinton-Cumberland County line in south-central Kentucky. For much of her life she had been unmarried, living a lonely life with her twin sister Viela, and one of her few pleasures had been to play on an old parlor organ that the family owned. When she died in 1963, the organ passed on to Mrs. Anderson's husband and they moved it to Bowling Green. The drawers of the organ were full of little scraps of paper, old poems, and scattered songbooks. Some of the books contained little notations written by the sisters: "It snowed today" or "I wish someone would come to visit" or "I sang this on August 14, 1936." In one of the books, a 1918 paperback songbook entitled *Redemption Songs*, in between pressed flowers half a century old, Mrs. Anderson found the sheet of tablet paper. Carrying it to the window, she could make out the faintly legible title: "A Song Ballad Pearl Bryant." As she scanned the neat lines, she remembered what she had learned about old ballads in her college courses in folklore, and began to wonder about the song and about what had possessed Ola Ashinhurst to preserve it so carefully all those years. Had it been sung to her some long-ago evening by her best beau? Had it been sent to her by some long-lost friend? Had she sung it in her lonely farmhouse, accompanying herself on the old pump organ? Faye Anderson knew that some of the personal questions about what the song meant to Ola could never be answered, but she knew that details about the song itself might be found. Her old teacher Dr. Guthrie could help.

Together Guthrie and his former student looked over the text of the old song:

A Song Ballad Pearl Bryant

Deep Deep in yondrous valley
  Where the flowers fade and Bloom
There sleeps my own Pearl Bryant
  In a Cold and Silent Tomb

She died not Broken Hearted
  Nor lingering Sickning Spell
But fore and instant Parted
  From the Home She loved so well

One Knight the moon shonn Brightly
  The stars was shining Too
When to Here cottag window
  Here Jealous lover Drew

Come Pearl lets take a ramble
  Through the meadow Soft and gaye
Where none can ever Disturbus
  We will name our wedding Day

Retrace your Steps no never
  There is sleep for every roam
For in these woods I have you
  Pearl Bryant you must Die

What have I done you Scott Jackson
  That you should take my Life
You Know I have always loved you
  And would have Been your wife

Down on Here Knees befor Him
  She Pleaded for Her Life
When deep in to Her Bosom
  He plunged the fatle Knife

I'll forgive you Walling
  was Here last and Dieing Breath
Here Heart had seased it Beeting
Here Eyes were closed in Death

Fare well Dear loving Parents
I'll greate you nevermore
For in these woods they have me
Fore nevermore to Roam

As Mrs. Anderson learned, her hand-written ballad was only the tip of an iceberg. For some twenty years students and teachers at Western Kentucky University had been collecting old songs like this and filing them in a cozy room on the third floor of the Cravens Library. Over the years they had gathered several dozen copies of the song about Pearl Bryan, some taken from old written sources, others directly from the singing of people who had learned them as children. The library also had printed collections of songs from other parts of the country with still more variations of the song, some published as early as 1913. In fact, folklorists had identified six distinct songs about Pearl Bryan that had circulated among people of Kentucky and the mid-South over the previous seventy-five years, songs still being sung and passed on today.

Though many of the people singing the ballad of Pearl Bryan did not know it, the song was an echo from one of the most sensational murders of the 1890s. It all began on a cold February day in 1896, when a farm boy near Fort Thomas, Kentucky, made a grisly discovery. Cutting across a field on his way to work, he came across the decapitated body of a woman. For several days police searched the field but found no trace of the victim's head; in spite of this, she was finally identified as one Pearl Bryan, the twenty-three-year-old daughter of a Greencastle, Indiana, farmer. Police were soon led to Scott Jackson, a young dental student living across the river in Cincinnati; he and his roommate, Alonzo Walling, were soon arrested and charged with Pearl's murder. In later months the prosecutors charged that Jackson had had an affair with Pearl and had agreed to arrange for an abortion after she announced that she was pregnant. For some reason he and Walling attempted to perform the abortion themselves. Either Pearl died or they thought she had died, and they took her across the river and beheaded her to prevent identification. The two men were convicted, and on March 20, 1897, still protesting their innocence, they were hanged at Newport, Kentucky.

For months newspapers in the mid-South carried details of the murder and the trial: the event was the sensation of the year. Even before the execution, songwriters were busy transmuting the events into song. In 1896 two different Cincinnati sheet music publishers issued "Pearl Bryan's Fate, Waltz Song and Chorus" by one Charles Kennedy, and "Pearl Bryan's Fate; or The Crime of the Century" by one "Add. J. Ressequie," and other poems appeared in local newspapers. These songs quickly lapsed into obscurity, though; the ones that survived were made by the less formal composers and were sung in parlors, on porches, and on street corners throughout Kentucky and Tennessee. Within ten years of the execution of Walling and Jackson, folk ballads about Pearl Bryan were being circulated by rural Kentuckians who were fascinated with the age-old theme of the jealous lover and the newer theme of the country girl done in by the evils of the big city.

Nobody in nineteenth-century Kentucky ever referred to "Pearl Bryan" as a folk song, as a country song, or even as a popular song. It was, in truth, a little of all three, but music in the 1800s was much less a victim of categories and genres than it is today. Certainly there were "old" songs and "new" songs, but if people liked the sentiment or the melody of a song they didn't worry too much about its source. Some songs that were written in New York, published in sheet music, and introduced on the vaudeville stage were learned by ear and passed on to another generation by word of mouth, in the manner of folk songs. Other songs, originally circulating among the people as folk songs, made a reverse journey when some tunesmith decided to write them down, "arrange" them, and publish them.

If a person of today could somehow miraculously be transported back into the Kentucky of 1850, he would find people across the state enjoying a wide variety of music, from square-dance fiddle tunes to hymns. Most of the people would be making the music themselves, not passively listening to it on a radio or record player, generally much more involved in it than most music fans today. Since there were few professional musicians and many amateur ones, the music might lack the polish or technical expertise of today's music. Many of the instruments—especially the fiddles and the banjos—were homemade, and little of the singing or playing style was learned from books of the time. It was, in a very real sense, a people's music, and for many it was, next to their religion, their only means for reflecting about their values, ideals, or aspirations.

The oldest songs in this nineteenth-century heritage were those that had been brought with the first settlers from England and Ireland and Scotland. Some had been old in England when the settlers left for the New World and trekked into "the Great Meadow" in the waning years of the eighteenth century. Many of the songs were thought of as a family heritage passed from parents to children. "Pap didn't have much to leave us," commented one old singer, "but he did leave us some fine songs, and I learned a lot of 'em." As far as we know, nobody tried systematically to collect or write down these songs in the nineteenth century, so there is no way of telling exactly what songs were favorites, or exactly what they meant to the people who made them favorites, or even how they were sung. All we can say is that a large number of these old English songs survived into the twentieth century, and we can infer that they were current in earlier days, as well.

Kentucky was by no means unique as a repository for the old British ballads (story songs) or lyrics (songs expressing emotions). These were found in other states, from Missouri to Maine. But Kentucky and the other Appalachian states had a special appeal; the mountains and highlands, it was thought, acted as a giant cultural deep freeze, preserving these old songs and singing methods better than in other parts of the country. The first generation of ballad hunters had a romantic image of mountain folk as noble survivors of Elizabethan England, uncontaminated by the evils of the modern world. Kentucky mountaineers fit this image better than Missouri farmers or Maine fishermen. While the sheer number of old ballads found in Kentucky may not have constituted a major influence on the later development of country music in the state, the amount of attention paid to ballad hunting in Kentucky certainly had an impact. Going into the age of mass media and commercialization in the 1920s, Kentucky had a popular reputation as the premier hunting ground for old ballads. No other state had as much national attention lavished on its folk music, and this attention had the effect of encouraging later commercial country music in Kentucky.

Popular interest in ballad study in America began in 1898 when a Harvard University professor named Francis James Child published the last volume of his massive five-volume study, *The English and Scottish Popular Ballads*. This was a collection of "case histories" of 305 ballads found in England and Scotland, and while it contained little about American ballads, students of the collection began to find that many of the songs were also still being sung in America. The American Folklore Society, formed in

1888, also began to stir interest in finding American versions of the old songs, and by the first decade of the twentieth century numerous local collectors around the country were starting to write down songs they were hearing. In 1907 Katherine Pettit, then a teacher at the Hindman Settlement School in Knott County, published "Ballads and Rhymes from Kentucky" in the *Journal of American Folklore*—the first real attempt to publish some of the old songs Kentuckians had been singing for over a hundred years. The collection includes seventeen songs and a handful of children's songs and rhymes, all but five of them with British pedigrees, that Katherine Pettit or her students had collected from the hills of southeastern Kentucky. In 1908 and 1909 James Watt Raine and Katherine Jackson, working out of Berea College, began to collect songs from people in that part of the state, initiating Berea's long and continued involvement in folk song study and collection. Two years later, in 1911, appeared the first book of Kentucky folk songs, *A Syllabus of Kentucky Folksongs*, including some 333 items from eastern and central Kentucky. The work was the result of research by Dr. Hubert G. Shearin, then a professor at Transylvania University in Lexington, and his precocious pupil, Josiah H. Combs, a native of Hazard who had trudged barefoot to the Hindman Settlement School, where he studied under Katherine Pettit. The book was published by Transylvania University, and was circulated well to area universities if not to the general public.

More popular with a general audience were books like *Lonesome Tunes* (1916), edited by Loraine Wyman and Howard Brockaway after an "expedition" into "the Kentucky wilds" of the southeastern hills. Brought out by a New York publisher, this book contained genuine songs and music, though edited and "touched up" by the collectors. The book was successful enough that the team worked up a sequel, *Twenty Mountain Songs*, for a Boston publisher four years later. Another music-and-words book was Josephine McGill's *Folk Songs of the Kentucky Mountains*, published in New York in 1917. It too was the result of an "expedition," this one also based at the Hindman Settlement School. By the time the famous English collector Cecil Sharp made his first collecting trips in Kentucky in 1916, the state had already generated a thriving local interest in folk songs. The Hindman and Pine Mountain settlement schools, Berea College, and Transylvania University were all serving as centers for collection and study of mountain ballads, and Sharp found numerous local collectors willing to help him in his quest for ballads. Sharp's international reputation meant that his published collections would call even more public attention to the Appalachian singing tradition. In his forty-six weeks in the mountains, from 1916 to 1918, he gathered over 500 songs from Kentucky—almost a third of his total collection. In less than a week at Hindman he was able to write down sixty-one songs, an indication of just how strong the ballad singing tradition was on the eve of World War I. There is evidence that Sharp was casual about writing down the entire text of some songs, but Oxford University's publication in 1932 of his massive *English Folk-Songs from the Southern Appalachians* fixed for generations to come the image of eastern Kentucky as a land of balladry and song.

As collectors and enthusiasts continued to harvest Kentucky's English ballad heritage, certain songs began to appear over and over in collections and lists. None of them were unique to Kentucky—all were found in other parts of the country as well—but certain ones were collected more frequently in Kentucky than in other states. One was "Little Matty Groves," a ballad about adultery and discovery that Professor Child dated back to the time of Shakespeare; another was "The Cherry Tree Carol," a religious ballad which describes the child Jesus performing his first miracle by bidding the tall cherry tree to bend down so Mary can get its fruit. "Lord Thomas" describes the eternal triangle, where a man must choose between a poor but beautiful woman and a rich but ugly one—a theme still found in modern country music. Next to "Barbara Allen," with its familiar account of the "hard-hearted" woman who refuses her love to Sweet William, "Lord Thomas" has proven the most popular of the old ballads still sung in the United States. Two other Kentucky favorites deal with Anglo-Turkish conflicts, probably dating from the sixteenth century and the Ottoman Empire—though few of the singers worried about such details. These songs were "Golden Willow Tree," about a young Englishman who single-handedly sinks a Turkish ship, and "Lord Bateman," about an Englishman who gets out of a Turkish prison by promising to wed a Turkish lady.

The most popular British-derived murder ballad seems to have been "Pretty Polly," a version of a 1750 English song entitled "The Gosport Tragedy." In the original song we learn of a young ship's carpenter who seduces the daughter of a mason; when she finds herself pregnant the carpenter leads her to a grave he has dug in the night and, in spite of her pleas for mercy, stabs her. His ship leaves the next day, but Polly's ghost follows him on board and eventually extracts a cruel revenge. The version collected by

Katherine Pettit before 1907 shows how Kentucky singers changed it: the song is made shorter and much more direct. This "Pretty Polly" omits entirely the courtship, seduction, and pregnancy, and focuses primarily on the murder itself; the supernatural elements have been played down and no ghost appears to demand vengeance. The death is presented with none of the effusive Victorian sentiment so common in popular literature and songs of the late nineteenth century; no golden-haired damsel here goes to her reward, nor do angels take her away. A few gritty details tell it all: "He threw a little dust over her, / And turned to go home, / Left nothing behind / But the small birds to mourn."

Using such songs as models, Kentuckians were soon making up their own songs about events that had special meaning to them. In this way dozens of native American ballads originated in Kentucky and were carried to other parts of the South and Midwest. Again, Kentucky was hardly unique in this: such local ballads sprang up in other states and were popular in Kentucky as well. But a look at some of the songs originated in the state suggests some of the concerns and events that were deemed vital enough to be preserved through several generations of song. The songs give us a hint of the image early working-class Kentuckians held of themselves, and of the events in social history they thought memorable.

There were a number of songs that, like "Pearl Bryan," told of the murder of a pregnant girlfriend by an angry suitor. "Stella Kinny" told of such a case in Fleming County in 1915, and "Lula Vower," in which the killer tied his victim to a railroad rail and threw her into the Ohio River, came from Floyd County at about the same time. "The Peddler and His Wife" was about a crime that shocked even the rough-and-ready citizens of Harlan County: three young men shot and killed an old German peddler and his wife for the few trinkets they had in their pack. The result was the last public hanging in Harlan County, in 1895. Feuds were also popular subjects in local ballads. "The Rowan County Crew" was about what was probably one of the most famous of Kentucky feuds, the Martin-Tolliver feud of 1884 near Morehead. "The Murder of J. B. Marcum" was about the assassination of a lawyer in Breathitt County in 1903. This murder and the song were so controversial that when collector Josiah Combs asked an informant to sing it in about 1915, he was told, "A fellow might get shot around here for singing that song." As late as 1920, a blind street singer was asked to leave the Breathitt County seat for fear he would stir up trouble by singing the song. Still, the ballad was kept alive and even recorded several times, once by famous pop composer Johnny Mercer. Many "badman" ballads were based on historical figures: "Talt Hall" told the tale of a famous Kentucky bandit who was hanged in 1900; "William Baker" was about the murderer of a man named Prewitt in Clay County; and "Bad Tom Smith" was composed by Smith himself, who sang it on the scaffold just before he was hanged at Jackson in 1895. Disasters were the subject of several ballads, as well; Kentucky saw no train songs as memorable as "The Wreck of the Old 97," but coal mining tragedies were memorialized in "Only a Miner," which seems to date from turn-of-the-century Harlan County, and "Shut Up in the Mines of Coal Creek," about a 1911 explosion that killed 150 in Briceville, Tennessee, just across the border from McCreary County.

One of the most distinctive Kentucky ballads involved a horse race. On July 4, 1878, Churchill Downs in Louisville, then called Louisville Racetrack, was the scene of the last grueling, four-mile horse race in American turf history. It was between the Kentucky thoroughbred Ten Broeck and the famous California mare Miss Mollie, and it was marked with cavil and controversy. The local favorite Ten Broeck won the race, but in the hours after the race Louisville was full of rumors: some said that Ten Broeck had been doped, others that Mollie had died. Ten Broeck continued to race and finally died in 1887; by that time people in Louisville were already singing a song about him and about the famous race:

Oh, the day was for racing and Tin Brook to run,
The hosses came marching in like prisoners to be hung;
The bell it did tap and the flag it did fall,
And Mollie went a-darting for the hole in the wall.

You'd better run, Mollie, run,
Run, Mollie, run.

This fragment was learned from a family servant by Mrs. Evelyn Polk Eldred in 1884 when she was a child in Louisville. Since many of the early Louisville jockeys were black, the Ten Broeck race was interesting to black and white audiences alike. Another fragment Mrs. Eldred recalled was:

"Old Marster, old Marster, I'm a-risking my life,
A-winning some money for you and your wife."
Says, "I wouldn't mind riding if it wasn't for my girl,
I'd mount on old Tin Brook and ride clean out of this world."

Versions of the song, called everything from "Old Timbrooks" to "Run Mollie Run" to "Tenbrook and Molly" to "Old Kimball," spread out across the land, carried by black and white singers. Many of the versions were based on an old Irish racehorse song of the 1820s, "Skew Ball," or "Stewball," which had made its way into America by 1829. As early as 1915 *The Journal of American Folklore* was printing these stanzas collected from a man in Louisville:

> Timbrook on the mountain, Mollie on the sea,
> Timbrook says to Mollie, "You can't get away with me."
>
> Timbrook says to Molly, "What makes your feet so round?
> Before I let you beat me, I'll never touch the ground!"
>
> Molly in the stable, weary and a-crying;
> Timbrook on the racetrack gone a-skipping and a-flying.

Between 1927 and 1929 the song was recorded on commercial phonograph records, first by an itinerant black minstrel named Henry Thomas, later by a black Louisville preacher named John Byrd, by a Barren County string band called the Carver Boys, and by a Tennessee duo named the Allen Brothers. These (especially the Allen version) made the song a modest "hit" in records, but in 1947 bluegrass star Bill Monroe recorded it and began singing it on the stage of the Grand Ole Opry, making it a bluegrass favorite and giving it yet another lease on life.

In modern country music the singer has become as important as the song, and most people are more aware of the "star" than of the individual songs he or she sings. The opposite is true when talking about country music in Kentucky in the 1800s: we have virtually no idea of who the great singers were, or who were key links in a song's transmission. All we have left is the songs themselves. We do have a few hints as to how the songs were sung in the old days. The popular concept of a ballad singer accompanying himself on a guitar is wrong; most classic balladeers sang unaccompanied, in a "high, lonesome" voice, freed from the steady rhythm of a guitar and able to vary meter to suit the dramatic needs of the song. Josiah Combs, in his 1925 *Folk-Songs of the Southern United States*, left descriptions of some of the singers he visited in Kentucky during his pioneer collecting days of 1907–1916. One man "stared vacantly into space" as he began to sing, removing himself from the present world and becoming totally absorbed in the song. At another cabin, an old woman, after complaining that the Civil War had caused her to forget most of her songs, began to sing. "Placing her hands in her lap, and fixing her eyes steadily on the ground, she literally chanted 'Vilikins and his Dinah' . . . 'Kate and her Horns,' 'Jack Williams,' and 'Come all ye jolly boatsman boys.'" Combs concludes, "If full and complete proof were needed of the oft-repeated assertion that the ballad singer is oblivious of his audience, that personality counts for nothing, this aged woman furnished it on this occasion." (One of the great changes in performing style that occurred as the music was commercialized lies in the fact that the modern country singer is far more eager to ingratiate himself with his audience.) A more romantic account of this singing style comes from a 1925 essay by Berea collector John F. Smith, who started collecting in 1915. "The story has seized the singer's imagination and drawn him out of himself. It has strongly stirred his emotions and for the moment his whole attention hangs upon the story. He is experiencing the adventures that he sings about. There is a directness about ballads, a simplicity, a naked nearness, that we do not find in any poetry. With this vividness there is often a mysterious echo from a lost world, a touch of the mystical and supernatural."

Instrumental traditions in nineteenth-century Kentucky were pretty much dominated by the fiddle and the banjo. It was not unusual to find a ballad singer accompanying himself on the fiddle, usually playing a melody line in unison with the singing. By the turn of the century, according to Combs, some banjoists were starting to adapt old ballads (such as "Pretty Polly") to their banjo styles. Since the early collectors were far more interested in noting down the words of ballads than the instrumental fiddle or banjo tunes, we lack a clear notion of what fiddle tunes were most popular. Based on the repertoires of twentieth-century fiddlers and their memories of what their fathers and grandfathers played, one can hazard a guess about which tunes were associated with Kentucky fiddlers. "Blackberry Blossom"—dating at least from the Civil War—and "Billy in the Low Ground" are two difficult and demanding pieces that have long pedigrees; "Grey Eagle," possibly named for the famous Kentucky race horse of 1839, seems always to have been popular, as have "Forked Deer" and "Humphrey's Jig" (drawn from a Scottish tune), especially in the eastern part of the state. These tunes joined such general southeastern favorites as "Sally Gooden," "Sourwood Mountain," "Cluck Old Hen," and "Soldier's Joy" in old Kentucky fiddlers' repertoires. Fiddlers often plied their trade at country dances, where they were usually the only source of music, keeping time by patting their feet and occasionally singing out a couplet or dance instruction. Many old fiddlers in the eastern part of the state held the instrument down on the chest rather than tucked under the chin, making it easier to sing but more difficult to maneuver the bow. Fiddlers' contests were routinely held in the county courthouses, often at the sessions of the quarterly circuit courts, where between six and a dozen local fiddlers would compete for little more than the honor of being thought "best in the county." In the western and central parts of the state, towns would hold a regular "jockey day," a day set aside for barter and trading of everything from horses to cedar buckets, and these special days attracted fiddlers and musicians as well as traders.

In the early days, if a fiddler had any accompaniment it was the banjo rather than the guitar; the guitar did not make its way into many parts of Kentucky until after the turn of the century, and the "string band" of the 1800s was usually a fiddle and a banjo. Banjos, which were probably brought into the country originally by slaves, were often homemade, with the head being made of groundhog hide or catskin. Five-string banjos (with a drone string) were popular in the eastern part of the state, four-string or tenor banjos in the west. Buell Kazee, growing up in Magoffin County shortly after the turn of the century, recalled how he learned the banjo: "Everybody played the banjo—not good but whacking at it, and you could find homemade banjoes around. . . . I started picking the banjo when I was five years old—a tack-head banjo. . . . I began to pick with [my] thumb. I'd hit the thumb string and then hit the melody (string). Then I began to frail—no melody at all. I learned to pick out the tune with my forefinger, picking down with the back of the nail. 'Lord Thomas and Fair Ellender' was the first tune I ever learned. Mother had sung that song ever since I could remember."

By the 1920s, when the recording companies began to document the music, eastern Kentucky musicians had developed a highly distinctive, driving banjo style which was defined through tunes like "Going Across the Sea," "Pretty Little Pink," "Blue-Eyed Gal," "Rock, Little Julie," "Buck Creek Girls," "Hook and Line." Some of the tunes featured frailing (downpicking), while others used a two-finger style, alternating thumb and index finger. Often the melody was broken into short, pulsing phrases.

Many times collectors found that old ballad singers would rather casually mix in with their versions of "Pretty Polly" or "Lord Thomas" old religious songs like "Been a Long Time Travelling Here Below" or "We Have Fathers Gone to Heaven."

Unfortunately these songs have not been studied as eagerly as the secular ballads, but many of them, like the ballads, seem to date from eighteenth-century England and to have been scattered via oral tradition by settlers on the frontier. There were more formal channels for the religious songs, though; they appeared in hymn books, were sung at church services, and played an important part in fundamentalist church dogma. Some were taught to congregations by travelling preachers, who, in the absence of songbooks, would "line out" the songs—shout out the words to a line before the congregation sang it.

At the dawn of the nineteenth century, the Great Revival swept over the settlements of Kentucky; it began on a Sunday in 1800 and one of its first leaders was a Logan County preacher named James McGready. The movement spread with such intensity and fervor that a year later some 25,000 gathered at the Cane Ridge church in Bourbon County to hear dozens of fundamentalist ministers. People would drive miles for these outdoor revival meetings, and often would have to camp out for the duration of the revival, giving the name "camp meeting" to the affairs. Group singing was an important part of these services, and in their fervor many groups "sung to pieces" many older hymns, learning them by heart, and putting them into oral tradition. The Cumberland Presbyterians, one of the new churches to emerge from the Great Revival, published one of the earliest songbooks to carry a Kentucky imprint: William Harris's *Hymn Book*, published in Russellville in 1824.

Other potent early sources for sacred songs were the various tune books published between 1815 and 1855 using shape notes, where one of four different shapes, rather than the position on the staff, indicated the pitch of the note. One of the first of these was called *Kentucky Harmony* (1815), but it was compiled by Ananias Davisson, a Presbyterian from Virginia; soon other similar books, such as Samuel Metcalf's *The Kentucky Harmonist* (Cincinnati, 1826) and the Silas Leonard-A.D. Filmore collaboration, *The Christian Psalmist* (Louisville, 1840s), were being published closer to home. Especially popular in the upper South was "Singing Billy" Walker's *Southern Harmony* (1835), a collection that proved so popular that it is still used today in the annual singings at Benton, Kentucky. Most of these tune books were, of course, collections of older songs, chosen and occasionally arranged by the compilers.

Church songbooks continued to spread old sacred songs through the state in the years following the Civil War, and many of the rural churches became bastions of tradition; old songs became part of the old, basic, fundamentalist ways of the churches, from the Primitive Baptists to the Holiness congregations. Under the protection of such strong social institutions, many of the old songs survived better than many of their secular counterparts. Their popularity formed the foundation for the strong gospel music flavor that country music in the state was later to acquire.

While the folk tradition was a strong influence on the development of country music in Kentucky, it was by no means the only one. The nineteenth century had its own brand of popular music, created by professional songwriters, published in sheet music, and copyrighted. Much of this music came out of "Tin Pan Alley" in New York, and it affected Kentuckians much as it affected other Americans. There were, though, certain pop songs and composers that came from Kentucky, or that made Kentucky their subject, and these had a special impact on the state's music and on the image the state presented to the country at large. Certain songs have been closely bound up with Kentucky history. After sharp-shooting Kentucky riflemen acquitted themselves so well at the Battle of New Orleans in 1815, they were glorified in a song called "The Hunters of Kentucky," written and published in 1824 by Samuel Woodworth. Woodworth was not a Kentuckian but a native of Massachusetts and a former newspaper editor who wrote a number of early patriotic songs in addition to the well-known "The Old Oaken Bucket." The lively song helped spread the image of the Daniel Boone-Davy Crockett type of pioneer hero:

> We are a hardy, free-born race,
>   Each man to fear a stranger;
> What'ere the game, we join in chace,
>   Despoiling time and danger.
> And if a daring foe annoys,
>   What'ere his strength and forces,
> We'll show him that Kentucky boys
>   Are alligator-horses.

The song achieved even wider circulation when it was used as the campaign song for Andrew Jackson a few years later.

By mid-century both Cincinnati and Louisville had become important regional centers for music publishing. William C. Peters (1805–1866) was an Englishman who had set up business in Cincinnati with branch offices in Louisville, and who was cited as early as 1839 as the third largest music publisher in the United

States. A gifted composer, he left behind several instrumental compositions, including the popular "Louisville March & Quick-Step," as well as a favorite parlor piano number called "Frankfort Belle" (1849). In 1848 his publishing company brought out (in both Louisville and Cincinnati) a series of five songs titled *Songs of the Sable Harmonists* and consisting of "The Lou'siana Belle," "Away Down South," "Susanna," "Uncle Ned," and "Wake up, Jake." The composer was a young friend of Peters's, then living in Cincinnati, and his name was Stephen Foster.

Foster (1826-1864), a Pittsburgh native, was on the threshold of a brief but brilliant career that was to produce dozens of well-known American songs. In spite of the pastoral or nostalgic themes of many of his works, he spent most of his adult life in New York; in spite of the fact that many of his most popular songs were later confused with folk songs, there is little evidence that Foster himself was ever exposed to any genuine folk music, aside from the occasional minstrel show tunes he learned as a child. Nonetheless, many of his songs have become symbolic of old southern life, and none more so than "My Old Kentucky Home." The original source of this song was Harriet Beecher Stowe's popular novel *Uncle Tom's Cabin* (1852), which Foster was reading as early as 1851 in its serial form. The book's popularity guaranteed that stage adaptations and musicals would be based on it, and Foster wrote several songs inspired by characters in the novel. One was for Uncle Tom himself, who early in the book has to leave his old Kentucky homestead to go with his new master, Simon Legree. By 1852 he had written a lament for Tom originally containing the refrain "Poor Uncle Tom, Good Night," but by the time the song was published (in New York in January 1853), he had dropped this and replaced it with the familiar chorus, "Weep no more my lady." During the next few years, several different musical versions of *Uncle Tom's Cabin* toured the east and midwest, many utilizing "My Old Kentucky Home" as one of the major songs. In later years it became popular with black concert singers, as well as with thousands of amateurs, who often thought of it as a folk song. Foster himself, who was no strong abolitionist, wrote several similar "plantation laments," such as "Old Folks at Home" and "Old Black Joe," but most of his later output was in the form of the popular parlor songs of the time.

Today, "My Old Kentucky Home" is one of the "official" Kentucky state songs, and is played before each running of the Kentucky derby. Popular legend has it that the song was inspired by Foster's visits to John Rowan's home, Federal Hill, in Bardstown. Judge Rowan was a cousin of Foster's father, and Foster's brother remembers them making "occasional" visits there, but modern researchers have found no positive evidence that Foster was directly inspired by Federal Hill. Foster's notebooks show that the song was written in New York, and a close reading of its lyrics, with its references to "little cabin floor" suggest that the "home" Foster had in mind was Uncle Tom's old cabin. In any event, the song is effective precisely because it does not refer to any specific house or time, but rather to an idealized, romanticized past for which "old Kentucky" is only a symbol. Not surprisingly, many later country songs were to use Kentucky in a similar way.

About the time Foster published "My Old Kentucky Home," another curious tune with roots in Kentucky was sweeping the country. This was "The Arkansas Traveller," perhaps the nation's best-known fiddle tune, interspersed with some of the nation's best-known jokes. The dialogue between the "sophisticated" traveller and the country bumpkin who makes a fool of him has taken hundreds of forms and has appealed to generations of rural Americans. Some of the jokes in the piece are among the most venerable items in American folklore. The exchange, "Say, stranger, your roof needs mending. Why don't you fix it?" "Can't mend it when it's raining. And when it's not raining, it don't leak" has even been found in print in German literature of the sixteenth century. Other researchers have found that the American version of the dialogue was in print at least as early as 1860, and that the tune was printed by 1847. One of the four claimants to authorship of "Arkansas Traveller" is Colonel Sanford C. Faulkner (1803-1874), a native of Scott County, Kentucky, who had moved to Arkansas and who claimed to have experienced the situation described in the song in 1840. In later years Faulkner gained fame as "The Arkansas Traveller" and regaled audiences throughout the Southwest with his story and his fiddle-playing to accompany it. Others argue that the piece was in fact originated by José Tasso, a Mexican-born violinist who lived in Kentucky and was known in the 1840s as the premier dance and concert fiddler up and down the Ohio River. Tasso, like Faulkner, certainly played the piece a lot and helped spread it, but whether he composed it or experienced the incidents the song describes has never been determined. Tasso died in Covington in 1887. Scholars tracing the history of the song have found other possible authors, but the final answer is still shrouded in mystery.

By the end of the Civil War, Kentucky could boast of having

its first really successful native-born songwriter. He was a colorful, flamboyant, and controversial character named William Shakespeare Hays (1837-1907). Born in Louisville, Hays grew up on the river and its lore, and for a time was a riverboat captain before he drifted into newspaper work, where he was to spend most of his career. He apparently wrote songs in his spare time. One story about him says that he wrote the words to his first published song, "Evangeline" (1862), with a charred stick on a fence during a party. His first real success was "The Drummer Boy of Shiloh" (Louisville, 1862), which became one of the most popular Civil War songs for both sides.

> On Shiloh's dark and bloody ground,
> The dead and wounded lay;
> Amongst them was a drummer boy,
> Who beat the drum that day.

The song was published in two editions: the "northern" one, in Louisville, showed a Union soldier on the cover; the "southern" one, from Georgia, showed the Confederate uniform. Hays apparently felt that a good song and strong sentiment outweighed political affiliation. The song spawned a number of imitations, and the theme is even echoed in the modern Christmas song, "Little Drummer Boy."

By 1866 Hays had established himself as a major popular writer, and his songs "Write Me a Letter from Home" and "We Parted by the River Side" each sold over 300,000 copies in sheet music—outstanding sales even by modern standards. Between 1869 and 1871 Hays published his most popular and enduring songs: "I'll Remember You, Love, in My Prayers," "Nobody's Darling," "Mollie Darling," and "The Little Old Log Cabin in the Lane." These songs are not as popular as, say, Foster's in modern mainstream music, but they were paid the ultimate tribute by the people themselves: they all went into folk tradition and were immortalized by generations of word-of-mouth tribute. In 1925 Josiah Combs remarked, "One is led to wonder what Will S. Hays would think, should he suddenly come to life and hear a Highland banjo picker metamorphosing that famous love song of his, 'I'll Remember You, Love, In My Prayers.'" "The Little Old Log Cabin in the Lane" was not only sung but was the victim of several parodies which also entered folk tradition. Settlers in the west had a version called "My Little Old Sod Shanty on the Plains," railroad men sang one called "The Little Red Caboose Behind the Train," and church singers favored a version called "The Lily of the Valley." It is not surprising that when a Georgia fiddler and singer named Fiddlin' John Carson made the first country record in 1923 he chose as one of his two selections "The Little Old Log Cabin."

Hays had a successful career in more formal music circles, as well. He eventually wrote over 300 songs, which apparently sold as many as twenty million copies. He often wrote nostalgic songs about the old South, such as "My Southern Sunny Home," "Oh, Give Me a Home in the South," and "Old Gate on the Hill," as well as many ethnic dialect songs and parodies. One popular song from 1871 was "Number Twenty-Nine," written for the Louisville and Nashville Railroad to celebrate the success of the new locomotive.

Hays died in 1907. Eighteen years later the next major chapter in Kentucky music was begun, not by a musician or writer, but by a young cave explorer named Floyd Collins. In February, 1925 Collins was exploring a sand cave he wanted to develop near Cave City, Kentucky. A rock fell on him and trapped him in a narrow passageway; for seventeen days rescuers labored to get him out, and his plight attracted national attention. Hundreds of newspapermen descended on the rescue site, and the story became front-page news. After seventeen days rescuers reached Collins, but it was too late. In Florida, Polk Brockman, a record company executive, sent a wire to his friend Andrew Jenkins, a blind Atlanta evangelist and songwriter, asking him to compose a song about the event. Within hours, Jenkins, who was a skilled and prolific songwriter, came up with "The Death of Floyd Collins" and sent it off to the record company executives for immediate recording. Soon several versions of the song were available on records, one by Fiddlin' John Carson, another by Vernon Dalhart. The records sold hundreds of thousands of copies, and the song spread across the South like wildfire. Within a few years, like so many of Hays's songs, "The Death of Floyd Collins" had become a folksong. For the first time the people were learning songs from a record, and for the first time in Kentucky the genres of pop music and folk music were joined by a third important element, the modern mass media. All three elements needed for commercial country music were now in place. The age of songs was ending; the age of singers was about to begin.

2 The New Minstrels

One evening in 1907, a man named Richard Daniel Burnett was walking home from his job in a barbershop in Stearns, Kentucky. He was twenty-four years old, a big strapping man with a reputation for knowing how to take care of himself in the rough-and-tumble oil fields and coal yards in the area. He was going home to his young wife and baby, and was cutting across the railroad yards of the CNO & TP line when he heard a noise in the shadows ahead. He stopped, and a man stepped out from behind a building and levelled a shotgun at him, demanding his money. Burnett had worked hard for his wages all his life: orphaned at twelve, one of nine children, he had been a wheat thrasher and a logger, then a driller and tool dresser in the oil fields up in the Aspen Valley. He wasn't about to surrender his earnings easily. Instinctively he lunged toward his assailant. The gun exploded, blasting a load of shot directly into Burnett's face. He crumpled to the ground unconscious, and the robber grappled in his pockets for his wallet.

Friends rushed Dick Burnett to a local hospital, where the doctor began picking the pellets out of his face; many of them had gone into his eyes and the doctor soon discovered that the optic nerve had been destroyed. When Burnett awoke in the hospital he was blind. In the days that followed he got used to the prospect that his days as a driller or tool dresser were over and that he would have to find some other way to support his family. Fortunately he had a musical background of sorts; as a boy in Wayne County he had learned "the rudiments of music" and had learned to play the dulcimer, banjo, and fiddle, and even the guitar, still relatively new in that part of the country. Music was one of the few vocations available to a blind man in rural turn-of-the-century America, and southern Kentucky was full of such minstrels, wandering from town to town, playing on street corners for nickels and dimes. In a couple of years Dick Burnett found himself joining their ranks.

The brutal assault on Dick Burnett by an anonymous railroad tramp, tragic though it was, in the end was to have a considerable impact on Kentucky music; it initiated a career that was to touch thousands of people in the mid-South and to preserve dozens of traditional songs and ballads. Working out of Monticello, Burnett began to travel to area towns, by rail when he could afford it, by foot when he could not. He became a familiar figure at fairs, at county courthouses, at train stations, on street corners—anywhere he could attract a crowd. A tin cup tied to his leg signalled contributions, and for those more interested in his songs he offered for sale "ballets"—small cards with the words to a song on them—or small songbooks. As he travelled his repertoire grew. He recalled, "You know, in travellin' everywhere, I'd meet people selling song ballets, other blind people in particular that way. We'd always swap ballets if somebody had a good one. I'd get them all. I'd get someone to hum the tune to it, I was always quick to catch the tune, I got the tune and then somebody . . . would read me the words on the ballet."

By 1913 he collected his best known songs in a little book he had printed in Danville. It included "The Lost Ship," one of several folk ballads about the sinking of the *Titanic* the year before; two old railroad songs, "The C & O Railroad" ("Along came the FFV") and "The Reckless Hobo"; a complaint against cheating merchants called "The Jolly Butchers," which Burnett claimed sold 4,000 copies; and two autobiographical songs, "The Song of the Orphan Boy," about how Burnett lost his sight, and the haunting "Farewell Song":

> I am a man of constant sorrow,
>   I've seen trouble all of my days;
> I'll bid farewell to old Kentucky,
>   The place where I was born and raised.
>
> Oh, six long years I've been blind, friends,
>   My pleasures here on earth are done,
> In this world I have to ramble,
>   For I have no parents to help me now.

So fare you well my own true lover,
    I fear I'll never see you again,
For I am bound to ride the Northern railroad,
    Perhaps I'll die upon the train.

Oh, you may bury me in some deep valley,
    For many years there I may lay,
Oh, when you're dreaming while you're slumbering,
    While I am sleeping in the clay.

Oh, fare you well to my native country,
    The place where I have loved so well,
For I have all kinds of trouble,
    In this vain world no tongue can tell.

Dear friends, although I may be a stranger,
    My face you may never see no more,
But there is a promise that is given,
    When we can meet on that beautiful shore.

Burnett apparently based his melody on an old Baptist hymn called "Wandering Boy," but his unique adaptation was to endure through the years as one of Kentucky's most famous lyric laments; in later decades it was recorded and popularized by Emry Arthur (in the 1920s), the Stanley Brothers (the 1940s), Bob Dylan (the 1960s) and even Waylon Jennings (the 1970s).

By the time World War I broke out, Dick Burnett was for all practical purposes a professional country musician, well before the era of the radio or the phonograph record. By now he had found a young apprentice to take with him, a fourteen-year-old boy from Somerset named Leonard Rutherford. Leonard helped Dick find his way around, and Dick taught him how to play the fiddle. Soon Leonard was performing regularly with Dick, learning a smooth, beautiful "rolling" fiddle bow technique that he picked up from other southern Kentucky fiddlers. It was the start of a thirty-five-year partnership, with Leonard playing the fiddle, Dick the banjo and guitar, and both singing. "The other people cut their music up so much with the fiddle bow, cut it all to pieces 'til it didn't sound good. Me and Leonard, we played every note exactly together. And, you see, that made it sound a heap better."

This "unison" style Dick described was an archaic survival from nineteenth-century Kentucky string music and sounded quite different from modern bluegrass or country music. On banjo and fiddle numbers the banjo picked out not a rhythm or an "embroidery" of the melody, but noted the lead right along with the fiddle; on vocal numbers the fiddle played the melody line right along with the voice. Many older traditional musicians in south-central Kentucky were still playing this "unison" style as late as the 1970s. During the following years the duo played all over the South. "There isn't a town this side of Nashville, from Cincinnati to Chattanooga, that's any size, what we been in," recalled Dick. Especially receptive to their music were the mining camps of eastern Kentucky and southwest Virginia; "I made good money at the coal camps. . . . The miners worked every day and didn't get to go nowhere." One day at the Bonnie Blue Coal Camp in Virginia they met a local record salesman who contacted Columbia Records and urged them to record the team; a few months later Frank Walker, the head of Columbia's "Old Familiar Tunes" series, wrote asking them to come to Atlanta to record. This was in early November 1926.

The country record industry was still in its infancy in 1926; it was only three years since Fiddlin' John Carson had made his first records for the General Phonograph Company, and recording executives were not yet sure how to meet the newly found demand for old-time songs and fiddle tunes. Columbia, who with Victor dominated the record market, had only recently begun to go into the South to do its recording and to hunt its talent. In its temporary studio in downtown Atlanta the company had recorded a handful of north Georgia musicians centering around a band called the Skillet Lickers, as well as a few gospel numbers; in their New York studios they had recorded North Carolinian singer Charlie Poole and Virginian Charley La Prade's Blue Ridge High-ballers. When Walker auditioned Burnett and Rutherford, he sensed not only that they were excellent musicians, but that they were authentic native minstrels—among the first to be recorded in his series and the first Kentucky artists to appear on a major label.

Those first six recordings for Columbia were made on Saturday, November 6, 1926, and included such Kentucky traditional favorites as "Pearl Bryan," "A Short Life of Trouble," "Lost John," and "Little Stream of Whiskey," as well as two sentimental songs, "Weeping Willow Tree" (recorded a year before the Carter Family made their famous version for Victor) and "I'll Be with You When the Roses Bloom Again." Released in early 1927, the records were all successful; Dick Burnett found he could sell them better than he could sell his old ballet cards and songbooks, and he simply replaced the older medium with the newer. Columbia paid them a flat rate of $50 per side—an all-too-common practice in those early years—but Burnett could buy records wholesale to sell retail and thereby gain back some money. Still, he was hardly aware of the quantum jump in popularity his records made over his old songbooks. Dick had felt very satisfied when he sold 6,000 copies of his little songbook over a period of ten years; he went to his grave never knowing that his Columbia recording of "Lost John" and "I'll Be with You When the Roses Bloom Again" (Columbia 15122) sold an astonishing 37,600 copies within three years, or that his recording of "Little Stream of Whiskey" racked up over 33,000 sales. When people had bought one of Dick's ballets they only had the words; when they bought one of his records they had the words, the music, and even the performing style they could copy. "It was naturally a better deal for 'em," he recalls. "That's why I went into the record selling business."

The Columbia company called Burnett and Rutherford back for two more sessions before a dispute over royalties caused them to move to the smaller Gennett Company in Richmond, Indiana. Among the remarkable recordings the team made for Columbia were "Ladies on the Steamboat" and "Billy in the Lowground" (1927), both among the finest known examples of the archaic Kentucky string band style featuring the fiddle and banjo (as opposed to the more modern fiddle and guitar). Between 1926 and 1930, Burnett and Rutherford went on to record over fifty songs, most by themselves but occasionally working with other partners; Dick recorded with Oscar Ruttledge, and Rutherford with another guitarist-singer, John Foster. With the coming of the Depression, record sales dropped and Dick suddenly found that he could no longer buy his records to sell; "I hadn't even kept copies for myself," he lamented. When the record business got back on its feet again, the old-time style of Dick and Leonard, once their strongest selling point, was out of fashion. The new music was smoother, more popular, or tinged with the new western swing coming out of the Southwest. Dick and Leonard returned to their old minstrel circuit, playing on street corners, at fairs, and for occasional dances. The people of south-central Kentucky and in the Cumberland mountains of Tennessee still liked their older music, and through the 1930s and 1940s the pair continued to make their way down dusty country roads in battered old cars. They made a few radio appearances from Cincinnati and Renfro Valley, but not regularly; Leonard developed a drinking problem, and this finally caught up with him in 1954. Dick lived on in his little house in Monticello, watching with amazement the musical trends and making chairs in a little shop out back; he lived to tell his story to historians and folklorists, who respected his old records and studied his old ballet cards. By the time he died in January 1977 he had seen most of his old records restored to print and had used his first royalty check in over forty years to buy his winter's supply of coal.

Burnett and Rutherford, for all their importance, were not the first Kentucky musicians to record the state's traditional music. That honor probably goes to an obscure fiddler named William B. Houchens (1884–ca. 1955), a native of Alton, Kentucky (Anderson County, just south of Frankfort), who recorded over a dozen fiddle tunes between 1922 and 1924 for the Starr Piano Company in Indiana. In fact, Houchens's first recordings were made on September 18, 1922, over nine months before Fiddlin' John Carson's initial recording, the one generally considered by many historians to be the first real country recording. Houchens was a trained musician—that is, he could read music—and some of the tunes he recorded were probably learned from old books of fiddle jigs and hornpipes; others, though, were probably learned from older native Kentucky fiddlers. These would include "Arkansas Traveller" (his first—and Kentucky's first—recording), "Bob Walker," "Hell in Georgia," and what is probably the first recording of "Flop Eared Mule," which Houchens called "Big-Eared Mule." A strong case could be made for Houchens being the very first to record southeastern tunes; history has ignored him partly because so little is known about him and partly because he ended his recording career in 1924, just at the time most other early musicians were starting theirs. Nor did he fit the stereotype of the mountain fiddler; he spent most of his life running his own music conservatory in Dayton, Ohio, where he taught a variety of stringed instruments. He did apparently learn a lot of his music from his mother, but we don't know what tunes he learned there, whether he plied his trade at square dances, or what possessed him to journey into the recording studios at such an early date and preserve his music in wax.

The first country singer from Kentucky was apparently a musician named Welby Toomey, who travelled to a recording studio in Richmond, Indiana, in the autumn of 1925 to record a half dozen songs for the Starr Piano Company. The son of a London immigrant, Toomey was born in Fayette County in 1897 and grew up in hilly Madison County, where he learned most of the songs he recorded, such as "Golden Willow Tree" and "I Wish I Was Single Again." Toomey soon dropped into obscurity, but his "back-up" band featured a man who was to become the

most prolific of all the old-time Kentucky musicians, a fiddler
named Doc Roberts. To fully appreciate the accomplishments of
this remarkable figure, however, requires a digression into the
nature of the record industry in the 1920s.

During the first decade of commercial country music recordings, most of the records were done "on location" in temporary
studios set up in cities around the South. The companies had
found that it was cheaper and easier to, in a sense, take the recording studio to the musicians rather than have the musicians make
long, difficult trips to New York or Chicago. It was also a fact that
many of the musicians who recorded during these early years were
basically amateurs who, though often highly gifted and innovative
folk artists, were not interested in pursuing a longer recording
career; many, therefore, recorded just a handful of sides and were
never heard from again. The most popular regional studio was
Atlanta, followed by Dallas. Of the dozens of others set up from
1925 to 1933, only two were in Kentucky. The first of these was
set up at Ashland in February 1928 by the Brunswick-Balke-
Collender Company, which had initiated its "Songs from Dixie"
series in April of 1927. In a month-long session the company
recorded over seventy sides by some ten artists, the works ranging
from gospel tunes to hot fiddle numbers. Unfortunately, virtually
all the musicians came from out of the state, many coming across
the river from West Virginia. Thus Kentucky's first recording
session was not of much help to Kentucky artists. The second
session was a much more elaborate affair staged in Louisville by
the Victor Company in June of 1931; here, in a vacant storeroom
on Main Street near Sixth, over sixty sides were recorded in conditions that one of the musicians described as "hot as blazes." This
session, too, did little to document old-time Kentucky music;
most of the sides recorded were blues and jug band numbers by
some of the many gifted black musicians who were part of the
thriving Louisville blues culture. A couple of white Kentucky
musicians were recorded, but most of the "hillbilly" product from
the session came from a series of joint recordings made by Jimmie
Rodgers and the Carter Family. Rodgers, then riding the crest of
popularity as country music's first real national star, also made
several records using local Louisville musicians. Some of these
featured blues fiddler Clifford Hayes's Louisville Jug Band ("My
Good Gal's Gone Blues"), two others featured WLAP staff pianist
Ruth Ann Moore, and two more featured young Cliff Carlisle and
Wilbur Ball, "The Lullaby Larkers," just starting to perform over
Louisville stations WLAP and WHAS. Efforts were made to keep

news of the session quiet lest hordes of aspiring recording stars mob the place, but the word leaked out anyway, and several Kentucky musicians, including Burnett and Rutherford, showed up and tried unsuccessfully to record.

Thus Kentucky musicians wanting to record were at a serious disadvantage. Lacking any local sessions, they either had to travel south to Tennessee or Atlanta for the regional sessions, or go north on their own to the studios. The net effect was that Kentucky generally was underrepresented on early country records, in comparison with Georgia, Tennessee, or North Carolina. Kentucky musicians had to make heroic efforts to get recorded in these early days. Seymour Penley, of Powderly, who was a tap dancer with one of the more famous western Kentucky bands, E.E. Hack's String Band, recalled the difficulties their band had: "They was trying to go to Atlanta, Georgia, to cut some records. . . . They had to get up two hundred dollars and it took them a long time to get up this two hundred dollars. And then they made arrangements with Dewey Hicks, who owned the ice company and had big trucks that hauled from one state to another, they hired him, hired him and one of his trucks. They put straw and stuff in the backs of the truck and he put a tarpolin over the cattle sides, and they all took their instruments and they got in the truck. And they was gone about three days and they cut two records. They was supposed to get royalty on the records, but I guess they never did sell very many 'cause I don't think they hardly recognized anything at all off of them."

For many musicians the closest recording studio proved to be the facility of the Gennett Recording Company (Starr Piano Company) at Richmond, Indiana, some sixty miles north of the Kentucky border. Unlike the bigger companies such as Victor, Columbia, and Brunswick, the Gennett Company was a relatively small, informal organization that was pleasantly receptive to fiddlers and singers who routinely arrived at their doorstep. From 1925 to 1933, Gennett recorded more country music from Kentucky than from any other state, and preserved many rare examples of the variety of traditional music in Kentucky. Unfortunately the technical quality of Gennett records left much to be desired; indifferently recorded to begin with, the discs quickly wore out on the old lathe-like Victrolas that customers played them on. They were distributed very poorly, so much so that many excellent recordings survive today only through one single copy; others have left no surviving copies at all. Gennett often leased its recordings for issue on various "stencil" labels to be sold mail order through Sears and Wards on such labels as Challenge,

Supertone, Champion, Superior, and others. These records did in fact gain fairly wide distribution, but in many cases the names of the artists had been changed to pseudonyms, thus depriving them of any degree of fame their "hits" might have brought them. Royalty rates on such stencil issues were minuscule, often amounting to no more than one-fourth cent per record sold.

In part because of these conditions, local record company talent scouts played a much greater role in developing early country music in Kentucky than they did in other states. While the image of a recording crew coming into a sleepy southern town, setting up, and advertising in the local paper for musicians to come in is partially accurate, the system quickly became more sophisticated. In some cases companies sent their own scouts around the South to audition performers months before the session was to be held; in other cases singers were told by mail what songs to "work up" weeks before the field unit arrived. Nearly all the companies relied on the local music store owners or record dealers to help them spot local talent, and some of these local merchants played important roles in getting Kentucky music on record. W.S. Carter of Ashland was responsible for getting artists such as Buell Kazee and B.F. Shelton to record. Dewey Golden, a dealer from Corbin, hauled fifteen or twenty musicians over the mountains to Johnson City, Tennessee, to record for Columbia in 1928. But perhaps the most important of these early entrepreneurs was a man from Richmond, Kentucky, named Dennis W. Taylor.

Taylor was a farmer who lived three miles from Richmond on Taylor's Fork Creek. He was by no means a musician—friends recalled that he could not even whistle a tune—but he liked old-time music, and began managing a local string band he called Taylor's Kentucky Boys, which played dances and local schools. About 1925 Taylor somehow got in touch with a Mr. Butt, who was the manager for the Starr-Gennett studio up at Richmond, Indiana, and learned that there was a growing demand for old-time music on record. Gennett, unlike the major companies, couldn't afford to send talent scouts or portable recording crews into the hills to find these musicians, and they were willing to contract this work out to independents like Taylor. For the next six years, then, Taylor began a second career as a talent manager for numerous musicians in eastern Kentucky. His widow later recalled that he would go into the mountains to "scout up" musicians, sign them to "management contracts," and as time for a recording session approached, bring them to the Taylor home in Richmond. There he would help them choose songs to be recorded, and Mrs. Taylor, who knew a good deal more about music than her husband, would help them with their timing and rhythm. Many rural musicians were used to playing long sets at country dances, where a tune would often go on for some twenty minutes, and getting them to cut their tunes down to the three-minute limit allowed by the phonograph record was sometimes a formidable task. Sometimes Taylor would board musicians for as long as three weeks before he finally took them to Indiana in his car to record.

Taylor would usually pay all expenses incurred in working up the tunes and making the trip to Richmond, and then pay the artists a flat fee of so much a side; in exchange for this the artists usually agreed to give Taylor any royalties that accrued from the record. This later occasionally led to bitterness between Taylor and his musicians, who often felt that their records sold more than they actually did, and that Taylor was enriching himself at their expense. During his peak years, in 1926 and 1927, Taylor would collect as much as $800 to $900 a month from Gennett, but this would represent royalties from dozens of records by a variety of musicians. Between 1925 and 1931 he scouted up about a hundred musicians from the area and got many of them to preserve their music on wax. They included men such as Fiddlin' Doc Roberts and Asa Martin; banjoist Marion Underwood, whose 1927 recording of "Coal Creek March" remains one of the finest examples of mountain finger-style banjo picking; Byrd Moore, a Virginia guitarist and singer whose style may well have influenced Maybelle Carter; Charlie Taylor from Irvine, Kentucky; guitarist-fiddler Edgar Boaz from Winchester; several black musicians, including fiddler Joe Booker from Camp Nelson, who was actually the fiddler for the recording band called Taylor's Kentucky Boys; and guitarist-singer John Foster, who later worked some with Leonard Rutherford. One of Taylor's last "discoveries" was a young man named Red Foley, but Taylor didn't like his voice and decided not to sign him up or take him for test recordings.

Taylor probably qualifies as Kentucky's—and one of country music's—first booking and recording agents. Through his efforts dozens of excellent Kentucky musicians committed their music to posterity, and even began professional careers in music. He probably would never have thought of himself as a folklorist, but in a very real sense he was, for he is responsible for a great deal of what we know about early eastern Kentucky old-time music. And this brings us back to that session featuring singer Welby Toomey in October 1925—Kentucky's first real country recording session.*

*The band arrived in Richmond in late September; on the thirtieth Toomey recorded three vocals, and on October first, Roberts and Boaz re-

Toomey recalled that the session was all Taylor's idea, that in the summer of 1925 Taylor was scouting the area trying to put together a recording orchestra. He finally settled on Toomey, whom he had known since Toomey was a boy, and paired him with a fiddler named Doc Roberts, whose farm adjoined Taylor's own. To fill out the band Taylor got Edgar Boaz, from Bourbon County, a guitarist and fiddler who already knew Roberts.

From this start Doc Roberts went on to become the most famous and widely recorded of all Kentucky fiddlers. Between 1925 and 1934 he recorded over eighty fiddle tunes for three different companies, and played back-up on at least eighty more recordings. His smooth bowing style and rich repertory of central Kentucky fiddle tunes won him thousands of fans and emulators, and only his aversion to travel (and thus a radio career) prevented his becoming a nationally known figure like the age's two other premier fiddlers, Arthur Smith and Clayton McMichen. Like them, Roberts began fiddling when still a boy in knee pants at his childhood home. This was an old log house on top of a hill in Madison County, where Phillip (Doc) Roberts was born on April 26, 1897. While growing up, Doc and his older brother Levert both learned to fiddle and listened a lot to Owen Walker, an older black fiddler from Madison County. Walker, born in 1857, became a well-known entertainer in the World War I era and was much in demand for social events in the region; he never recorded but he passed on much of his repertoire and style to the Roberts brothers, including such tunes as "Old Buzzard," "Brickyard Joe," and "All I Got's Gone," all of which Doc later recorded. In fact, researcher Gus Meade has estimated that as much as 70 percent of Roberts's recorded repertory came from Owen Walker. Years later Doc acknowledged this debt to Walker: "He helped me in every way in the world," he said. In addition, recent research indicates that in 1927 Doc recorded with black guitarist John Booker and his brother Joe, a fiddler—probably country music's first integrated recording session.

Possibly because of this influence, Doc Roberts's repertoire contained a surprising number of "blues" tunes; many of these, he admitted, had been learned from local black fiddlers and "reworked" to fit his own style. This was a style that was characterized by the "long bow" technique—featuring long, graceful, flowing lines—that later came to characterize Texas fiddling, and

corded four fiddle tunes. For some reason the vocals were all rejected, but the four fiddle tunes were issued. The band returned for remakes on November 13-14, and this time Toomey's vocals were accepted.

that contrasted markedly with the "jiggy" bow style of many other mountain fiddlers. Doc's repertoire was also a uniquely Kentuckian one; he apparently paid little attention to music on the radio or phonograph records, for almost all of his tunes are indigenous to the east-central part of Kentucky and many are seldom heard outside that area. These include "Deer Walk," "Waynesburgh," "New Money," "Hawk's Got a Chicken," "Coal Tipple Blues," and others.

Doc's very first recording was "Martha Campbell," an old Kentucky frolic tune known widely throughout the eastern part of the state; along with "Shortenin' Bread," "Dixie," and "Billy in the Low Ground," it was reasonably successful, but the company officials told him that, regardless of how good their instrumentals were, vocal numbers would sell better. He soon parted company with his "manager" Taylor and organized a band called the Kentucky Thoroughbreds that featured singing—the singing of Charles "Dick" Parman, a railroad switchman from Corbin, and Charles "Ted" Chesnut from London, Kentucky. This trio recorded a strange variety of songs at their 1927 sessions for the Paramount Company, including "Only a Miner," one of the most effective and widespread occupational folk songs, old sentimental songs like "In the Shade of the Old Apple Tree," sacred songs like "He Cometh," and fiddle tunes such as the venerable "Rocky Mountain Goat."

Later that same year Doc found another partner, one who was as skilled a back-up man as he was a singer. He was Asa Martin, born in Clark County in 1900, the son of a piano teacher and an old-time trick fiddler who wanted their son to go to medical school at Louisville. The money didn't hold out, though, and Asa dropped out of school about 1920 to take to the vaudeville stage, plying his trade as a musician. A lot of his work came from silent movie houses, which needed bands to play for intermissions and to make mood music for the likes of Charlie Chaplin, the Keystone Cops, and Rudolph Valentino. When talkies came in, Asa felt his career was washed up, but about that time he met Doc at a fiddling contest and learned all about the record business.

For seven years Asa and Doc worked together, recording dozens of tunes, playing contests, schoolhouses, vaudeville stages, and some radio over WHAS, Louisville. (Doc was taken up to Chicago by Bradley Kincaid about this time to be on the WLS Barn Dance, but he returned to Madison County a couple of weeks later, complaining that he could not sleep in the city.) A few years before his death, Asa recalled the type of songs he and Doc would perform: "Now when I first started recording, the sadder songs you were doing, the better they were. Such as 'The Knoxville Girl,' 'Kitty Wells,' and 'Gentle Annie' and those old numbers. . . . Then it went into kind of the railroad songs, like 'East Bound Train,' 'Old 97' . . . and mining songs, about the north, 'Dingy Miner's Cabin'—my sister wrote that song, it was a true happening. . . . And then it came right in from the railroad songs that they had comic and bootlegging songs and all that."

To their third recording session, in 1928, Doc brought his eleven-year-old son, James Roberts. He sang soprano with Asa on a couple of numbers, and everybody was pleased with the way the two voices blended; he and Asa thus began a series of close-harmony recordings that featured Doc playing mandolin instead of fiddling. By the early 1930s these vocals—usually of sentimental songs like "Ninety Nine Years" and "There's a Little Box of Pine on the 7:29"—were becoming more popular than Doc's fiddle tunes. By 1934 Doc was becoming discouraged with the record and music business, and made what were to be his last records for many years. He had never really considered himself a professional musician but rather a farmer, and as his son and his old friend Asa continued to work in the music they loved, Doc contented himself with playing rural dances around Madison County, keeping alive the distinctive central Kentucky fiddle repertory that had first brought him fame. He was "rediscovered" by folklorists in the 1960s and coaxed out of retirement in the 1970s for occasional performances at Berea College. He died in 1978.

Asa, for his part, had been somewhat frustrated by Doc's unwillingness to travel, and was much more interested in trying to make it as a full-time professional. Certainly, records could not provide a livable income. Their records on the actual Gennett label averaged sales in the hundreds, not thousands, of copies; the Super-tone and Champion releases of their material, often under pseudonymns, averaged 4,000–5,000 sales per disc, with occasional Champion best-sellers peaking out at around 20,000 copies—far fewer than those sold by stars like Jimmie Rodgers, the Carter Family, and the Skillet Lickers recording on major labels. Asa had to turn to radio for livelihood, and he had done this as early as 1930, even before he broke with Doc. As we shall see, local Kentucky radio stations were slow in getting into the country music business, but by 1930 Asa was starting to work on stations like Louisville's WHAS. He eventually formed a larger group called the Kentucky Hillbillies, and headed up a "Morning Round-Up Show" over WLAP (Lexington) that featured a troupe of about twenty other performers. Throughout the 1940s he remained a major figure in local country music, often acting as a talent spotter. He was responsible for getting many fine traditional musicians, such as singer Green Bailey, fiddler Charlie Wilson, mandolinist Roy Hobbs, and the Hatton Brothers, into the Gennett recording studios, and he played an important role in "discovering" later acts like the Ledford Sisters (the Coon Creek Girls), Granny Harper (of Renfro Valley fame), and David "Stringbean" Akeman. For a time in the 1940s he was a talent director for several stations in the Mutual Southern radio network. Like Doc, Asa lived to see his old-time music vindicated by scholars and students; his last band, the Cumberland Rangers, made a couple of stereo albums and some television shows, and played a healthy number of festivals. Asa even visited Japan. In between engagements he entertained countless visitors wanting to know about "the good old days." He died August 15, 1979, at the age of 79.

The third member of the Doc Roberts trio, James Roberts, went on to have an equally interesting career in professional music. In spite of the success of his duets with Asa Martin, James became discouraged with music and joined the navy in 1937. On his return he married Irene Amburgey, one of the three Amburgey sisters from Neon, Kentucky, who were making a name for themselves in regional radio. With them, he moved to the "Renfro Valley Barn Dance" and then in 1940 to WSB in Atlanta. There he and his wife began to sing duets, using the stage names "James and Martha Carson, the Barn Dance Sweethearts," and specializing in gospel numbers. Martha could read shape notes, and the two plundered the rich storehouse of sacred songs in the paperback Stamps-Baxter songbooks so beloved of gospel quartets. Their 1947 version of "The Sweetest Gift, a Mother's Smile" helped establish that song as a bluegrass classic, and James's original composition "Man of Galilee" became a favorite. By 1949 they were recording for one of the country's leading pop labels, Capitol, but split up when Martha decided to try to make it as a mainstream country singer. James continued to lend his sparkling mandolin work to the recording sessions of other singers, but eventually retired to Lexington, where today he still performs occasionally and does evangelical work.

Both the Burnett-Rutherford and the Doc Roberts groups made their marks in early recordings by emphasizing the instrumental traditions of the region's music. But a third major figure in early recording emphasized singing. He was Buell Kazee, a banjo-playing minister who has been called "the greatest white male folk singer in the United States." To one listening to his records, Buell Kazee sounds like the epitome of the Kentucky mountain songster: in a high, tight, "lonesome" voice, accompanied only by a banjo "geared" to unusual tunings, Buell performed ancient ballads like "Lady Gay" (Child 79) and "The Butcher's Boy," many of which he had learned as a boy. To one listening to his recorded skit "A Mountain Boy Makes His First Record," he appeared as a bumpkin, wandering into the Chicago studios armed with a jug of white lightning, a homemade banjo with a cat-skin head, and utter astonishment that his voice could be carried along little wires from the microphone to the control room. To the young folk song enthusiasts who rediscovered Buell in the 1960s, he seemed to be the "real thing," the authentic Kentucky mountain sound, as opposed to the smoother, more "commercial" purveyors of folk songs like Bradley Kincaid. Yet a closer look at his career yields quite a different story, a story that reveals a complex struggle between a sensitive and articulate musician and the stereotyped image the outside world wanted to foist on him.

To start with, Buell Kazee's background wasn't much different from that of other early eastern Kentucky recording artists. Born August 29, 1900, at the head of Burton Fork in Magoffin County, about sixty miles east of Richmond, he learned old songs and hymns from both parents. "We just sang by nature," he recalled. "Everybody sang and nobody thought there was anything unusual about it. And a good many people around us did. Down the road almost in sight was Preacher Caudill's family. They were all singers. They had a banjo, the first one I ever saw." By the time he was five, Buell was whacking away at a little banjo, and he spent the rest of his childhood hearing and learning the music in his rural society; he experienced the "frolics," the brush arbor meetings, the bean stringings, the customs that any mountain boy at the time encountered.

The stereotype began to break up when Buell, thinking he was preparing for the ministry, continued his education on into high school and then to Georgetown College in central Kentucky. There he majored in English, Greek, and Latin; he began to understand some of the cultural significance of the old ballads and songs he knew. Some of the "old English" ballads in his literature books were similar to those he had heard at home. He also began to study voice and music, and to replace his "mountain" voice with a formal, cultured voice style. For a time he studied with a tenor from New York who summered in Ashland. He was quick to merge his newer formal musical training with his mountain music background; in 1925, after he had graduated from Georgetown, he presented a concert of "folk music" at the University of Kentucky. It was a formal affair, with young Buell in tie and tails, playing the banjo, singing to piano accompaniment, and even lecturing about mountain songs. For the next few years he staged several such recitals in the area. Thus when he was talked into travelling to New York to make his first Brunswick records, in April of 1927, he expected the sophisticated New York recording executives to want much the same thing.

They didn't. They listened politely as Buell sang parlor songs and religious songs in his "formal" voice, but didn't really perk up until he got out his banjo and began to sing some of the old mountain ballads. Years later he recalled: "I had to make a record seven or eight times to get it bad enough to sell. They'd say, 'Buell, that's fine, but it won't ring on a cash register.' I'd ask, 'Well, what do you want?' 'Well, that vibrato and resonance, if you can cut that out.' If you want to sound country, you sing with a tight throat." He found that to get this "country" voice he had to sing with a tight voice, high in the throat, not from the diaphragm as trained singers are taught to do. He finally good a good enough mountain sound to "John Hardy" and "Roll on John" to satisfy the Brunswick people, and his record career was under way. During the next two years he was to record over fifty songs. A fifth of them were religious numbers, reflecting Buell's career in the ministry; others were pop tunes and sentimental laments where Buell was backed by New York studio musicians. But well over half were strong, forceful performances of some of the best traditional ballads, including what is perhaps the finest recorded rendition of "Lady Gay" (1928). Others included "East Virginia," "The Sporting Bachelors" (probably a nineteenth-century song), "The Wagoner's Lad," and "The Orphan Girl."

During this time, Buell returned to his hometown and overheard someone say, "There's Buell Kazee. He'll never have to work another lick—making all that money on records." This was a common belief of people in the 1920s, thinking that record-making was a way to wealth. In truth, Buell, like most others, got only a flat fee for recording—in his case, $60 to $75 per record—and no royalties. He was surprised to find that his best seller, "Little Mohee" and "Roving Cowboy," topped out at around 15,000 and was selling strongest in Texas. ("Little Mohee" was an early variant on the well-known "On Top of Old Smoky" tune.) Buell's affected singing style even won critical acclaim from the national press. A writer for *Billboard* in February 1933 saw Buell as a possibility for radio, and explained: "Buell Kazee—probably a phony moniker of a better known personality making recordings for Brunswick. Hillbilly character, accompanied by guitar. An honestto-goodness sample of soul-tearing keoboy [sic] lamentation. Marvelous delivery on the disc, this being particularly noticeable in recordings of *The Blind Man* and *The Butcher's Boy*." The company wanted Buell to tour the Southwest, "plugging" his records and doing concerts, but he had just married and, like Doc Roberts, really didn't want to professionalize his music any further. Still, his records continued to spread his music, and some of his more successful ones were issued even in England, Australia, Japan, and Ireland. The Depression curtailed the spread of these original issues of his records, but in 1951 they were included in Harry Smith's *Anthology of American Folk Music*, a huge set of old recordings reissued by a New York company, and found new audiences.

Buell became a minister, serving one church in Morehead for twenty-two years, and singing at revival meetings. In later years he also wrote a number of formal pieces using folk music themes, including a cantata based on the old *Sacred Harp* piece "The White Pilgrim," and an operetta entitled *The Wagoner Lad*, containing a number of his favorite folk melodies. Like Doc Roberts and Asa Martin, he lived into the era of the folk festivals and was one of the first authentic performers to appear at the Newport Folk Festival in the 1960s. He also did a lot of writing, including three books on religion, a book on banjo techniques, and an unpublished autobiography. When he died in August 1976 he left behind all this, some splendid recordings, old and new, a son who has the skill and interest to keep his father's music alive, and a somewhat perplexed cadre of admirers who have still not entirely come to grips with the man who was the most complex, demanding, and multi-faceted of Kentucky's traditional musicians.

There were other pioneer Kentucky singers who worked primarily through the medium of the phonograph, and one of them in particular offers a striking contrast to Kazee, both in his attitude toward his musical heritage and in his attempt to commercialize it. His name was Emry Arthur. By many measures, Emry Arthur's career was a failure; though he was one of the more prolific early record makers—he eventually accounted for some 78 sides—his name is hardly known today by fans who lionized Buell Kazee, Doc Roberts, or Bradley Kincaid. Indeed, the basic facts of his biography are sketchy. He was born about the turn of the century in the Elk Spring Valley in Wayne County. His family were known throughout the area for their singing, and his brothers Sam and Henry were noted songsters and easy hands with the fiddle, guitar, and banjo. A hunting accident took one of Emry's fingers, forcing him to adopt a rather plain, straightforward guitar style that, paradoxically, was to become fashionable a few years later. His family shared many of their old songs with Dick Burnett, the other famous Wayne County singer, and freely swapped back and forth; they taught Dick a version of "Going Across the Sea," and he taught them his "Farewell Song," which Emry began calling "Man of Constant Sorrow." "The White Rose," which Emry recorded, was a favorite on the wide courthouse lawns of Monticello, where both the Arthurs and Burnett and Rutherford held forth on Saturday afternoons.

In the mid-1920s Arthur moved to Indianapolis, where he found work at a variety of jobs before journeying to Chicago to make his first records for the Brunswick-Vocalion Company in 1928. His jaunty versions of "I Am a Man of Constant Sorrow" and old gospel hymns like "Shining for the Master" sold very well, and he began a hectic three-year period of recording. Many of the tunes were commonplace sentimental songs and sacred pieces, but there were more interesting ballads like "Ethan Lang," "The Bluefield Murder," "Down in Tennessee Valley," and a two-part, six-minute version of "Frankie and Johnnie" that he called "Frankie Baker." Arthur was also interested in the blues and in original songs. Some of these Arthur himself wrote, and others, such as "Sunshine and Shadows" and "True Love Divine," were written by his manager and part-time sponsor, W.E. Myer, a remarkable Virginia lawyer with a keen interest in old-time music. For a time Arthur lived in Port Washington, Wisconsin, where he worked in the factory that made Paramount Records; naturally he recorded his share of Paramounts before the Depression overtook the business. One of his letters to Myer, dated March 18, 1930, reflects the near desperation that he and other would-be recording artists must have felt during these times:

> I should have wrote you before now, but I have just been waiting, thinking that something would turn up so I could get to record one or 2 records, but that good luck must have went some other way. I have got the songs ready to record but there is no use to try to get this co. to let me record them unless some one else pays me to record them. It don't seem like they are very busy just now. We have been cut down to 8 hours a day and things sure do look bad just now. If they don't get some work to do in the factory before long I am looking to get layed off but if i could get to record one or 2 records it would sure help out.

As it turned out, Arthur did get a chance to record some more songs, but they sold poorly and he gradually drifted out of the music business. He died in Indianapolis in 1966.

Unlike Doc Roberts or Buell Kazee, Emry Arthur was certainly aggressive enough in pursuing his career as a musician; he was constantly trying out new songs and setting up "deals" with recording executives. He had a pleasant if not exceptional voice and a good ear for songs; he sensed that many of the old songs had to be smoothed out and simplified if they were ever to reach a wider audience. But he was dogged with personal misfortune: he married three times before he was thirty and once left Kentucky on the run, begging his friends not to give out his location. He had little education and spent much of his time in the North doing the most menial of jobs. There is no evidence that he appeared very much on radio—certainly not on major stations, at least—and thus had no steady source of income with which to support a full-time career. He left behind no songbooks, no autobiography, no rich taped interviews with folklorists. His sole legacy was his records, which are mostly out of print today and deserving of more recognition than they have received.

While the majority of Kentucky's first generation of country musicians came from the eastern part of the state, there were several other centers of musical activity in the late 1920s. One, as we have seen, was Wayne County and its environs in south-central Kentucky, which produced Richard Burnett, Leonard Rutherford, the Arthur boys, and others, such as sacred singer William Rexroat, who was close to seventy years old when he led his Cedar Crest Singers on a splendid series of gospel recordings for the Vocalion label. Another fertile pocket of music was the Corbin-Knox County-Laurel County axis in the southeastern part of the state. Corbin's population in the 1920s was only slightly over 3,500, but the town did have as an attraction the big L & N Railroad shops, where more than a few musicians found work. Except for this, it is difficult to explain the fact that over a dozen bands or singers from this region made records between 1927 and 1934. None of them had the kind of long-range success or commercial impact of Doc Roberts or Asa Martin, but many of the individual records were quite popular and influential, and the recorded work from the Corbin area comprises a documented cross-section of regional traditional music that is almost unrivaled in American music history.

To begin with, there were some of old-time music's most intense gospel singers. Alfred G. Karnes (1891–1958), though a

Virginian by birth, spent most of his life around London and Corbin, where he was first a barber and then a Baptist minister. He was always a singer, and for years had a "family band" that gave "courthouse steps" concerts each Sunday in the area. In fact, many Sundays they gave concerts in four different towns, rotating between Mt. Vernon, Brodhead, Lancaster, and Stanford. Residents of these towns still today remember these concerts and the band's theme song, "This Is My Day, My Happy Day." But record buyers across the country remember Karnes's 1927–1928 efforts for Victor. Driving to Bristol, Tennessee, one summer day in 1927, Karnes became a part of the historic recording session that "discovered" the Carter Family and Jimmie Rodgers. Karnes took with him his then-new $375 Gibson harp-guitar, an unusual instrument which allowed him to make difficult bass runs and achieve a rich, full tonal effect. He recorded a total of eight sides (in 1927 and at a later session in 1928), including his most popular song, "Called to the Foreign Field." He also made some of the first country recordings of standards like "I Am Bound for the Promised Land," "Where We'll Never Grow Old," and "When They Ring Those Golden Bells for You and Me." Karnes probably also played on the recordings of Ernest Phipps and his Holiness Singers, who recorded a dozen songs at the same Bristol sessions. Phipps (ca. 1900–ca. 1968) was a preacher in the Free Holiness Pentecostal church who brought into the studios several members of his congregation and recorded some rare examples of the exuberant, ragged, hand-clapping rural Holiness music. Their Victor recordings of "Do Lord, Remember Me," "Old Ship of Zion" (using the tune of "She'll Be Comin' Round the Mountain"), and "If the Light Has Gone in Your Soul" sold surprisingly well and some stayed in print into the 1930s. There is nothing in the history of early white recorded gospel music that can match the Phipps recordings for sheer drive and feeling, though the handful of records made on Paramount by yet another Corbin group, the Joe Reed Family, would come close; though little is known about the Reed Family, they exhibit the same style of fervent, emotional gospel music.

Corbin was also quite a nest for banjo players, especially those reflecting the hard-driving "banjo song" style so characteristic of eastern Kentucky, with the high-pitched voice floating over a frailed banjo. The best known of these was George "Shortbuckle" Roark, from nearby Pineville. Roark was a slim, curly-headed lad with a growing family of small children who all seemed to be able to sing old-time music. He recorded with these children for Victor in 1928 (yielding the remarkable lyric "I Truly Understand You Love Another Man," resurrected in the 1960s by young folk-singers), and for Columbia in the same year. In the mid-1930s he was one of the "sources" for Bradley Kincaid's song-hunting trips, and in 1937 and 1938 he recorded some pieces for the Library of Congress. He was more of a comic entertainer than an out-standing banjoist, and in 1937–1938 seemed much under the influence of the Grand Ole Opry's Uncle Dave Macon.

More subtle with his music was B.F. (Frank) Shelton, a Corbin barber whose four lone recordings (1927) are considered by many experts to represent the epitome of the eastern Kentucky banjo song style. For some reason Victor allowed him to put two of his ballads on twelve-inch discs, giving him a full four minutes of recording time. These ballads, "Pretty Polly" and "Darling Cora," feature Shelton's lonesome, nasal voice singing in an eerie minor key, delivering the old English ballad "Pretty Polly," with its bleak, naturalistic account of Polly's murder. Two other pieces of Shelton's were unusual examples of "mountain blues": "O Molly Dear" is an early rendering of the song that came to be known as "East Virginia Blues," while "Cold Penitentiary Blues" (which Shelton himself may have learned in prison) is a variant of a "blues ballad" that has been collected from black singers in both Kentucky and Texas. Shelton (1902–1963) was born in Clay County and came from a family of musicians; he played har-monica and guitar in addition to the banjo, and though he com-posed few songs he became an excellent interpreter of traditional and old-time material. Edd Ward, who knew Shelton in Corbin in the 1920s, remembers that just across the street from Shelton's barbershop was "a restaurant and they had some kind of record player and would play a number from time to time which Frank was trying to learn, and every time this record came on Frank would rush out on the sidewalk with pencil and tablet and jot down a stanza or two." Shelton knew Alfred Karnes and probably travelled with him to the Bristol recording sessions.

Another area banjoist whose style may well reflect the influ-ence of black string band music is Hays Shepherd, "The Appa-lachia Vagabond," from Jenkins. Shepherd's 1930 recordings of "Hard For to Love" (later popularized by Woody Guthrie) and "Peddler and His Wife" (about the 1896 murder of a peddler which resulted in the last public hanging in Harlan County) were his only solo recordings, but they are exceptional. His brothers Will and Bill were also unusually good musicians with a love for the blues, but the only record they ever made together survives in one sole battered copy. Hays and Will spent much of their time working in the mines at Appalachia, Virginia, appearing at local fiddling contests and delighting those few who had the good fortune to hear them in person.

Corbin's premier fiddle band was that of John V. Walker (1891–1980), an L & N railroad fireman. Walker's band was an offshoot of an earlier Corbin group called Bond's String Band, a six- to eight-piece group that was composed almost entirely of railroaders. It specialized in playing blues (such as "St. Louis Blues," "Memphis Blues," and "Joe Turner Blues") and was generally considered the best of all the Corbin bands. Unfortunately it never recorded. Walker's band did, though, travelling to Knoxville (1930) and New York (1934) to preserve a legacy of some eighteen sides which reflected an easy-going mixture of old string band tunes ("Stone Mountain Toddle," "Ned Went a Fishing") and dance tunes from the 1920s ("Darktown Strutters' Ball," "I Had a Dream"). Walker's mandolin player and guitarist was Larry Hensley (1912–1973), a skilled and innovative virtuoso who was among the first in a long line of Kentucky mandolin and guitar soloists. His guitar masterpiece, "Match Box Blues," a cover of bluesman Blind Lemon Jefferson's classic, is one of the finer examples of recorded white blues. Friends give him credit for composing "Mandolin King Rag."

Other early Corbin area artists to record included Blind Jim Howard (Victor, Library of Congress), Alec Hood (Paramount, Vocalion), Dick Parman (Paramount), Ancil McVay and Roland Johnson (Columbia), and Faye Cole (Paramount).

In western Kentucky, the center of much activity was radio station WFIW in Hopkinsville, near the Tennessee border. Though licensed to broadcast at only 1,000 watts, the station was rather informally managed by Plug Kendrick, a jazz band drummer, who would lock the doors at night and illegally boost the power so high that the station could be heard throughout most of the country. Jack Jackson, a singer who worked for the station, called it "one of the most old-time music stations in the whole country." "There were a whole flock of us, we were on 24 hours a day, and anything you can think of doing, we'd just do it." Between 1927 and 1933 the station broadcast a wild Saturday night barn dance which went on till the wee hours and featured local talent and string bands. Three of the more important bands that appeared on this program were those headed by E.E. Hack, Ted Gossett, and Noble Carver.

The best known early string band in western Kentucky was

that of E.E. Hack. The band worked out of Central City, in Muhlenberg County, and most of its members worked in the mines around there. Hack himself, who was more of a manager than a musician, had earlier led a brass band in the area, and when string band music became fashionable in the mid-1920s he organized a large (eight- to nine-piece) string band. Virgil "Cricket" Garrett was the lead fiddler for the band, while Charlie Underwood (guitar) and Walter Cobb (tenor banjo) did much of the singing. In addition to a regular program over WFIW, the band played routinely at the big Selby Theater in Central City, and sponsored fiddling and string-band contests throughout the area. With its two fiddles, big "doghouse" string bass, and tenor (not five-string) banjo, the band had a strikingly different sound from many bands in the east; the repertoire featured a number of marches, rags, and waltzes, tune types quite different from those featured by mountain bands. (The Hack band, in this respect, was generally reflective of the western Kentucky string band style; other groups, such as the Green Brothers band from Henderson County, and the Madisonville String Band, used similar styles and repertoires.) Hack's band left a dozen records, made in 1929–1930, including the splendid "Western Kentucky Limited" (known in the area as "The Limit"), a tribute to a local L & N train. Hack himself later moved to Kansas City, where he died, but his musicians continued to perform in the area after the band's breakup in 1932. Walter Cobb, who later teamed with legendary guitarist Ike Everly, was still performing as recently as 1978 in Chicago.

The band led by Ted Gossett, also from Muhlenberg County, was tight, precise, and built around the fiddle, in some ways the antithesis of the Hack band. "The Fox Chasers," as they were called, were headed up by Graham native Gossett (born in 1904), and were known throughout the area for two "imitative" numbers Gossett played, "The Fox Chase" and "Wild Geese." Southern fiddlers for generations have delighted their audiences by doing imitations on the instrument—everything from a train to a mocking bird—and a fairly extensive repertory of these pieces exists in folk tradition. Most, however, have little musical substance; Gossett's, which he learned from a neighborhood fiddler named Charlie Jones, do, and the "effects" are deftly blended into a driving, elaborate melody. Some of the band's 1930 recordings remained in print for over ten years.

Two counties over from Gossett's territory, in Barren County, the band to beat in fiddle contests was that of the Carver Boys: brothers Noble and Warner Carver, along with their cousin Robert

Carver. The Carver clan had deep musical roots, and forbears of the Carver Boys, known as the Carver Brothers, played concerts and dances in central Kentucky and northern Tennessee in the early years of the century. Noble (born in Barren County in 1891) was later called "Uncle Bozo" and seems to have been the band's banjoist and sparkplug. When they recorded ten selections for Paramount in 1929 (as a lark) they became the first in their area to record, and the local people lapped up their records: a dealer at the Glasgow County Fair sold 1,400 of their records in one week. The tunes recorded included one of the first recorded versions of "Molly and Tenbrooks" (they called it "Tim Brooks," or at least that's what the company put on the label), a brace of fiddle tunes, and some sentimental songs like "The Brave Engineer" and the Burnett-Rutherford favorite "I'll Be with You When the Roses Bloom Again." On Halloween night in 1931 Noble and Warner left Kentucky to seek their fortunes in music. Like so many other aspiring musicians, they landed in Chicago, but found they had to pay a $105 fee to join the union before they could broadcast. This forced them to move on to Council Bluffs, Iowa, and Kansas City, Missouri, where they began successful radio careers. Warner eventually gave up, but Noble—"Bozo"—kept at it and eventually joined the Grand Ole Opry. In later years Bozo turned to life insurance and for a time sponsored his own show on radio "in order to advertise the policy that I was a sellin'." He also helped to get started the most famous of all the Carver clan, cousin Cynthia May, who became known nationally in the 1940s as Cousin Emmy.

As the 1920s drew to a close, other scattered musicians around Kentucky began to make tentative, isolated inroads into radio and recording. The Bird Family, probably from the Covington area, made several excellent recordings featuring twin mandolin work and soulful singing. Henry Bandy from Petroleum, an old-time fiddler, became one of the pioneers on the early Grand Ole Opry, and Blind Joe Mangrum (born in Paducah in 1853), a personal friend of Kentucky humorist Irvin S. Cobb, won fame on the Opry and in Henry Ford's fiddling contests. In the northern part of the state, Jimmie Johnson's String Band, featuring the fiddle of Andy Palmer, recorded and broadcast in the early 1930s. Pa and Ma McCormick from Boone County initiated a "Top O The Morning" show over WLW, Cincinnati, that ran from 1928 to 1933 and featured daily old-time music. The sister team of Jo and Alma Taylor, "the Kentucky Girls," probably the state's first successful female country singers, recorded rather extensively in the late

1920s and early 1930s and appeared regularly on Cincinnati radio. They were from the Barrens and specialized in close-harmony sentimental pieces like "Sweet Golden Daisies" and "Old and In the Way." But by and large the musicians in the state who wanted to professionalize their music were hampered by not having any really satisfactory locus for their operations. There was no real radio center and no recording center. Tennessee musicians had centers like Knoxville or Nashville, and Georgia musicians had Atlanta, where people serious about music could congregate, exchange ideas, develop a sense of identity. Kentucky musicians seemed to lack this throughout much of the 1920s, but as the Depression began to change forever the face of America, the musical focus was to sharpen in ways none of the fiddlers or singers could imagine.

3 The Radio Kids

DETROIT, 1933. The Great Depression was at its deepest point, some 75,000 people in the city were out of work, and a grim joke was circulating around the bread lines and union halls. "To crash a job at a plant, one man I know practiced up on the southern dialect and drawl, then presented himself at the factory gates. He was hired as soon as he opened his mouth." Nervous over ideas of unionism in their regular workers, the big auto companies had for months been chartering buses and bringing loads of young south-erners from Kentucky, Tennessee, even Alabama, into Detroit to work on the assembly lines at fifty cents an hour. By 1934 there were between 15,000 and 30,000 "hillbillies" in Detroit alone, with more coming. Nor was this case unusual; young workers were also fleeing to Indianapolis, Chicago, Pittsburgh, Cincinnati, and Cleveland, looking for work in manufacturing, looking for escape from their rural poverty and rocky farms. Kentucky was especially hard hit by this exodus. Between 1920 and 1930, over 188,000 of Kentucky's native white population left the state, a greater loss by far than any other southern state—in fact, it amounted to al-most 9 percent of the state's 1920 population. Another 83,000 left during the next ten years. Many of these people, of course, carried with them not only their "hillbilly drawl" that so irritated the auto workers, but their culture and values, as well. And part of that culture was their music.

A case in point was Joe Steen. Born about 1910 in the Ken-tucky Barrens, near Glasgow, Joe was the grandson of a local patriarch named Captain Jim Bybee. His mother, Molly, was the only girl in a family that included boys named Joe, Charley, Judge, and Doc, and the five of them were known throughout the area as a family string band. They carried their instruments to threshing bees as well as dances, and entertained into the night with "The Wreck of Number Nine," "Red Wing," and "The Ship That Never Returned." A friend recalled, "Even pious people who condemned them for their devil-may-care ways could not deny the power and charm of their music." Molly married Clay Steen, but he died young, leaving her with four children, ages two to twelve, to raise. Joe was one of those children. He learned to play the guitar and sing, and showed a special fondness for the records of America's "Blue Yodeller," Jimmie Rodgers. But he left home in 1928 to seek his fortune, looking for work that would provide a decent living and satisfy his interest in mechanics and aviation. He found it working for Henry Ford in Detroit, where he was to stay throughout the 1930s. He never gave up on his old-time music, though, and made a name for himself singing to other southern workers around the area, both in person and on the radio. He even recorded a few songs for Victor—they are rare collector's items today—including an original piece which he called "Kentucky, My Home":

> When I return to old Kentuck,
> I'll find my sweetheart there,
> My heart it yearns, I'm in good luck,
> She said for me she would care.
>
> I'll meet her in the garden 'neath the willow,
> I'll make love to her beneath the stars,
> The old Kentucky moon shines bright and mellow,
> I'm sorry now I ever roamed afar.
>
> And when she names the day, I'll be so happy,
> It's the same old story that's told o'er and o'er,
> We'll build a little cottage by the roadside,
> For my old Kentucky home I'll weep no more.

Awkward, full of sentiment, full of stale phrases though it is, the song, and many others like it, spoke for a generation of Kentuckians who found themselves in exile from their farms and homesteads and families. For them, and for generations to come, country music was to be a cherished link with this past, with their heritage, and with a way of life that many of them would never see again. Joe Steen, for instance, left WHAS in 1932 after being voted the most popular entertainer of the year there, and went to Detroit. In later years he formed a band and appeared as Jack West and the Golden West Cowboys; he worked for the Ford Motor Company until 1942, when he died from a childhood heart condition.

The medium for music in the cities was not the barn dance or the phonograph record but the radio. The Depression had wrecked the phonograph record industry; in 1931, the entire industry sold barely 10 million records, as opposed to 34 million in 1928. Many well-known performers saw their 1930–1931 releases sell as few as 500 copies, and the few who were serious about making a living in music sensed that radio was the only way to do it. By 1930 there were 14 million radio sets in the country—seven times as many as there had been just five years earlier—and over 600 stations; though many of these stations were beginning to affiliate with the newly-formed national networks (such as NBC or Columbia), there was still plenty of room in the daily schedule for local programming, especially in the early morning and at noon. Many stations were finding that the most popular type of local programming was country music. By 1935 there were some 5,000 different programs around the country that featured "hillbilly" music, and they generated an estimated $25 million a year in business. Of course, the musicians themselves got little of that; they struggled along on fifteen or thirty dollars a week, making their real money from personal appearances that they were allowed to plug on their radio shows. For many it was quite a grind; they did daily radio shows live and then got in their old cars to drive perhaps seventy-five miles along narrow highways to play a local schoolhouse or auditorium. After a couple of years of this, fans in the area would tire of them, the region would be "played out," and they would move on to another station and start all over again. In between, they tried to find time for their wives, their families, and a little fishing.

But much of this was not even possible for Kentucky musicians. In 1932 there were only five radio stations broadcasting in the state. In the southwest there was Hopkinsville's WFIW, which, as we have seen, was interested in old-time music but was licensed for only 1,000 watts; even less powerful was tiny 100-watt WPAD in Paducah. To the north, WCKY in Covington held forth at 5,000 watts, sponsoring an early barn dance program that for a time featured Riley Puckett. The state's powerhouse was WHAS, licensed at 25,000 watts and already an NBC affiliate; like many early radio stations, it was owned by the local newspaper, in this case the *Courier-Journal* and *Louisville Times*. Also in Louisville was tiny WLAP, broadcasting at 250 watts. (The station later moved to Lexington.) Many Kentuckians listened to other stations, of course; Grandpa Jones, growing up in Niagra, liked WOS in Jefferson City, Missouri; along the southern border listeners tuned in to WSM and the "Grand Ole Opry"; stations in Cincinnati and Charleston, West Virginia, appealed to people in the northern and eastern parts of the state. But the station that seemed to have the most influence was the powerhouse station WLS in Chicago, a 50,000-watt station owned by Sears-Roebuck Company. And it was from that station that Kentucky musicians established their dominance of country music in the 1930s.

A week after it went on the air in April 1924, WLS started a barn dance program, inspired by the success of an earlier show over WOS in Jefferson City, Missouri. At first the show featured as much old pop and sentimental tunes as genuine folk songs or country music, but through the efforts of several Kentucky musicians this was to change. Walter Peterson, who billed himself as "The Kentucky Wonder Bean," played guitar and rigged up a rack to hold his harmonica while he sang songs like "The Boston Burglar" and "The Farmer Is the Man Who Feeds Them All." Chubby Parker, a moon-faced young man from Kentucky, played the banjo and delivered nonsense songs like "Nickety, Nackety, Now, Now, Now" (derived from a British ballad some 200 years old), "Bib-A-Lollie-Boo," and a version of "Frog Went a-Courtin'" called "King Kong Kitchie Ki-me-o." Next to the Grand Ole Opry's Uncle Dave Macon, Chubby Parker was the best known comic banjoist of his day. He is best remembered for his version of the old Will Hays song that Chubby called "The Little Old Sod Shanty on the Plains." Parker left WLS abruptly in 1926, reportedly upset at the greater success young Bradley Kincaid was having with the same kind of material. Attempts to document his later career have proven fruitless, except for a report that he was working in some sort of non-music business in Chicago in the 1930s.

A third Kentuckian, the one who was to have greatest impact on the show, originally came to the station as part of a YMCA quartet in 1926. Bradley Kincaid was no farm boy, trooping into the studio in overalls and high-top shoes, but a neatly dressed, bespectacled young man in a bow tie and suit who had been singing with the quartet at Chicago area luncheon clubs and conventions. The quartet manager made Bradley go to the WLS music director and tell him that he knew some of the "old folk songs" that the Barn Dance specialized in. "Well," the manager, Don

Malin, replied, "how would you like to come down and sing a few of them on the Barn Dance on Saturday night?" It meant fifteen dollars for Bradley, so he went out and borrowed a guitar, practiced up on a few chords, and appeared before the microphones Saturday night singing "Barbara Allen" and a few other old-time standards he had learned as a boy. "They were so impressed that they asked me to be on their regular staff for $15 every Saturday night," recalled Bradley later. "Well, for a college student that had donuts and coffee for breakfast, that was pretty good." His clear, warm tenor and straightforward delivery also appealed to listeners. "One day after I'd been singing there for three or four weeks, I went down one Saturday afternoon a little early, and the girl at the outer desk said, 'Bradley, there's some mail back there in the back room for you.' Well, it never occurred to me that anyone would ever write and say anything about Bradley Kincaid. I went back there. You've seen these big laundry baskets about the size of a desk? Here was this basket full of fan mail. I took all I could carry home with me, and everywhere I read where they said, 'You're the best singer on the air.'"

Bradley had been born some thirty-one years earlier, in 1895, near the Cumberland foothill town of Lancaster, just a county away from the farms of Dennis Taylor and Doc Roberts, and just eighteen miles from Berea College. His father, William Kincaid, led singing in the Campbellite church, reading with ease from the old shape-note songbooks and getting his pitch by striking a tuning fork. In his spare time he liked to sing songs like "After the Ball" from the gay 90s. Bradley's mother, Elizabeth Hurt Kincaid, sang too, but, Bradley recalls, "she went farther back. She sang the old English ballads. I learned a lot of ballads from her, like 'Fair Ellender,' 'The Two Sisters,' and any number of English ballads. . . . My mother never did show too much musical ability, though she used to—in a very lamentable voice—sing some of the old blood curdlers to me, and my hair would stand straight up on my head." Later Bradley guessed that he had learned as many as eighty old songs while he was growing up. Most of these songs were performed unaccompanied, until the day when Bradley's father, an ardent fox hunter, traded one of his old fox hounds to a Negro friend for an old dilapidated guitar. It was the first musical instrument in the Kincaid family (Bradley had nine siblings), and Bradley soon learned how to strum it as he sang. In later years he would make much of his "Hound Dog Guitar" and Sears would give the name to a cheap copy which was sold by the thousands throughout the South and Midwest. In fact, there would come a time when Bradley, going deep into the mountains to hunt up new songs, would be amazed to find one of his informants proudly holding a "Hound Dog Guitar."

As a teenager Bradley tried a little farming and seemed destined to lead the life of an average hill country boy at that time. But one summer, after working hard to harvest a crop of tobacco, he figured up that he had made only forty dollars for his year's work. A religious experience also caused him to want to make something of himself, and he enrolled in Berea College in 1914. There he worked toward his high school degree and gained his first inkling of the history of the old ballads he knew by working with pioneer collector John F. Smith. He also got some formal musical training and fell in love with his music teacher, Irma Foreman, a native of Brooklyn, New York. They were married in 1922 and two years later moved to Chicago, where Irma worked for the YMCA and Bradley began attending YMCA College (later George Williams College) at night. It was at this point that he auditioned for WLS.

Within months, Bradley became the most popular figure on the "Barn Dance." The fan mail continued, and booking agents began to call wanting to put him on the stage in the area. On the first of these personal appearances, in Peoria, Illinois, Bradley arrived to find a line of people several blocks long trying to get into the theater. "That radio singer from WLS is going to be here," a man told him. While he made only $15 a night on the Barn Dance, he found he could get $300 for a personal appearance. He began to think he might make a living out of his singing. He also began to print up little songbooks, which he could sell by mail and at theater doors for fifty cents each. His first book, published in 1928, sold over 100,000 copies, and from 1929 to 1934 he issued five other songbooks.

These songbooks offer interesting clues to Bradley's popularity, and to the "image" he was, consciously or subconsciously, presenting to his public. This is important, for many listeners today, hearing the old records Bradley made in the late 1920s, cannot understand his appeal. The singing on these records seems to modern ears rather stiff and formal, containing little of the expressiveness heard in Buell Kazee's or B.F. Shelton's best work. The records, of course, capture none of Bradley's "personality"; he is not heard introducing the songs, chatting with his listeners, speaking with sincerity and conviction about his family and his home. He wrote in one of his later songbooks: "When I sing for you on the air, I always visualize you, a family group, sitting around the table or the radio, listening and commenting on my program. Some of you have written in and said that I seem to be talking right to you, and I am. If I did not feel your presence, though you be a thousand miles away, the radio would be cold and unresponsive to me, and I in turn would sound the same way to you." His simple style also allowed listeners to hear the words of the old songs he sang, and his rather formal enunciation made it easy for listeners in the Midwest and East to understand him. His manner might have been a step removed from the genuine mountain singing style of eastern Kentucky, but it made the songs far more accessible to a wide audience than they would have been had B.F. Shelton or Dick Burnett wandered into the WLS studio. Even the distinguished Burridge Butler, publisher of the *Prairie Farmer*, which came to own WLS, admitted that "when I hear Bradley sing on WLS I drop my book and listen. . . . After a busy day his songs bring to mind the beauty and restful charm of his Kentucky mountains. . . . His work on the radio is an inspiration to the farm boys and girls."

The image also involved emphasizing the "folk" quality of the songs Bradley sang. His 1929 songbook, for instance, contained no less than four separate introductions by various people, including Berea folk song collector John F. Smith, all stressing the authenticity of Bradley's songs and their uniqueness in the so-called "Jazz Age." Smith wrote: "In these days of made-to-order music it is refreshing to be able to hear the songs that come direct from the soil and which still lie close to the hearts of the singers. . . . Many of these songs and ballads were brought by our pioneer forefathers from their homelands across the sea, where they had long been sung as an expression of the souls of a rugged people." As Bradley's popularity began to exhaust his repertoire, he began to spend his vacations combing the mountains for other songs, making collecting trips not only to eastern Kentucky but to north Georgia and North Carolina. He printed photos from these trips in his 1930 songbook, where readers saw a smartly dressed Kincaid, with tie, straw hat, glasses, and two-tone shoes sitting on the porch next to a mountain fiddler in overalls and old leggins.

In truth, Bradley's repertoire in these early years was almost entirely composed of genuine traditional songs; his first songbook contained "Barbara Allen," which became his most popular piece, a song whose pedigree extends back to the England of 1666, where it is mentioned in Boswell's *Journal.* (It was so popular, in fact, that Bradley reputedly sang it every Saturday night for four years on "The National Barn Dance.") Others included some favorite

Kentucky songs like "Pearl Bryan," "The Hunters of Kentucky," and "The Fatal Derby Day," as well as English ballads like "The House Carpenter" (Child #243), "Two Sisters" (Child #10), and "Fair Ellen" (Child #73). At personal appearances Bradley liked to do comedy songs that would "get the audience stirred up," and pieces like "Liza Up a Simmon Tree," "The Little Shirt My Mother Made for Me," "I Was Born Four Thousand Years Ago," and "Gooseberry Pie" became favorites. Even those were old, if a bit updated. And, to his credit, Bradley did not abandon these old songs as his career continued to flourish.

And flourish it did. In 1928 he began recording his old songs, with fair success. Sears ran a special section in their catalogue for records by "The Kentucky Mountain Boy" and sold hundreds by mail. By the end of 1930 he had recorded some sixty-two songs on a variety of labels. Still, however, he considered himself a "radio artist," and while he continued to record prolifically through 1934, his real success was on radio. In the 1934 *Radio Guide* "Star Poll," conducted on a nationwide basis, Bradley was the only male country singer to even place on this list, and while he got nowhere near as many votes as Bing Crosby, he did outpoint other pop music legends like Al Jolson and Gene Austin.

By this time Bradley had left WLS, and from 1930 to 1941 began a dizzying round-robin series of one-year stays at radio stations in the east: WKDA (Pittsburgh), WGY (Schenectady), WEAF (New York), and finally WBZ in Boston. Here he continued to do the same kind of "mountain songs" he had done in Chicago, with the same kind of success. One of the young apprentice musicians who worked with him, Marshall (Grandpa) Jones, recalled of his Boston years: "They say that people in the East didn't appreciate country music until just the last few years here, but the people in those small New England towns were as crazy about it as anybody in Kentucky or Tennessee. Lots of times up there after a show people would even invite us home to take supper with them."

Bradley continued to remain a major draw in professional country music throughout the 1940s, doing successful stints at WLW and even for a time at WSM Nashville's Grand Ole Opry. He weathered the new and different fads in country music, the blue yodels of Jimmie Rodgers, the western swing of Bob Wills, the honky-tonk songs of Ted Daffan, and continued to sing what his songbooks described as "mountain ballads and old-time songs." In the late 1940s he made a couple of tentative inroads into country music, writing and recording songs like "The Legend of the Robin

Red Breast" (1945) and "Brush the Dust from That Old Bible" (1950), a topical song about the atomic bomb. But he chose to retire in 1950 and run a music store rather than compete in the Nashville hit market. In 1963 he recorded 162 songs for the Bluebonnet Recording Company of Ft. Worth, a sort of "collected works of Bradley Kincaid," but the company soon went bankrupt and the records are unavailable today. In later years Bradley often returned to his alma mater, Berea College, to participate in folk festivals and to talk with students of his music.

Though Bradley Kincaid became the most famous of Kentucky's old-time singers, it was an ironic twist that hardly any of his extensive radio career was spent broadcasting over Kentucky stations, and that his many fans in the state had to settle for hearing him over WLS or the NBC network from WEAF or from the Grand Ole Opry. Yet this was to be the pattern for the next decade, as other Kentucky musicians carried their rich native music outside the state and broadcast it to an increasingly large national and even international audience.

Though he was at WLS only four years, Bradley Kincaid generated an interest at the station in genuine folk music and in its commercial potential. A key man in developing this interest was another Kentuckian, John Lair, who had come to the station in 1927 as a program director and later as the music librarian. Lair had a genuine interest in old songs, and considerable first-hand knowledge of them; within a few years he was writing a monthly column about them for the WLS magazine *Stand By*, a column in which he traced the histories of old songs and printed different variants sent in by readers. By 1936, WLS publicity was referring to him as an "outstanding authority on American folk music," which was not much of an exaggeration. But Lair also influenced the music on the station in more direct ways.

Lair had been born in 1894 in Livingston, Kentucky, in a valley near the junctions of the Big and Little Renfro creeks. Though Lair was never highly skilled as a musician, he organized neighborhood string bands as a child, usually in secret because his grandfather, an old southern judge, believed that "There's no good in a man who plays the fiddle or parts his hair in the middle." (To his credit, Lair never did the latter.) Young Lair did his hitch in World War I and came back to run the family farm for a time. Discouraged at the way his valley was being modernized, he left for the North and eventually found his way to an art institute at Battle Creek, Michigan. After a stint at other odd jobs, he came to WLS. Once established, he began to import into the WLS "Barn Dance" an imposing array of musicians from his native Renfro

Valley area. Most of these musicians were formed into a string band called the Cumberland Ridge Runners. Though the band went through several early personnel changes, it eventually stabilized to include Linda Parker, a young vocalist born in Covington, Kentucky, but reared in Indiana; Karl Davis and Hartford Taylor, a guitar-mandolin duo from Mt. Vernon, Kentucky; Red Foley, from Bluelick, Kentucky, then a twenty-year-old youth playing the bass fiddle and occasionally singing; Doc Hopkins, a guitarist and vocalist born in Harlan County but reared in Renfro Valley; and Homer "Slim" Miller, a fiddler who was born in Lisbon, Indiana, but reared in Renfro Valley. The only member who had not grown up playing Kentucky music was Hugh Cross from Oliver Springs, Tennessee. Lair was the leader and announcer for the group, and occasionally played the harmonica or jug.

It was a young, spirited group—Lair was about the only member over thirty—and it soon became the favorite band on the "Barn Dance" in the early 1930s. Though the publicity photos of the time show the crew dressed in stylized "hillbilly" costumes and sitting on bales of straw, the members were not exactly fresh from the mountains. Hopkins had had ten years' experience working with medicine shows, wandering around the country and playing Hawaiian music. Cross had worked with Riley Puckett and the Skillet Lickers in Georgia, as well as other Tennessee acts. Karl and Harty had appeared on WHAS in Louisville. Possibly because of this, the Cumberland Ridge Runners served as one of the most successful training schools in country music history; almost every one of its members later went on to stardom in his own right. This is reflected in the recordings the band made; there were only forty-two of them, done between 1933 and 1935, but of these only six really feature the overall band. The rest feature various members of the band doing specialties, backed by the Cumberland Ridge Runners. The band itself featured instrumentals like "Goofus" and "shout tunes" like "Ole Rattler" (later to be immortalized by Grandpa Jones); young Red Foley did things like "I Traced Her Little Footsteps in the Snow," later a favorite with Bill Monroe; Linda Parker sang "Take Me Back to Renfro Valley" and "I'll Be All Smiles Tonight"; and Karl and Harty specialized in close harmony duets of old sacred and sentimental songs.

Karl Davis (1905-1979) and Harty Taylor (1905-1963) grew up together in Mount Vernon. Harty, whose real name was Hartford Connecticut Taylor,* grew up listening to the mountain

---

*In later years John Lair delighted in telling audiences the story of how Harty got his name. "Harty's Uncle John Taylor was a blacksmith, and

musicians who would come into their town—the county seat—on Saturday to shop or attend court; one in particular was a big bare-foot man named Willie St. John, who played the five-string banjo and sang "I'm As Free a Little Bird As I Can Be." The boys also learned songs from their folks, and from a man named Brag Thompson, who played "mood music" on an old piano for the town's silent movies. Karl began to play mandolin, Harty guitar, in private because they were so shy; "I had a $10 catalogue mando-lin, and Harty had a $12 catalogue guitar," recalled Karl. After they graduated from high school, the boys joined with Doc Hop-kins to form the Kentucky Krazy Kats, a string band that per-formed as early as 1929 over WHAS in Louisville. It was a unique band, though, because it was also part of a basketball team that would barnstorm the state, play a local team, and then during the half go out into center court and entertain the fans with string band versions of 1920s favorites like "Five Foot Two." "We would dress in these Spanish costumes," Karl recalled, "and I remember how hard it was to have to put that costume on right over my basketball uniform after we had been playing for a half hour."

In 1930 Bradley Kincaid got the boys to WLS, where they became members of Lair's group and were featured on the early morning farm program as well as the "Barn Dance." They soon found that the daily radio grind devoured repertoire, and they began to hunt out more songs. Their methods make an interesting case history of how old traditional songs got into the mass media. "The first thing I did," said Karl, "was to write my mother and have her go see some of the people we had known from back in the hills and get some of their songs." Another source for them was the old records by The Carter Family. "I bet we used 50 of their songs. They were a great source for real authentic, colorful songs with a punch, with beautiful melodies, and we would go to the Montgomery Wards catalogue store here and order their Blue-bird records." Still another source was the old gospel songbooks that their families had used; they would take the old songs written in shape notes and designed for quartets or congregations, and turn them into haunting duets. Two of these were songs by James D. Vaughan, the Tennessee publisher who helped popularize the idea of the gospel quartet, and they became two of the team's

he ordered all of his horseshoe nails and supplies from this place in Hartford, Connecticut. The night he was born, his father looked up at the wall and saw a calendar there from this company, with the name and address, and said, 'We'll call him Hartford Connecticut.' It's a good thing he didn't look over at the opposite wall, cause there was a calendar there from Lydia Pinkham."

biggest hits when recorded in 1934 and 1936: "I Dreamed I
Searched Heaven for You" and "I Need the Prayers of Those I
Love." But their best source of songs was ultimately to be themselves. In 1933, after driving the WLS minister up to Madison,
Wisconsin, Karl thought up the words and music to "I'm Here to
Get My Baby Out of Jail." For years after, this remained their
most popular song, and their 1934 recording of it was imitated by
almost every country duet in the nation. As recently as the 1950s,
when Karl met George Gobel, a former "Barn Dance" star who
had made it big in Hollywood, Gobel greeted him by singing the
first line of the song.

Karl and Harty were also in the vanguard of the singing style
which was to dominate all of country music in the 1930s: the
close harmony duet style. The new carbon microphone technology
had made it possible to sing softly and still be heard both on radio
and in theaters; the older mountain shouting style was now no
longer necessary. Usually with mandolin and guitar accompaniment, groups like the Blue Sky Boys, the Callahan Brothers, the
Monroe Brothers, and the Delmore Brothers quickly established
themselves as favorites of a generation. But Karl and Harty were
among the first and best of this new breed, and their songs can be
seen in the repertoires of nearly all the others. Harty's tenor and
Karl's lead graced hundreds of programs on the WLS "Barn Dance"
and, after 1937, on rival Chicago station WJJD's "Suppertime
Frolic." They appealed not only to southerners and rural mid-
westerners, but to Finns from Wisconsin, Indians from Michigan's
upper peninsula, and Pennsylvania Dutch.

In the mid-1940s the pair became victims of changing times.
The record companies were now concentrating more on the juke-
box market than on home sales, and they encouraged Karl and
Harty to start doing more modern "honky-tonk songs" like
"Seven Beers with the Wrong Woman," "Don't Mix Whiskey with
Women," and "Blondes, Brunettes, and Redheads." Karl recalled:
"I remember once we were in Henderson, Kentucky, and we
walked down the street and we heard our records—I think, 'Don't
Mix Whiskey with Women'—coming out of a couple of places that
were kind of wild. Well, that's what we had turned to, but on the
air our best songs were things like 'Read the Bible' and 'Wreck on
the Highway,' those good old substantial religious and sentimental
songs." The gap between their records and their radio shows became greater. "We were like Dr. Jekyll and Mr. Hyde, and we
didn't much like that either." In the 1950s, as live radio declined
and country music in Chicago died out, Karl and Harty gracefully

retired from performing, though Karl continued to be a successful
songwriter and to see his works recorded by people like Emmylou
Harris and Linda Ronstadt. At the end, Harty was working as a
toll-gate collector and Karl was a "record turner" for WLS.

It was during the trying times of the 1940s that Karl wrote his
most famous and enduring song: "Kentucky" (1941). "I wrote the
song as a tribute to my home state," Karl said simply, but it
became much more than that.

> Kentucky, you are the dearest land outside of Heaven to me,
> Kentucky, your laurel and your redbud trees,
> When I die, I want to rest upon a graceful mountain so high,
> For that is where God will look for me."

Karl and Harty recorded the song first in January 1941 for the
Columbia label, and the record was especially popular with lonely
southern servicemen who found themselves thousands of miles
from the land they loved. But in 1947 the Blue Sky Boys (the
Bolick Brothers) recorded the song, and it really became a best-
seller, reportedly running up sales of almost half a million copies;
it has since been recorded by dozens of country singers, including
later Kentucky groups like the Osborne Brothers and the Everly
Brothers. On the strength of its beauty, and its popularity, Karl
Davis was made a Kentucky Colonel in 1970. It was one of the
few tokens of recognition he received in later life for his immense
contributions to country music.

Just as Kentucky singers made their names in other parts of
the country, so did Kentucky string bands. The most successful of
these was the Prairie Ramblers, who emerged to become the most
popular country music ensemble of the 1930s and a fixture on
Chicago station WLS for some twenty years. Whereas many singers
found they had to simplify the vocal styles they brought out of
Kentucky in order to achieve commercial success, the Ramblers
did quite the opposite: they took the older string band square-
dance style, added sophisticated elements like take-off solos and
key changes, and adapted the style to pop styles of the day. The
result was a delightful mixture of playing and singing that found
favor from New York to Hollywood.

The two men who formed the keystone of the Prairie
Ramblers, and who were to remain with the group through all its
years, were Charles "Chick" Hurt (1901-1967) and Jack Taylor
(*ca.* 1900-1962). Chick, the mandolin player, was born in

Summershade, Kentucky, near Glasgow, into a musical family that taught and encouraged him. As a young man, Chick moved with his family to Kewanne, Illinois, where he organized his first band. A few years later, though, he got together with Jack Taylor, who had been a neighbor and childhood friend, and two other boys from the same western Kentucky region, to form the first version of the Prairie Ramblers, then called the Kentucky Ramblers. The other two members were Shelby David "Tex" Atchison, a fiddler and later lead vocalist, who was born in 1912 near Rosine in Ohio County, on a farm adjoining that owned by Bill Monroe's father, and Floyd "Salty" Holmes, a harmonica and jug player from the same area. The band's first radio job was on WOC in Davenport, Iowa, in 1931 or 1932, but in the fall of 1932 they moved to Chicago, where they began appearing on the WLS "Merry-Go-Round" and later the "National Barn Dance."

In December 1933, the band, now known as the Prairie Ramblers, made their first recordings in a session for Victor's new low-priced Bluebird label. There is still much of the old-time Kentucky string band feeling on these records, which included several blues, traditional songs like "Shady Grove" and "Gonna Have a Feast Here Tonight," fiddle breakdowns like "Tex's Dance" and "Blue River," and early versions of two songs that were to become Ramblers' standards, "Rollin' On," and "D Blues." The latter was a showcase for Chick's dazzling mandolin work—some of the first really dexterous mandolin solos on record.* By this time the band had also met and joined forces with a young western singer from Arkansas, Rubye Blevins, who was soon to become known as Patsy Montana and was to establish herself as the first real national female country singing star. She joined the Ramblers in this first session, recording the original version of one of her western hits, "Montana Plains."

In 1934 the Ramblers took a temporary leave of absence from WLS and moved to New York, where they appeared for six months over WOR, with Hal O'Halloran as their emcee. This sojourn in New York was to become crucial in the band's development. "We left Chicago as an old-time string band," recalls Tex Atchison, "and we came back from New York as a cowboy band." The New York stay fully exposed the band to pop and swing music, and especially to the pop-styled cowboy songs that were

---

*Hurt actually played a mandola, larger than a regular mandolin and with a deeper, richer tone.

starting to sweep the country. Never really a naive or archaic band, the individual Ramblers had always had some interest in pop music, and their immense instrumental and vocal talent was still pliable enough to be molded into new forms—forms that would win them far more popularity than their older style would have. They also began recording for the American Record Company, one of the country's largest, and one which supplied records to Sears and Wards for catalogue sales. These first sessions were still full of hot string band stuff like "Lefty's Breakdown" and "Jug Rag," but the band began to find that their slower, sentimental songs featuring their smooth close-harmony singing were selling better. They had their biggest hit with one such sweet number, "Nobody's Darling But Mine," an old song that had been re-worked by country singer Jimmie Davis, but pop pieces like "That Old Town of Mine," "Isle of Capri," and "When I Grow Too Old to Dream" were about as popular with their wide, diverse audiences. While in New York they also recorded as the back-up band for some of the most popular Gene Autry records, including "Tumbling Tumbleweeds" and "Old Faithful," as well as "That Silver Haired Daddy of Mine," Autry's greatest early hit.

By the end of 1936 the group had recorded almost 100 songs, and their repertoire was gradually shifting away from the tough instrumental blues and fiddle breakdowns to the smoother sounds of cowboy music—or at least the popular cowboy music so much in vogue then. In fact, "Riding Down the Canyon" became the band's theme, and publicity poses made after their return from New York to WLS showed them in western garb; at state fair appearances throughout the midwest they appeared on horseback, waving their hats to the fans. They continued to use some of the old Kentucky folk songs they knew as kids—"Beaver Creek" is their version of the old Chubby Parker nonsense song "King Kong Kitchee Ki-me-o," and "Sugar Hill" is a redaction of an old banjo tune—but they added smooth complex harmonies to the vocals, and even on occasion drums and a hot piano solo. They also successfully added many old sacred songs to their repertoire, and actually had hits with "This World Is Not My Home" and "How Beautiful Heaven Must Be." On the other hand, they were persuaded to record a series of off-color songs, such as "There's a Man who Comes to Our House" (1937) and "Sweet Violets" (1935), which came out under the pseudonum the Sweet Violet Boys. Hurt recalled that the band sought to disguise their sound on these records by featuring the clarinet and vocals of Bill "Willie" Thawl—features they did not use on their radio or personal appearances—but that the identity of the Sweet Violet Boys was an open secret. In fact, the record company once even issued a record with the Prairie Ramblers' name on one side and the Sweet Violet Boys listed on the other. Bob Miller, the famous Memphis-born songwriter who played piano for the Ramblers on many recordings, authored several of the off-color Sweet Violet Boys songs and joined in the attempted deception by copyrighting the songs under what is perhaps the most transparent of pseudonyms, Trebor Rellim.

In 1938 Tex Atchison, the popular lead singer and left-handed fiddler, left the band to go to California. There he continued to perform with Jimmy Wakeley and his band on the CBS "Hollywood Barn Dance" during World War II, and with other west coast stars such as cowboy singer Ray Whitley, western swing star Spade Cooley, and fellow Kentuckian Merle Travis. He appeared in over thirty singing cowboy films, often with Charles Starret. From 1949 to 1960 he was on the staff of KXLA in Los Angeles, and recorded for several labels under his own name, having hits with "Somebody's Rose" (1947) and "Tennessee Hound Dog" (1964). Among the songs he has written are "Sleepy-Eyed John" (1961), probably based on an old Kentucky fiddle tune but recorded by Johnny Horton and accepted today as a bluegrass standard, and "Sick, Sober, and Sorry" (1951). He retired to his native Rosine about 1975, but continued to appear at local fiddlers' contests (he had won the Kentucky championship in 1933), where he astounded young musicians with his skill and his ability to play left-handed on a regular "right-hand" fiddle.

About the same time, Salty Holmes temporarily left the band and Hurt had to find two replacements. "They always went back down to Kentucky to get their replacements," Hurt's daughter recalls. "They wanted to try to get someone from their old home base if they could." To replace Salty they chose Kenneth Houchens, a singer and guitarist who had earlier recorded for Gennett; to replace Tex they chose Alan Crockett, a brilliant young fiddler then living in California. Alan Crockett was formerly a member of Crockett's Kentucky Mountaineers. Though Alan left few recordings of his fiddle style, some transcriptions made in 1944 feature him in several tunes playing in a lean, modernistic style that was years ahead of its time. He took his own life in 1947.

In the early 1940s the band modernized even more and now established a major national act with an audience as much urban as rural. An accordion (played by Augie Kline) was added, and jazz guitarist George Barnes added his electric guitar to the outfit. Ralph "Rusty" Gill, one of the WLS Hoosier Sod Busters, joined in 1941, about the time that Patsy Montana left to go out completely on her own. By the end of the war the band was doing all kinds of material, including forgetable topical pieces like "Have a Heart, Taft Hartley," and was demonstrating the truth of one of their other songs, "You Ain't Got No Hillbilly Anymore." Chick and Jack Taylor continued to job around Chicago after the Ramblers broke up, appearing in one of their last jobs as the backup for Stan Wallowick and his Polka Chips. It had been a long road from Summershade.

Many of the new radio stars from Kentucky were quite young—most were in their twenties—but none was as young as the state's premier child star of the 1930s, Little Jimmy Sizemore. Americans have always been fond of child performers (especially if they were presented with their families), and just as little Shirley Temple won the hearts of the movie public in the 1930s, Little Jimmy won the hearts of the country music radio fans. Thousands of listeners can still remember sitting in their front rooms on an early evening in 1936 and picking up the transcribed "Asher and Little Jimmy Program":

> *Theme song* (sung by Asher and Little Jimmy): Way down in old Kentucky, where skies are never gray . . .
> *Announcer:* Once again, ladies and gentlemen, the familiar strains of "Memories of Old Kentucky" is your invitation to set aside fifteen minutes and join in a transcribed meeting with Asher and Little Jimmy, the singing Sizemores. Mother and dad have been about their usual duties of the home and family, but little Jimmy and his younger brother Buddy have had a day of fun and frolic. But now we see them ready to greet all their friends by way of your loudspeaker.
> *Theme song* (concludes): Kentucky, I love you today.
> *Asher:* Hello, everyone, mighty happy to be here. And right here he is, little Jimmy boy.
> *Jimmy:* Hello, everybody. Hope everybody's feeling fine.
> *Asher:* Hope everybody's feeling fine. Well, it wouldn't be little Jim if it didn't hope everybody's feeling fine.

Much of Little Jimmy's success came from the fertile brain of his father Asher Sizemore (1906–*ca.* 1973), a pleasant if undistinguished singer who was one of the great innovators in country music promotion. He was quick to follow Bradley Kincaid's lead in pioneering the use of paperback songbooks to sell over the air (in his long career he produced about as many as Kincaid), and through a complex system of "leasing wires" and cutting entire fifteen-minute programs onto large 16-inch transcription discs, Asher was able to syndicate his programs throughout the South and Midwest. He also watched his copyrights on songs carefully, and worked to place songs he owned or published with other acts, such as Frankie Moore's Log Cabin Boys.

Asher was a genuine eastern Kentucky product, born in Manchester and working in his youth as a bookkeeper for a coal mining company in Pike County. He married Odessa Foley, the daughter of a minister, and their first son, Jimmy, was born in 1928 at Paintsville, on the Big Sandy River. By 1931 Asher himself, singing old-time songs and cowboy ballads, had a radio show in Huntington, West Virginia, then on WCKY Cincinnati, and finally on WHAS Louisville. By 1933 five-year-old Jimmy had joined him, and the duo was splitting its time between the WSM "Grand Ole Opry" and WHAS Louisville. Little Jimmy soon developed a repertoire of radio favorites including "The Booger Bear," "Chewing Gum," "Has Anybody Seen My Kitty?" "My Little Rooster," and the old Sunday school favorite, "Little Feet." Little Jimmy actually had a hit record of sorts in 1934 when he recorded "Little Jimmy's Goodbye to Jimmie Rodgers" for Bluebird.

By the time Jimmy was five, his father boasted that "he can sing from memory more than two hundred songs and there are numerous others that he can join in with dad on the chorus." In some of the publicity, Asher also reported that "After each engagement Little Jimmy always asks the question, 'Dad, how much dough did we make tonight?'" George Hay, announcer and founding father of the "Grand Ole Opry," was not used to seeing so young a child enter upon so professional a career, and worried "for fear the emotional strain would be too much for Jimmy." Little Jimmy survived quite well, though, and by the late 1930s the act had expanded to include his younger brother, Buddy. For a time the group was on the NBC network, and in the 1940s worked successfully in the Midwest. By 1950 they were back in Louisville, at WKLO, with Asher's daughter Nancy Louise added to the show; both Jimmy and Buddy served in the army in the Korean War, but Buddy was lost in action in November 1950. In later years both Asher and Little Jimmy moved to Arkansas, to work in radio, and Jimmy still lives there today.

By the early 1930s it was possible for performers to work from a musical base that depended less on a folk tradition than on a commercial country music tradition. One of the first Kentuckians to do this was Cliff Carlisle, whose extensive work on radio and records from 1930 to 1950 made him one of the most visible country singers in the nation. For a time Carlisle was the heir apparent to the mantle of Jimmie Rodgers, whose premature death in 1933 had robbed country music of its first national star. Later Carlisle's career took more complex turns as he sought to merge a variety of styles into his work and to create a music that was among the most distinctive in country music history.

Like many early string band professionals, Cliff began his career playing Hawaiian music. When he was growing up in Spencer County, Kentucky, where he was born near Mt. Eden in 1904, Hawaiian music was a national craze. Guitarists like Sol Hoopi and Frank Ferera made early records that had a wide appeal, especially in the South. "I always did like the Hawaiian steel guitar," recalled Carlisle. "I bought every record of this instrument I could get, and I played them until they scratched so badly you couldn't hear them." Unlike many guitarists who played Hawaiian style, Carlisle did not start out playing standard guitar; early in his career he inserted a steel nut under the strings of his little Sears guitar, and he liked the sound so well that he never tried to play any other way. He became, in the words of his discographer, Gene Earle, "one of the few artists to successfully use the steel guitar as a solo accompanying instrument."

By 1920, when Cliff was sixteen, he had teamed up with another guitarist and singer, Wilbur Ball, a Louisville native who worked at the construction trade. For the next ten years these two toured with various vaudeville groups and travelling tent shows, including the Continental Red Path Chautauquas, the B.F. Keith shows, and Happy Roy's Company. When they were in the South, Carlisle and Ball would do a sort of "hillbilly" show; in northern states, where country songs were less appreciated, they would do an all-Hawaiian show, wearing white costumes with leis around their necks. As radio began to grow, the two turned to that medium, and as "The Lullaby Larkers" landed a spot on Louisville's WHAS in 1930.

It was the heyday of Jimmie Rodgers, and young men all over the South were trying to copy Rodgers's songs and style; it was a style that merged three-line blues stanzas and vague double entendre with a high, clear "blue yodel." Cliff found that he was especially adept at this sort of thing, and when he made his trip to the Starr Piano Company studios in Richmond, Indiana, to try out for Gennett Records, he delighted Manager L.A. Butt with his Rodgers imitation. Rodgers was so popular and was selling so many records for Victor that rival record companies were stumbling over themselves to find someone with the Rodgers sound. Yodelling itself was so popular that some companies were putting on record labels legends like "Singing with Guitar and Yodel," suspecting that a good many customers only wanted songs featuring yodels. In Cliff Carlisle, Gennett felt they had a premier Rodgers clone, and by the end of 1930 Carlisle and Ball had recorded sixteen songs, almost all of them cover versions of Rodgers's hits like "T for Texas" and "Desert Blues." (A year later, Cliff and Ball actually backed Rodgers on two of his 1931 Louisville recordings.)

It wasn't long before Carlisle began to find his own style. A 1932 record advertisement bills him as "The Yodellin' Hobo" and describes his latest releases as "new song stories." A few of Cliff's new songs were traditional ballads, such as "Shot the Innocent Man" (1938), about a Madison County murder, but most were pithy vignettes describing modern rough-and-tumble working-class life. "Seven Years with the Wrong Woman" (1932), one of his first non-Rodgers hits, was one of the first country songs to deal forthrightly with divorce, and his biggest hit, "Pay Day Fight" (1937), described a husband and wife assaulting each other over who got the pay envelope. "The Hobo's Fate" was an effective commentary on hobo life, and "Wildcat Woman and a Tomcat Man" (1936) is a blow-by-blow account of a domestic brawl. While he continued throughout the 1930s to sing about hobos—a subject he and thousands of other American men during the Depression had had some experience with—his real specialty during this period was the risqué, double-entendre blues song. Jimmie Rodgers had recorded items like "High Powered Mama" and "Let Me Be Your Side Track" a few years earlier, but Carlisle took this style several steps further. As a boy he had heard black guitar players near the courthouse in Taylorsville, Kentucky, and now found ways to utilize these ideas. "My music," he said later, "is a cross between hillbilly and blues—even Hawaiian music has sort of blues to it."

At first the sexual innuendo in Carlisle's songs was masked by animal references—a well-worn technique among rural Americans who wanted to joke about sex but whose morality prohibited them from being too specific. "Shanghai Rooster Yodel" (1931) and "Tom Cat Blues" (1932) were two of his early big hits in this mode, and the latter, with its well-known lines, "Here comes a

Ring Tail Tom, / He's boss around the town, / And if you got your heat turned up, / You better turn your damper down," even became a new hit in the 1960s when it was recorded by the Rooftop Singers. Chickens were favorite images, showing up again in later songs like "Chicken Roost Blues" (1934) and "It Takes the Old Hen to Deliver the Goods" (1937). The title of "When I Feel Froggie, I'm Gonna Hop" speaks for itself. As he developed the genre, Cliff's songs became even more specific: two 1933 songs, "Mouse's Ear Blues" and "Sal's Got a Meatskin," were about deflowering virgins: "My gal, she's got a mouse's ear, / But she's gonna lose it when I shift my gear." "That Nasty Swing" updated these older erotic images by using the phonograph record itself as a symbol of fornication: "Place the needle in that hole and do that nasty swing." Not surprisingly, many of these off-color songs were released under a pseudonym ("Bob Clifford"), a practice which didn't seem to affect their sales. With his brother Bill, at one session in 1934, Cliff did successive recordings of "Sugar Cane Mama," "String Bean Mama," "Copper Head Mama," and "Onion Eating Mama," songs designed to put to rest forever the prim, idealized woman of the sentimental songs favored by an earlier generation of country singers.

Cliff's brother Bill, born in Wakefield, Kentucky, in 1908, had emerged as a "straight" guitarist and good singer, and in 1933 Cliff secured a recording try-out for him, as well. Bill's first recording under his own name, "Rattlesnake Daddy" (July 1933), was a surprising success and was later rerecorded several times, emerging as a bluegrass standard in the late 1940s. "Smilin' Bill," as he was called, could rip off runs on the flat-top guitar with stunning accuracy, and soon was rivaling his brother in popularity. By 1937 he was working on "The Carlisle Family Barn Dance" over station WLAP (the station had moved from Louisville to Lexington), at the same time that Cliff headed up his Rambling Cowboys over WWNC in Asheville, North Carolina. Bill and Cliff continued to record together, and in 1936 signed with Victor Records, then one of the country's most prestigious.

About this time the brothers' repertoire began to shift somewhat away from the off-color songs to cowboy and even sacred songs. Cliff's little boy Tommy began working in his father's act when he was three, and this may have prompted the change. Though the acts ran afoul of the child labor laws in some states, children, following the lead of Little Jimmy Sizemore, were very much a part of the family groups of the 1930s. Sonny Boy Tommy made his first record ("My Lovin' Cathleen") in 1936, and was part of the show thereafter until he joined the army in World War II. The Carlisles found themselves now recording pieces like "The Blind Child's Prayer," "Will You Meet Me Just Inside," and "That Great Judgement Day." Cliff had a hit with his "Valley of Peace" and another with his 1939 version of "The Unclouded Day," an old hymn from the Billy Sunday era.

During the 1940s the brothers generally worked together, centering their activities on Knoxville and Memphis. They had a last big hit on the King label, "Rainbow at Midnight," in 1946 before Cliff gradually drifted into retirement in the early 1950s. Bill organized a new group called the Carlisles, and returned to Knoxville, where he did shows with Don Gibson, Chet Atkins, Homer and Jethro, and others before joining the Grand Ole Opry in 1953. In Knoxville he developed his own antic, supercharged style that won him the nickname "Bounding Billy." Bill's leaping stunts grew out of a comic figure he created in the 1940s named "Hot Shot Elmer" who toured with the Carlisles and succeeded in disrupting the show by flying over chairs, tumbling, and so forth. His later hit songs reflected this manic energy: "Too Old to Cut the Mustard," "What Kinda Deal Is This?," "No Help Wanted" and "Poke Salat Annie." He has continued to be a regular on the Opry since 1954, and has won over sixty music industry awards of various kinds. His children Sheila and Billy, currently in the act, seem destined to carry on the Carlisle brand of music for yet another generation.

The Carlisles were among Kentucky's first successful full-time country musicians, and their accomplishments are impressive by any standard: Cliff has written over 500 songs (he is still active as a songwriter today) and has recorded almost 300 for virtually every major record company. Bill has recorded over 90 pre-1947 singles and numerous LPs since then. The pair have worked on almost every major radio station in the southeast. Cliff has appeared with major pop stars like the Andrews Sisters and Rudy Vallee. In the 1960s young folksingers rediscovered some of Cliff's songs and began singing them, leading to the rerelease of several of the old masters. Bill's group remains one of the Opry's cherished links with older country music.

4 Take Me Back to Renfro Valley

While many of Kentucky's finest young musicians were going to the big cities to make a living with country music in the 1930s, the rich tradition of folk music that had nourished them began to attract national attention in its own right. Through a series of popular books, festivals, and radio broadcasts, Americans during this era began to learn about folk music and "colorful" folk performers, and more often than not they began to associate this sort of music with Kentucky. The picture of this music that Americans sometimes received was not entirely accurate—it was often romanticized or based on unfortunate stereotypes—but it did offer at least a glimpse of genuine traditional culture to thousands who had heretofore not appreciated it, and it offered welcome relief from the Tin Pan Alley music of the day and the grotesque Hollywood musicals that were the rage. More important, this new interest in Kentucky grassroots music eventually made it possible to set up the commercial outlets that would permit Kentucky musicians to ply their trade in their home state rather than in the studios of Chicago or Cincinnati.

The era started with two unlikely partners: an old hill country minstrel named Blind Bill Day and a former Hollywood script writer and publicist named Jean Thomas. James William Day (1860–1942), known throughout eastern Kentucky as Blind Bill, had been born in Rowan County and was blind from childhood. As a young man, he took up the life of a wandering minstrel, playing his fiddle and singing on courthouse lawns and street corners throughout the area. Living in Morehead, he was himself composing topical broadside ballads on local events as early as 1884, and either composed or popularized well-known songs like "The Rowan County Feud," "The Coal Creek Troubles," and "The Murder of J.B. Marcum." Day made his living by playing for handouts on the street, and he would occasionally bring home to his wife as much as five dollars on a good day. One summer afternoon in 1926 he was playing "The Lady Went A-Hunting" in front of the Morehead courthouse when he attracted the attention of a middle-aged court stenographer with an interest in old songs. They struck up a conversation, and a few days later the woman visited Day and his wife, bringing a portable typewriter and impressing them both by transcribing on it the words to some of Day's old ballads.

The woman's full name was Jeanette Mary Francis de Assisi Aloysius Narcissus Garfield Bell Thomas, and she had been born in 1881 to the Bell family in Ashland, Kentucky. The daughter of a retired engineer and a schoolteacher, she had been interested as a teenager in noting down some of the folk songs of the region. In 1913 she married a New York accountant named Albert Thomas, but the marriage was unsuccessful and for the next thirteen years she travelled widely, working in show business (though not as a performer) in New York and Hollywood. She was a script girl on the set of Cecil B. DeMille's 1923 silent epic *The Ten Commandments*, but shortly after that she returned to Ashland where she worked as a court stenographer.

By the time she met Blind Bill Day in 1926, Thomas herself was forty-five years old, she had a lot of contacts in the national media, and she saw show business potential in the colorful old fiddler and his music. She signed him to a management contract and talked him into changing his name to "Jilson Setters," a name she apparently thought was more colorful or authentic sounding. Dressing him up in homespun clothes and outfitting him with a couple of key props (a ladderback hickory chair and handmade egg basket), Thomas and "Jilson" travelled to New York in February 1928 to introduce to the nation a typical Kentucky mountain sage. A few months before this, Day had travelled to Louisville for an operation which had removed cataracts and restored his sight, and he was suitably impressed with New York. He appeared at Loew's Theater, broadcast over the radio, and recorded ten titles for the Victor phonograph company. Uncertain about his "new" name, the Victor executives put both "Jilson Setters" and "J.W. Day" on the artist credits of the records. But they were far more interested in Jilson's fiddle breakdowns than his ancient ballads, and they teamed him with one of the nation's leading pop songwriters and studio musicians, Carson J. Robison, who provided excellent guitar backing to Jilson's tunes. It is quite possible that the Victor executives looked on Jilson as an answer to the successful recordings by fellow Kentuckian Doc Roberts, since many of the tunes he recorded had been hits earlier for Roberts: "Forked Deer," "Marthie Campbell," "Billy in the Lowland." (Jilson's records were not best sellers, averaging between 5,000 and 10,000 copies each.) In a later article, Thomas quoted from a broadcast that had introduced him: "Jilson Setters, whose Elizabethan ballads broadcast over a hook-up from coast to coast and relayed round the world, delighted millions last night . . . is a modern survival of the ancient minstrel. . . . Who knows but that his primitive tunes have blazed the trail for American grand opera! Blind for more than half a century, he opens his eyes in a great, modern world."

The spectacle of an old mountain man encountering the wonders of the modern world was to become a standard motif in Thomas's writings about Setters. First appearing in places like *American Magazine* and the New York *World*, many of them, as well as many of Jilson's songs, appeared in book form in 1931 when Thomas published *Devil's Ditties*. This book was so popular that it was chosen as an alternate selection of the Book-of-the-Month Club. This book began a series of Thomas volumes about the Kentucky mountain folk and their culture, which was eventually to include a whole volume about Jilson, *The Singin' Fiddler of Lost Hope Hollow* (1938). Though some critics have referred to these books as "novels" because of their excessive dramatization and Thomas's unfortunate tendency to use false names for all of her informants, they were very popular in their day, and their success spawned a curious second career for Jilson, who was 78 when *The Singin' Fiddler* came out. He recorded for the Library of Congress in 1937 (though Thomas's voice can be heard prompting him in some of the ballads), and he became a well-known fixture at another of Jean Thomas's creations, the American Folk Song Festival.

As a young woman, Thomas had been out riding with friends one June afternoon when she came by accident upon a "singing gatherin'" of local mountain folks, a regular custom of the people in the area that allowed them to get together and swap old songs. Now, years later, flushed with the success with Jilson Setters and finishing her manuscript for *Devil's Ditties*, she found herself acting as local consultant for an NBC radio personality named

Dorothy Gordon. In September 1930 she staged for Gordon's benefit an informal private festival in the Thomas back yard, for which she gathered several local singers and musicians, including Bill Day, to perform. Also in attendance was Mrs. Susan Steele Sampson, the wife of the governor of Kentucky, as well as other dignitaries. It was so well received that Thomas began to think about doing it on a regular basis.

> If, I argued, seventy-five or a hundred people from my home town will turn out on a cold September day to see and hear an old mountain minstrel . . . perhaps, if I selected a warm June day and a place "nigher the county seat," more people would come. Why not try it then on the next second Sunday in June?
>
> Then, too, I reasoned that these old minstrels were fast passing. There would be no one to take their place. The children in the valleys, in the foothills, and in the mountains should be given the opportunity of hearing the ballads of their forbears, as the old minstrels, like Jilson Setters, sing them; the jig and frolic tunes of Elizabeth's time, as he plays them on his ancient fiddle.
>
> It was high time that our nation had an organization to preserve our folk music and songs, and folklorists everywhere agreed. England had had a similar organization since 1878. Of course, there was the American Folklore Society, founded in 1888, the outgrowth of the work of Professor Child of Harvard; but I felt that research and printed journals were not sufficient in themselves. There should be a living, a vital presentation of the song of our fathers. I believed, too, that in an annual American Folk Song Festival only those mountain minstrels to whom the ballads had been handed down by word of mouth should participate. Only those untrained fiddlers and musicians who had learned their art from their forbears should take part.

Kentucky's First Lady, Mrs. Sampson, proved receptive to the idea, and in August 1931 joined Thomas in incorporating the American Folk Song Society, the organization that would direct the festival. In order to attract the kind of national publicity needed, the women drew upon their own contacts as well as the prestige of the governor's office to form an Advisory Board which included some of the nation's most popular writers: Sigmund

Spaeth, the popular music historian; Dorothy Scarborough, then known for her popular *On the Trail of Negro Folk-Songs* (1925) and later for her collection from Virginia, *A Song Catcher in the Southern Mountains* (1937); William Allen White, the famous journalist from Kansas; Carl Sandburg, the modernist poet and amateur folk song collector; Stephen Vincent Benét, a popular poet; best-selling novelist Erskine Caldwell; and others. In her haste to assure national attention for the festival, though, Jean Thomas neglected to involve any local Ashland area people in the planning of the festival, and this was later to cause resentment and hard feelings among local civic and business leaders.

On June 12, 1932, the first American Folk Song Festival was held at Bolts Fork on the Mayo Trail near Ashland. This initial festival, which is described in detail in Thomas's 1933 book *The Traipsin' Woman*, featured some eighteen acts, including children dancing and singing play-party songs, balladeers (one singing from a typewritten copy of his "ballet"), banjoists, guitarists, fiddlers, dulcimer players, and one "Bonaparte Tufts" playing an old accordion and singing "Nellie Grey." A motion picture camera recorded some of the action and the Louisville papers sent a photographer. "This is history," a local judge was quoted as saying. "For the first time in the annals of our nation, America's musical history has been portrayed by authentic minstrels."

During the next ten years the festival continued to grow and to attract attention. By 1938, the program contained forty-two items, including a large number of costume pieces and dances; it had, in fact, become as much pageant as festival. Marshall Portnoy has offered the following account of the opening of a typical festival:

> Every festival began with a loud series of blasts on a fox horn that had been the property of Devil Anse Hatfield of the famous feuding family. At that point, a covered wagon would emerge from behind a hill with a man, his wife, and two children, representing the early settlers of the Kentucky mountains. They would be welcomed by a female performer dressed as a Cherokee Indian. An old English country dance would then be performed by a dozen children and a piper. An historical prologue would be a costumed lady attended by eighteen or more ladies in waiting attired similarly in long black Elizabethan gowns complete with white ruffles at the neck and sleeves.

It didn't seem to matter to the audience that many of the "mountain children" were in fact bused in from the nearby industrial city of Ashland, or that the "natural" event was skillfully and carefully orchestrated. They continued to pour into the area every June, attracted by glowing articles in the *New York Times, Time, Newsweek,* the St. Louis *Post-Dispatch,* the Baltimore *Sun,* and slick magazines like *Travel.* The last commented, "Quite possibly no other regional event in the country retains, year in and year out, the native simplicity of this folk song festival." By 1938 attendance was up past 20,000, a high point, and Bradley Kincaid, then at Cincinnati and one of the country's most popular singers, was the master of ceremonies.

Few of the performers at the festival were able to parlay their success there into careers as entertainers, but that was not the intent of the festival's organizers, nor the motives of many of the participants. The festival's publicity did do a lot toward stimulating public awareness of folk music—it emerged at the same time that fellow Kentuckian Sarah Gertrude Knott was beginning to stage the National Folk Festival in various cities around the country—and it drew attention to the need to preserve and document this music. In 1937 the Library of Congress sent pioneer folklorists Alan and Elizabeth Lomax to Ashland with portable recording equipment to record dozens of discs of festival performers singing, playing, and talking about their lives. Preserved in the library's Archive of American Folksong, they represent some of the earliest attempts to capture, for noncommercial motives, the traditional music of the state. Sadly, few of them have been reissued and are available for public consumption today. During the Depression, the Federal Music Project of the Works Progress Administration (WPA), formed to develop work projects for the jobless, provided employment for people to assist with the festival.

From 1935 until 1949, the festival took place on the Mayo Trail, about eighteen miles south of Ashland, and remained primarily a Kentucky festival, though participants from Ohio and West Virginia also took part. The festival was discontinued in 1943, and not revived until 1948, when country singer Kenny Roberts was the main attraction, with Bradley Kincaid acting as Master of Ceremonies. Moved in 1950 to a wooded area on Cogan Street in Ashland, with the citizens of Ashland for the first time taking an active role in staging it, the festival continued to attract national attention. It appeared on the *Today* show in 1955, and was often televised in its entirety by WSAZ-TV in Ashland. As the older performers from the 1930s began to die off, they were replaced with younger musicians like J.P. and Annadeene Fraley. No one, however, came forth to replace Jean Thomas, and when she retired from the festival in 1972, it literally marked the end of an era.*

Jean Thomas was by no means the only conduit between Kentucky's traditional culture and the popular or formal culture of the American 1930s. Other writers, performers, and collectors added to the mystique that was developing about Kentucky music. One of the most colorful and controversial was John Jacob Niles (1892–1980), a Louisville native who won fame in education circles and concert halls as a singer of and lecturer on old English ballads. Though he had genuine roots in the traditional folk music of the area through his grandfather, Niles also studied classical piano and later studied at the Schola Cantorum in Paris and the Lyons (France) Conservatory. Throughout the 1930s and 1940s he made concert tours, accompanying himself on a homemade dulcimer and delivering his Child ballads in a high-pitched, highly mannerized style that owed little to Kentucky tradition. He said, "I soon discovered the electric effect of a male alto C-sharp, and this led me to compose a melodic line involving the highest notes in my range." Some of Niles's "folk" songs, such as "Venezuela," "Black Is the Color of My True Love's Hair," and "I Wonder as I Wander," have become popular with folk revival audiences over the years. But Niles had little appeal to the average Kentuckian of the day; his 1940 Victor recordings were issued in the "Red Seal" or classical catalogue, and the catalogue entry for Niles reads: "Mr. Niles' songs are by no means to be confused with the modern 'Hillbilly' songs, with which they have nothing in common. Mr. Niles' voice and style are so far as can be established absolutely authentic, and they have a strange and beautiful charm." History, unfortunately, has not vindicated this assertion, but Niles does have a genuine place as a stylist and popularizer, and he did make some ballads palatable to devotees of formal music who were unable to accept the rough-hewn voices of some of Jean Thomas's discoveries.

A conduit of a different sort was one of the state's premier poets and novelists of the time, Jesse Stuart. Growing up in rugged Greenup County during the waning days of World War I, Stuart experienced at first hand the country frolics, the singing gather-

*In 1973, Hubert Rogers began staging a Kentucky Folk Song Festival that eventually settled at Grayson, Kentucky. Rogers had performed at many of Thomas's festivals and utilized in the new festival many of the performers who had worked with Thomas.

ings, and the court day minstrels that were the sources for the hill country music. As a young graduate student at Vanderbilt University in Nashville, Stuart came under the spell of the Fugitives, a group of authors and intellectuals who were trying to instill in the South a sense of pride in its own traditional culture, and who were advising southerners to turn off their radios and take their fiddles down from the wall. Inspired by the interest of his teachers—especially Donald Davidson—in folk music and folk poetry, Stuart went on an eighteen-month writing binge in 1932–1933 which eventually produced his autobiographical *Beyond Dark Hills* (1938), his famous sonnet cycle, *Man with a Bull-Tongue Plow* (1934), and a giant unpublished manuscript entitled "Cradle of Copperheads." Each of these was rich in references to Kentucky traditional music. *Beyond Dark Hills* contains an especially lengthy section about a singing revival meeting, and another about court day in Greenup, with its street-corner singers. "I wished Donald Davidson could be in Greenup then. He could hear plenty of the old songs now. Only drop a nickel, a dime, a quarter into the hat. 'Doc, I want you to play and sing, "The Little Mohee." Can you play that?'" "Cradle of Copperheads" contains similar passages, including a first-hand description of the Grand Ole Opry as it was in 1930. Stuart knew this aspect of old-time music well, since for a time he courted Elizabeth Hale, one of the daughters of Opry band leader Theron Hale, who appeared regularly on the show playing piano for her father's band.

In fact, *Man with a Bull-Tongue Plow* is dedicated to Elizabeth Hale. This book, a collection of 703 sonnets about Kentucky rural life which created a sensation when it was first published, has won fame not only as a literary classic but as a rich storehouse of authentic Kentucky folklife. There are many references to music in the book, but the most memorable are a series of sonnets about a fiddler Stuart often saw in Greenup, Blind Ed Haley. In the sonnets he is known as Blind Frailey.

> When old "Blind" Frailey starts his magic fiddle
> And a Plum Grove man is there by chance,
> You ought to watch this man step out and dance.
> Of course he has some patches on his pants
> And by his side the old men jig a little
> And laugh and listen to the talking fiddle.
> "Blind" Frailey stops for resin on his bow
> And when he starts to fiddle up he cries:
> "'Girl With the Blue Dress On!' Boys, let's go!"

And then coarse shoes like mauls thug on the ground
Until they nearly drown the fiddle sound,
And soon a jolly crowd is gathered there
With best of drink upon the courthouse square
And talk about dancing and the fiddling there!

And if one Plum Grove man has gone to Heaven
And if he hears this fiddle by a chance,
He will call out the angels here in Heaven;
The sweet fair maids here all white-robed in Heaven,
And they'll renew again the old square dance—
The old Kentucky mountain "Waltz the Hall"—
The most Kentuckian of all dance calls—
The Lord will sit in his high golden chair
And watch "Blind" Frailey from Kentucky there,
The Lord will sit wistfully a-looking on,
But surely He won't say a word at all,
Not when he sees his angels "Waltz the Hall—"
And hears "Blind" Frailey from Kentucky there,
He will sit back and laugh from his golden chair.

Stuart's praise was neither misdirected nor exaggerated. Students of Kentucky fiddle styles now agree that Haley (1883–1951) was perhaps the most influential of all the early eastern Kentucky traditional fiddlers. Though he was born in Logan County, West Virginia, he lived all of his life in Ashland, where he and his wife, also blind and a native of Morehead, managed to put six children through school and make ends meet by performing at local fiddlers' contests, at dances, and most especially on court days in various county seats. Blinded with an untreated case of measles when a boy, Ed learned to play the fiddle in the archaic way preferred by mountain men in the region: instead of tucking the instrument under his chin, he would hold it against his upper arm and chest, supported by his left hand. By rocking the instrument back and forth, in addition to bowing, he could achieve a breathtaking dexterity and establish an excellent sense of timing. By 1914 Ed was widely known as one of the prime fiddlers in eastern Kentucky and West Virginia. His wife was related to Blind Bill Day, and in fact Haley was Jean Thomas's original candidate to be "Jilson Setters." Haley's family says, though, that he would have no part in such humbug, and turned Thomas down. She later mentioned him briefly in *Ballad Makin' in Kentucky*. Haley was intensely proud of his fiddling, and was wary of people he felt were trying to exploit it or commercialize it. He repeatedly refused to make commercial records, or even to record for the various Library of Congress teams that came through the area. Finally in 1946 his sons convinced him to make a series of home recordings to preserve his music, and these are all that remain today of his legacy.

Haley's most famous tune—his "signature piece"—was "Blackberry Blossom," an old tune dating from the Civil War and carried all over eastern Kentucky by Haley. Another was "Ladies on the Steamboat," recorded commercially by Burnett and Rutherford, and another was "Parkersburg Landing." "Girl with the Blue Dress On," mentioned in Stuart's sonnet, is a West Virginia tune Haley played often. His repertoire contained dozens of unusual tunes, from schottisches and jigs to fast rags, from blues ballads like "Stackolee" to complex cross-tuned pieces like "Lost Indian." One old-timer, after hearing Haley play "Bonaparte's Retreat," declared that "if two armies could come together and hear him play that tune, they'd kill themselves in piles." In addition to Dick Burnett and Blind Bill Day, other fiddlers learned from Haley: Fiddlin' Cowan Powers from Virginia, who made many early records, learned some from him, and "Georgia Slim" Rutland, the leading fiddler on radio in the 1940s, spent a year in Ashland learning from him, as well. Today younger musicians remember Haley as a misty legend, though in 1976 Rounder Records issued an LP collection of some of his home recordings that made his music available to a wide audience for the first time, and the music on the album fully justifies the Haley mystique.

In addition to works by Jean Thomas and Jesse Stuart, the 1930s saw other books about Kentucky folk music achieve national and even international popularity. Some were "singing books"—song texts with music designed for singing rather than for history or folklore—such as the eight collections by John Jacob Niles (starting with *Seven Kentucky Mountain Songs* in 1929), and the popular collections by Mary Wheeler (*Kentucky Mountain Folk-Songs* in 1937). Other more substantial collections of songs were Harvey Fuson's *Ballads of the Kentucky Highlands* (1931) and Josiah H. Combs's *Folksongs from the Kentucky Highlands* (1939). Combs (1886–1960) was a native of Hazard who had been interested in Kentucky folk songs since 1911, and whose interest continued throughout a long and distinguished academic career that ranged from the University of Paris to the University of Virginia. He is perhaps Kentucky's most important collector and student of native speech and songs, and one of the most colorful characters in the ranks of folklorists.

Starting in 1937 the Library of Congress began to collect songs in a different way: on ten- and twelve-inch audio discs, recorded on portable equipment set up in front rooms, in remote general stores, and on front porches throughout eastern and central Kentucky. While many performers only sang two or three songs for the microphones, and while others did inferior versions of songs they had learned from radio or records, several were important and influential folk artists who offered to the microphones a rich repertory of unique songs and instrumental tunes. In Hazard, Alan and Elizabeth Lomax found ballad singers Jimmy Morris and Justus Begley, who still performed Child ballads unaccompanied, and in nearby Harlan, singer G.D. Vowell along with fiddler-singer Jim Howard. Salyersville, in Magoffin County, was found to be a veritable nest of ballad singers, including Clay Walters, Winnie Prater, Uncle Branch Higgins, and Nell Hampton. The Lomaxes found and recorded excellent instrumentalists, as well: fiddlers W.M. Stepp from Lakeville and Luther Strong from Dalesburg, as well as banjoist-singer Pete Steele, who had spent eighteen years as a miner in Harlan County and had developed an interesting finger-picking banjo style. In 1938 Mary Elizabeth Barnicle visited the Pineville area and recorded some fascinating church music and sacred songs, as well as more banjo songs from George Roark. A year later still another folklorist, Herbert Halpert, spent time in the state, recording balladeer Finley Adams from Durham, among others. In 1943 Artus Moser made yet another trip, recording among others Pleaz Mobley of Manchester, a fine singer who later joined the Renfro Valley Barn Dance. Over the years, many of these early field recordings have been issued on discs from the Library of Congress as unparalleled examples of American folk music.

Watching all this folklore activity with great interest from his berth in Chicago was John Lair. Throughout the 1930s he had been busy forging links between the commercial radio/country music industry and the developing interest in folk music. His "Music Notes" column in *Stand By* continued to act as a clearinghouse for people interested in tracking down or exchanging old songs, and his other writings in the magazine paid homage to figures like Bascom Lamar Lunsford and topics like the 1937 National Folk Festival, which was held in Chicago. Lair and his friends, though, were somewhat bothered by the trend toward cowboy music that was influencing country music in the mid-1930s. Figures like Gene Autry and Bob Wills dominated the industry, and the western image was becoming popular on a lot of the big country radio shows, including the "National Barn Dance" and "The Grand Ole Opry." The programs, for their part, were trying to appeal to a wider audience—WLS especially had always insisted that its country music was not southern but "prairie ballads"—but some felt that in turning to so much cowboy music the stations were turning their backs on their original audience, the people of the Southeast and Midwest. As Lair watched the success of the American Folk Song Festival and noted its ability to draw crowds down in Kentucky, he began to think seriously about starting a show that would take country music out of the big-city theaters and put it back in the countryside where it had started. "Closely studying the audiences from week to week I noticed that a great many folks who attended the theater came from out of town, apparently combining the show with a trip to the city and a general outing for the party. This set me to thinking that it might work the other way around: that city folks might enjoy a trip to the country to see a show." Furthermore, as he wrote later in a publicity release, "the barn dance type of program which he had helped to develop didn't ring true, somehow it didn't remind him enough of the real things as he had known them in the good old days in Renfro Valley. He felt that what radio needed was a little realism—a little less showmanship and a little more heart-felt sincerity." As a young man returning to his native Renfro Valley after World War I, Lair had been dismayed to see how "progress" was changing the face of the area, and he had wished he could do something about it. Now, perhaps, was a chance to kill two birds with one stone.

Lair took his idea to another Renfro Valley native who was making it big in music, Red Foley, and he liked the idea as well. Foley then took it to his brother, Cotton, and they had a third investor. Whitey Ford (a Kentuckian by vocation, though born in Missouri), well-known as "The Duke of Paducah," rounded out the group, and they bought a tract of land in 1937 in Rockcastle County, about 100 miles southwest of the American Folk Song Festival site, with the idea of building a music barn and camp-ground that would house their own barn dance. History conspired with them; at that same time, WLW in Cincinnati decided to boost its power and enter the national radio market. For a time it was broadcasting at the unheard-of power of 500,000 watts, and getting to every farm in the Midwest and most of the South; in fact, some farmers claimed they were picking up broadcasts on their milking machines and others insisted they were getting it on their barbed wire fences. In the 1937–1938 season, the station was broadcasting over a dozen hours of country programs per week, many of them featuring Kentucky artists: "The Drifting Pioneers" (with a young guitarist named Merle Travis), "Top O the Morning," "Boone County Caravan," "Brown County Revellers," "The Happy Valley Girls," and others. To bolster this staff they approached John Lair, and he helped effect a massive shift of country artists from WLS to WLW. With him came Bill McCluskey, one of the key announcers for the WLS "Barn Dance"; the Girls of the Golden West, two sisters from downstate Illinois who were named Millie and Dolly Good and did close-harmony duet singing; Whitey Ford, who had been emcee for Gene Autry's part of the "Barn Dance"; and important Kentucky musicians like the Owens Sisters, Red Foley, Lily May Ledford, and Slim Miller. Using this roster, Lair formed his new show, "The Renfro Valley Barn Dance," even though he had not had time to prepare his Renfro Valley site. On October 9, 1937, the show's flagship broadcast took place, but from the cavernous Cincinnati Music Hall before a wildly enthusiastic crowd and a huge listening audience. Within months, touring groups from the roster were hitting the small theaters around the South, often playing before movies like Darryl Zanuck's *In Old Chicago*. A year later, in the fall of 1938, the show moved its base to the Memorial Auditorium in Dayton, Ohio. Finally things were ready in Renfro Valley itself, and on November 4, 1939, the first show went on the air from rural Kentucky. Since the roster included some of the nation's leading stars, network affiliation was quick in coming, and WHAS in Louisville was soon originating the remote broadcast and feeding it to the NBC network.

That first night when Lair stepped before the microphones, he said, "This is the Renfro Valley Barn Dance, coming to you direct from a big barn in Renfro Valley, Kentucky—the first and only barn dance on the air presented by the actual residents of an actual community." Historically speaking Lair was right, and throughout the years local residents of central and eastern Kentucky did get a chance to appear before the microphones alongside Lair's well-known stars. But to prove his point to a skeptical radio audience, Lair offered to send out a free photograph of the barn to any doubters who cared to drop him a postcard. He only made the announcement once, but within a few weeks he had received an astounding 253,000 requests for the photos. A good many of the audience soon made plans to drive over and see for themselves, and before long the 1,000-seat barn was being filled to capacity and local boys were finding extra work directing traffic.

The physical setting of Renfro Valley, which soon included a "little red schoolhouse" and a museum in addition to the big barn, certainly helped its claims to "authenticity" and aided in its success. So did Lair's insistence on "mountain dress" for the participants, as opposed to fancier costumes. "Cowboy garments are considered in bad taste—except for cowboys," one early reporter noted. Some of the most popular acts, including Red Foley and the Girls of the Golden West, left after 1939, but enough remained to establish the show as one of the leading national shows, and certainly Kentucky's premier barn dance show. The 1940 cast included Jerry Byrd and Ernie Lee, each of whom was to achieve fame on his own in the 1950s, but who were then known as the Happy Valley Boys; the Amburgey Sisters, a popular girls' vocal trio from Neon, Kentucky;* a trio composed of fiddler Guy Blakeman (from the Mammoth Cave area), Roland Gaines, and Jerry Behrens, who were known as the Range Riders; comedy teams of mandolin player Shorty Hobbs and Little Eller, from central Kentucky, and Granny Harper (nee Williams, from Camp Nelson) and Little Clifford; Elsie Behrens, who played the dulcimer and sang old folk songs; and the Pine Ridge Boys (Marvin Taylor and Doug Spivey), who were popular as duet singers. But two of the most popular acts were built around two strong Kentucky traditional musicians, fiddler Slim Miller and banjoist Lily May Ledford.

Homer "Slim" Miller (1898-1962) was for over twenty years the cornerstone of the program's string band and one of the show's most colorful characters. He was a tall, laconic character who always dressed in an old checked shirt and tiny gray hat, with oversized trousers ornamented with a giant safety pin from which he hung his bow. Though most of his fans assumed he was a Kentucky native, Slim had been born in Lisbon, Indiana. He learned fiddling from the local musicians, and by the time he was twelve he was accomplished. In 1930 he joined Hugh Cross's band in Knoxville, the Smoky Mountain Ramblers, and made his first records with them. He was an early member of the Cumberland Ridge Runners, and later followed Lair to the Renfro Valley show. In 1933 he had recorded what were to be the only records on which he was featured, "Goofus" (in a version that became very influential with later fiddlers) and "Roundin' Up the Yearlings"; he also backed other members of Lair's band—Red Foley, Linda

---

*Irene Amburgey soon married James Roberts, and later won fame on her own singing country gospel music as Martha Carson.

Parker, Doc Hopkins, and Karl and Harty. His fans heard plenty of him, though, on the weekly Renfro Valley radio shows, and on the thousands of tour dates he played. John Lair later noted just how big Slim's role on the "Barn Dance" was: "Unquestionably, 'Ole Slim,' as he was known to his friends (he never had an enemy) was the life of the Barn Dance. Where other performers, and we had some of the best, would come out and do their act and leave the stage, Slim was out there every minute of the time, leading the backup band, mugging for the audience, and keeping them convulsed with laughter." Slim's musicianship also impressed people; he had a loose, rolling style that was beautifully adapted to the 2/4 rhythm of the string bass that was becoming a fixture in country bands, and for years his playing was the standard of excellence against which amateur fiddlers in Kentucky measured themselves. "He plays like Slim Miller" was a supreme compliment—and still is. In later years, Slim's health began to fail, but he stayed in Renfro Valley. He and his wife for a time owned and operated the Scenic View Motel in the Valley.

Another group that remained a fixture on the "Barn Dance" for over fifteen years was the Coon Creek Girls, a remarkable all-girl string band built around the awesome talents of Lily May Ledford. Lily May grew up on a tenant farm in Powell County, about fifty miles east of Lexington, and made string band music with her family; by the time she was a teenager she had joined her sister Rosie and brother Cayen in a band they called the Red River Ramblers, which played for local square dances up and down the wooded, hilly Red River Gorge area. Lily May had become skilled on both banjo and fiddle, and picked up old traditional songs and ballads from her father, her aunt, and her brother Kelly, who had picked up banjo styles and a lot of old songs while working in the mines of Pike County. In 1936 the band auditioned for one of the touring WLS talent scouts, and Lily May was chosen to come to Chicago and be on the WLS "Barn Dance." She was only nineteen and John Lair signed her to a five-year personal management contract, designed in part to placate her nervous parents. Lily May recalled, "Papa signed it at once, but mama was tougher to deal with. Poor thing had read terrible stories where girls had gone to the city and were captured and sold into white slavery and came to horrible ends, and at first she could not bring herself to sign."

Soon after Lily May got to WLS, Lair began talking to her about his dream of having a barn dance in the country. One of the ideas he was toying with was forming an all-girl string band, and when he made the move to Cincinnati he brought together Lily May, her sister Rosie, and two new musicians from the Chicago area, "Daisy" Lange and "Violet" Koehler. (By design, all the girls were to have stage names of flowers.) In many ways the group was a studio band; only Rosie and Lily May had performed together before. The girls were all energetic and versatile musicians, though, and soon developed a distinctive sound. Lily May recalls:

> Since we had not yet been named, we got the bright idea of calling ourselves the "Wildwood Flowers." We went straight to Mr. Lair and asked him if we could do this. He was kind and tactful, but laughed a little and said "Girls, I had thought a more country name might be better. How about 'Coon Creek Girls'? Any one hearing that name would know at once the type of music to be expected from you. Don't you believe that would be more appropriate?" So Coon Creek Girls we became. My part of the country hadn't a Coon Creek in it, but there is one in Pike County and I believe one in western Kentucky.

Finally the band made its debut on the famous broadcast from the Cincinnati Music Hall on October 9, 1937. As Lily May remembers, "Then it was our time. We startled the audience by being all girls—our sound was drowned out by the uproar of applause and yelling."

In 1937 there was nothing new about women playing country music. Patsy Montana was as popular as any country singer in the nation, and the Girls of the Golden West (Millie and Dolly Good) were attracting huge, devoted audiences: Sara and Maybelle were continuing to serve as the foundation of the Carter Family and the Three Little Maids—the Oversteak Sisters—were serving as a training ground for a couple of the best women songwriters of the time. But by and large women's country music was either romantically "western" or gushingly sentimental and "sweet." When the Coon Creek Girls, with Lily May's clawhammer banjo, Violet's mandolin, Daisy's bass, Rosie's guitar, and their high mountain harmony burst on this scene, ears perked and heads turned. Here were no sentimental parlor songs about mother, and no Tin Pan Alley odes to prairie sweethearts. Here was mountain music coming in the front door: "Banjo Pickin' Girl," "Sowing on the Mountain," "Pretty Polly." John Lair's prefabricated image aside, the Coon Creek Girls developed into genuine exemplars of old-time music. They represented the tradition well in 1939, when Eleanor Roosevelt asked them to play before the king and queen of England.

At a time when the country was swept up in the jazzy rhythms of western swing or the smooth harmonics of cowboy trios, the music of the Coon Creek Girls almost seemed to be a throwback to the string band style of the 1920s. Almost—for the Coon Creek sound always had a unique swing and lilt about it, generated in part by their pulsing string bass. Many of the songs were modifications of traditional material from the eastern Kentucky hills. Lily May described their act this way:

> We were writing songs at this point. We did vocal duets, trios and even quartets, with me singing bass. We did fiddle duets, mandolin duets with Violet and Daisy. Violet would do songs and poems and old ballads—I played banjo, Rosie would sing tenor and do an occasional Jimmy Rodgers solo—yodelling her best. I had the best rollicking guitar backup behind my banjo breakdowns I've ever had. What a good time we had on stage, playing mostly fast pieces, jumping up and down, sometimes ruining some of our songs by laughing at each other. Sis, when carried away by a fast fiddle tune, would let out a yell so high pitched that it sounded like a whistle. Sometimes, when playing an outdoor event, fair or picnic, we would go barefooted. We were so happy back then. Daisy and Sis, being good fighters, would make short work of anybody in the more polished groups who would tease or torment us. We all made short work of the "wolves" as they were called, who tried to follow us home or get us in their cars.

All this drew them forty dollars a week apiece, for radio work and bookings nearly every night. After 1939, when Violet Koehler and Daisy Lange left, they were replaced by a third Ledford sister, young Minnie (dubbed "Black-eyed Susie"), making the group a family string band. For some eighteen years the Ledfords nurtured their distinctive style, appearing regularly on the Renfro Valley Barn Dance and raising their own families. Their only concession to changing times was to gradually add to their repertoire, as a balance to the frolic tunes and mountain ballads, a selection of gospel and sentimental songs, like "Going Down the Valley" and "I Have No Mother Now." Even in this, though, they emulated the older string bands of the 1920s and 1930s. By 1957 the formal career of the Coon Creek Girls came to an end, but during the folk revival of the 1960s they, like many earlier groups, found themselves getting back together to play at various folk festivals.

By 1944 the Renfro Valley Barn Dance was the lead success

story in *Billboard*'s feature about the amazing success of "folk-shows." Even in wartime, the Barn Dance was able to keep two touring units on the road, each one averaging about $5,000 a week playing small towns in West Virginia, Indiana, Kentucky, Ohio, and the South. As for the personal attendance at the Barn Dance itself, Lair had reason to be well pleased. He told *Billboard*: "During 1942 we showed to more than 10,000 paid admissions on three different Saturday nights and averaged around 5,000 each Saturday night during the year. Since our barn will accommodate only 1,000 people we found it necessary to give many shows each Saturday afternoon and night. When peak crowds hit here, we often start around two o'clock on Saturday afternoon and run continuous shows until after daylight Sunday morning. Many people get discouraged and leave, but, on the other hand, many of them, including women with small children, stay in line most of the night to get in. People have visited the Renfro Valley Barn from every state in the union." (The Renfro Valley attendance looks even more impressive when one considers that the maximum attendance at the Grand Ole Opry in that year was only 3,000.) To accommodate these hordes of visitors the organization built dozens of new cabins, and other motels sprang up in a radius of twenty-five miles around Renfro Valley. A grandstand and stable for show horses later went up, as did a museum, a country store, and even a walnut cracking plant which Lair hoped would stimulate cottage industry in the area.

Much of this success, of course, was a result of the show's success on radio. Early sponsors over WLW and later WHAS included companies who pitched their products to a rural audience—Allis-Chalmers, Pinex, Wildroot Creame Oil. But, Lair recalled, "Our first big break came when Ballard and Ballard, of Louisville, decided to give us a chance to sell Ballard's Obelisk Flour and other products." Ballard and Ballard, who had earlier sponsored one of Louisville's best jug bands on radio, helped to sponsor a daily morning broadcast from Renfro Valley over the CBS network, a fifteen- to thirty-minute show called "Renfro Valley Merrymakin'." A little later the flour company agreed to sponsor a Sunday morning show, "Sunday Morning Gatherin'," a pleasant, low-keyed show that was heavily scripted and narrated by Lair and which featured Renfro Valley artists doing old sacred and sentimental songs. Each program was devoted to a common theme, such as "Changing Times," "The Old Homestead," or "Memories of Mother." Lair intended to start the show by ringing an old church bell, but quickly found that a real church bell made an awful sound over the air; for years, therefore, faithful listeners heard a "church bell sound" over the air that was actually created by striking an old brake shoe with a hammer. Lair took such "actuality" broadcasting even a step further when he did a series of Monday broadcasts over NBC designed to carry to city listeners the sounds of country life and customs. "When we put on a hay-ride program we were riding in an old farm wagon filled with hay and drawn over rocky roads by a team of horses. We put on the air direct from the banks of Renfro Creek a fish fry, and the listeners could hear the creek frogs in the meadow and the fish frying in the pan. We had a 'possum hunt one night and actually took to the woods with lantern and dogs and caught a 'possum. We, of course, carried portable broadcasting equipment with us to present these broadcasts from real life."

For over fifteen years the Renfro Valley formula was wildly successful, and the program, as well as the valley itself, was known nationwide. During its golden years almost every major country star did guest stints on the show, and the program itself fostered numerous country acts that achieved stardom: comedy team Homer and Jethro, singer Little Jimmy Dickens, Cincinnati favorite Ernie Lee, gospel singer Martha Carson, singer Pete Stamper, comedian Whitey Ford, Red Foley, banjoist and disc jockey for the Renfro Valley station Old Joe Clark, harmonica virtuoso Lonnie Glosson, guitarist Jerry Byrd (later a pioneer in developing the "Nashville sound"), and country gospel great Molly O'Day. Throughout this time, though, the program featured a bed-rock of talent drawn from eastern Kentucky, and Lair continued to make talent hunts throughout the area. Even the musicians who did not achieve national stardom, or even fully professional status, continued to use Renfro Valley as a much-needed outlet for their talent. Even today, with Lair still owning the Valley and its show, the program continues to have a strong local-color element in its cast, and still adheres to the purer forms of country music. In 1962 Kentucky Governor Bert Combs issued a proclamation on the twenty-fifth anniversary of the Barn Dance, declaring it "a Kentucky institution." But the Barn Dance was also an important local clearinghouse for the hundreds of talented Kentucky musicians who now were finding they no longer had to leave the state to find an audience for their art.

Meanwhile the radio scene in Louisville was starting to generate its own excitement. WHAS now became powerful enough to reach far into the hollows and coal towns of eastern Kentucky as well as the plains of the Midwest, and developed its own roster of talented performers. One of the earliest bands to win fame over Louisville radio was Lonesome Luke and His Farm Boys, the area's most popular string band from about 1927 to about 1935. It was led by D.C. "Luke" Decker (1900-1964), a native of Breckinridge County who grew up in Grayson County. Decker's father was Lodic Decker, a noted fiddler and banjo player in the area, who taught his sons all manner of old tunes and breakdowns. Many of them, Luke's brother Ira recalls, did not even have names as such. "He'd say something like, 'Let's play that tune in D and A,' and we'd know what he meant." About 1918 the family moved to Louisville, but by this time Luke was already travelling around the South, working as a fiddler and singer throughout Tennessee and Kentucky. By 1927 he had organized a band and had a sustaining program on tiny WLAP, then located in an old Victorian house in Louisville, and soon moved on to the more powerful WHAS. Ira Decker recalls: "We were one of the first bands around to dress up in a costume, in overalls and red bandanas." At the peak of his popularity, in the early 1930s, Luke's radio band generated baskets of fan mail and filled the large dance hall at the old Sennings Park in Louisville. A local newspaper reviewer wrote in 1931: "Wailing blues may appeal to many persons, but Lonesome Luke and his Farm Boys have a type of plaintive melody that is likely to draw tears to the most hardened fan." In February 1931, C.W. Johnson, a local booker and talent manager, got the boys a recording date with the Starr Piano Company, and Luke, his brother Ira on tenor banjo, guitarist Lee Day, and one other guitarist whose name has been forgotten, went to Richmond, Indiana, to cut their only commercial records, including two of their favorites, "Halfway to Arkansas" and "Dogs in the Ashcan."

Friends feel that Luke had the potential to become Louisville's first really big country star. "He was too easy going," recalls his brother. "He wasn't particular enough about his back-up band. Anyone who was his good buddy could get on in his band, whether he could play well or not. He didn't demand the high caliber sidemen that he deserved." Personnel in Luke's band changed often and casually, and Luke didn't seem anxious to push the band much beyond the Louisville area, beyond one-night stands at local fairs and dances. Luke was never able to make a living full time at his music and spent much of his life working at Gamble's woodworking plant in Louisville to make ends meet. Later he appeared on WLAP again and, after that station moved to Lexington, over WAVE. But by the 1930s Luke's brand of old-time music, solidly grounded in Kentucky fiddle tradition, was becoming passé and the new cowboy style bands were becoming the rage.

A local band that displayed the ambition, initiative, and flashy showmanship that Lonesome Luke lacked was the band that replaced him as Louisville's favorite: Uncle Henry's Original Kentucky Mountaineers. "Uncle Henry"—Henry Warren—was of Luke's generation and, like him, came from a background of rural music-making. He was born in Taylor County, hardly mountain country, in 1903, and worked as a blacksmith, soldier, boxer, and dairyman before deciding to go into the music business. He did not play an instrument but was an astute manager, a clever emcee, and a skillful comedian. For five years, starting in 1928 over a radio station in Rockford, Illinos, he led a band that was a combination modern dance band and string band throughout the Midwest. Then in 1933 he modified his act, adopting for himself a costume that featured a long frock coat, a dark goatee, and wire-rimmed specacles, giving him the appearance of a rube Abe Lincoln. He renamed members of his band: his wife became Sally the Original Mountain Gal, and his brother Grady Warren assumed a character known simply as the Coonhunter. For a time, the band became a stage company, presenting "hillbilly musicals" like "Zeb Turney's Gal" in and around Lexington. Soon he won a place on WLAP and then WHAS, where he held forth between 1936 and 1940 on the "WHAS Morning Jamboree" program as well as "Kentucky Play Party," with Cousin Emmy, the Rangers, and fiddler Clark Kessinger. His programs were an eclectic mixture of the old and the new; Sally and the Coonhunter did older sentimental country ballads, and Johnny Ford featured fiddle breakdowns, while Curly Bradshaw played harmonica. This early band never recorded commercially, and established itself solely on the basis of radio work and personals. In 1941 they were lured away, like so many earlier Kentucky bands, to Chicago, where they were featured for ten years on the WJJD "Suppertime Frolic," alongside other Kentuckians like Karl and Harty. In Chicago the band was joined by songwriter Paul South, by Casey Jones, a superb Kentucky fiddler, by "Grandpa Nerit" (Ballard Taylor), another Kentuckian who could "rap" the banjo in the old style, by instrumentalist Del Remick, and by Warren's son, Jimmy Dale Warren, who specialized in modern country heart songs. After the Mountaineers broke up, Dale Warren went west where in 1952 he joined the Sons of the Pioneers, eventually becoming their lead singer. Henry died in 1968.

Rivaling Uncle Henry in popularity in the mid-1930s was

Frankie Moore's Log Cabin Boys, for years a fixture on WHAS. This too was a hybrid string band that included an accordion and a trumpet in addition to banjos, fiddles, and guitars, played music that appealed to the Midwest as well as the South, and featured polkas and waltzes in addition to breakdowns and ballads. The band's recorded output was meager: they did four songs for the American Recording Company in October 1934, and eight songs for the new Decca Company in 1935. None of the records was a hit, or really even a unique song or performance: most were old gospel standards, versions of old Kentucky folk songs like "Crawdad Song," or sentimental songs like "Please Papa Come Home." Their 1936 songbook reflected a similar mixture, adding such favorites as "The White Rose" and "My Old Coon Dog." Moore broke up the band about 1936—he went into managing and booking, for a time managing Roy Acuff—and it is remembered today best as a training school for several other musicians who later established names for themselves. Bill and Joe Callahan, an important early brother duo from North Carolina, worked with Moore before going west to appear in films. Roy "Shorty" Hobbs, one of Kentucky's finest mandolin players and a former colleague of Asa Martin, worked with Moore before going on to even greater fame as half of the comedy team of Shorty and Little Eller at Renfro Valley. The most famous Moore alumnus was undoubtedly Pee Wee King, who was with him between 1934 and 1936 on the way to a career that was later to take him to the stage of the Grand Ole Opry and eventually the Country Music Hall of Fame. But probably the most colorful graduate was a dynamic musician and comedienne named Cynthia May Carver (1903-1980), who went by the stage name of Cousin Emmy.

Born near Glasgow, Cynthia May began her career playing the five-string banjo with her cousins, Bozo and Warner Carver, in a band heard over Kansas City radio station WHB. The next-to-youngest of eight children born to sharecroppers, she herself never fully understood how she developed her considerable talents; she was always a show-off and she told interviewer Mike Seeger that when her mother would leave her in the tobacco patch and assign her one row, she'd dance and sing and entertain the other seven children to get them to do her work. By the time she became a featured act with Frankie Moore in the mid-1930s she was adept with some fifteen musical instruments, including unusual ones like the twelve-string guitar, the hand saw, and the rubber glove (played in a strange kazoo-like fashion).

With her cascades of platinum hair, her wide mouth, piercing voice and exuberant delivery, Cousin Emmy was soon drawing in sacks of fan mail for her driving renditions of old shout tunes like "Groundhog." In one sense she was out of place in the increasingly sophisticated country music of the late 1930s, and was a throwback to the early days of the medicine show "buskers" who had higher regard for flair and showmanship than for subtlety or original songs. Yet the rural audiences loved it. By 1938 Cousin Emmy had her own show and touring group. "It's fantastic how popular she was," recalls Linda Lou Eastwood, a former band member. "She was really something in Hazard and all those mountain towns; those mountain people, they'd come up and hand her a $20 to play something on the banjo. . . . She had this big Cadillac and four of us girls rode in the front, and five guys and a bass fiddle in the back seat. One thing I remember about the shows we did was that everybody on stage had to dance." A few years later Cousin Emmy gave this description of her show to a reporter from *Time* magazine: "First, I hits it up on my banjo, and I wow 'em. Then I do a number with the *guit*-tar and play the French harp and sing, all at the same time. Then somebody hollers, 'Let's see her yodel,' and I obliges. And then somebody hollers 'Let's see her dance,' and I obliges. After that we come to the sweetest part of our program—hymns."

In 1941 Cousin Emmy was hired by KMOX in St. Louis, a 50,000 watt station with listeners from Canada to Mexico, and established a national audience with a daily radio show that, in spite of its 5:25 A.M. hour, attracted over 2.5 million listeners. During the war years she remained the leading radio act in the country and even appeared in a couple of Hollywood films with titles like *Swing in the Saddle*. In the late 1940s she finally got around to recording, producing an early bluegrass classic with her version of "Ruby," an exciting old song propelled by Emmy's twelve-inch S.S. Stewart open-back banjo. In 1947 folklorist Alan Lomax recorded an album by her called *Kentucky Mountain Ballads*, one of the finest collections of traditional Kentucky music recorded. In her later years Emmy moved to the west coast, and in the 1960s made a comeback working with the New Lost City Ramblers. When she died in 1980, Cousin Emmy had received only a fraction of the recognition due her for her contribution to American music: as an instrumentalist whose skill inspired other performers like Grandpa Jones; as a pioneer woman performer in a field that had been all too much dominated by men; and as a Kentucky folk artist who refused to sell out or compromise the music that she saw at once as her birthright and her heritage.

An unidentified family poses with homemade instruments, about 1935.
Jean Thomas, The Traipsin' Woman, Collection, University of Louisville Photographic Archives

Leonard Rutherford and Dick Burnett

Uncredited photos are from the author's collection.

Unknown Kentucky fiddlers at a contest sponsored by Henry Ford in Louisville, 1925. *Caufield and Shook Collection, University of Louisville Photographic Archives*

Edgar Boaz, Welby Toomey, Dennis W. Taylor, and Fiddlin' Doc Roberts at an early recording session at the Gennett studio, Richmond, Indiana, 1925

James Roberts *(left)* and Irene Amburgey *(right)* performing as James and Martha Carson about 1948 on the WSB Barnyard Jamboree, Atlanta. *Courtesy of James Roberts*

Asa Martin, about 1975
The Pepiot Studio

Left: Buell Kazee, 1970
The Pepiot Studio

Below left: Emry Arthur
Don Nelson and John Edwards
Memorial Foundation

Below right: Ted Gossett

Above: Guitarist
Joe Steen and band

Right: Blind Joe Mangrum
Caufield and Shook Collection,
University of Louisville
Photographic Archives

Joe Troyan, Bradley Kincaid, and Grandpa Jones in Boston in the mid-1930s

The Cumberland Ridge Runners in 1931. *Left to right:* Harty Taylor, Doc Hopkins, Karl Davis, and "Slim" Miller. *R.R. Powell*

Karl and Harty

Above: The Prairie Ramblers

Left: The cover of Asher and Little Jimmie Sizemore's "Hearth & Home Songs" (1935)

Above: Wilbur Ball and Cliff Carlisle, 1921
Below: Bill Carlisle, Shannon Grayson, and Cliff Carlisle
Photos courtesy of the Country Music Foundation Library and Media Center

Jean Thomas, founder of the American Folk Song Festival *(above)*, and Jilson Setters *(below)*, one of her discoveries. *Jean Thomas, The Traipsin' Woman, Collection, University of Louisville Photographic Archives*

Above: John Lair *(at mike)* and the Renfro Valley Gang. *Left to right, back row:* Slim Miller, Lynn Davis, Jack Holden, Fairley Holden, Jerry Behrens, Marvin Taylor, Ernie Lee; *middle row:* Shorty Hobbs, Bob Simmons; *front row:* Little Eller Long, Jean Dickerson, Molly O'Day, and Judy Dickerson. *R.R. Powell*

Right: John Jacob Niles, 1967 *The Pepiot Studio*

The Coon Creek Girls: Rosie Ledford, Violet Koehler, Lily May Ledford, and Daisy Lange

THE COURIER-JOURNAL, LOUISVILLE, TUESDAY MORNING, JANUARY 25, 1938.

Behind the Scenes At Flood Gratitude Show

—(C.-J. Photo.

Cousin Emmy of WHAS rehearses in the dressing-room at the Armory. Her audience consists of Sarie, left, and Sallie, right, of WSM, Nashville.

Cousin Emmy (Cynthia May Carver)

Left: Renfro Valley founder
John Lair, 1975
The Pepiot Studio

Below: Lonesome Luke and His Farm
Boys, about 1930. *Left to right,
standing:* Luke Decker, J.C. "Red"
Sumter, Rex Grant, unknown; *seated:*
Ed Grant, Jimmy Eliu, Ira "Happy"
Decker, and Joe Steen

The Bluegrass Hawaiian Trio, 1925. *Left to right:*
Kermit Whalen, Evelyn Jackson, and J. Eldon Whalen

Cliff Gross and His Texas Cowboys, about 1941. *University of Louisville Photographic Archives*

Above: Clayton McMichen's Georgia Wildcats at WAVE in the late 1940s. *Left to right:* Ordie Lee Day, Bob Simmons, McMichen, Tony Sheeler, Claude Cobb, and Bernie Smith

Left: Pee Wee King, about 1937

Charlie and Bill Monroe, 1936
Photo courtesy of the Country Music Foundation Library and Media Center

Above: Birch Monroe, with brother
Bill in the background, 1975
Carl Fleischhauer photo

Left: Kenny Baker, 1982
Julie Aiken photo

Bobby and Sonny, the Osborne Brothers, 1970
Carl Fleischhauer photo

J.D. Crowe and Red Allen, 1968. *Marty Godbey photo*

Ricky Skaggs, J.D. Crowe, and Tony Rice of The New South, 1975.
Marty Godbey photo

The only known photograph
of Arnold Schultz *(left)*,
shown here with Clarence
Wilson, probably late
1920s. *John Edwards
Memorial Foundation*

Left: Merle Travis
Below: Grandpa Jones
Photos courtesy of the
Country Music Foundation
Library and Media Center

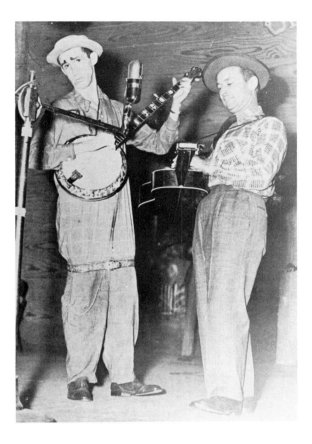

Above: Stringbean (David Akeman)
and Lew Childre, 1936

Left: Red Foley

Lonzo and Oscar, about 1973

Lynn Davis and Molly O'Day

Roscoe Holcomb, 1975. *Loyal Jones photo*

The Rambos: Reba, Buck, and Dottie

Loretta Lynn, 1965

Jean Ritchie, 1974
Carl Fleischhauer photo

Much of the national success of Louisville radio stars in the mid- and late 1930s stemmed from their association with J.L. Frank (1900–1952), an Alabama native who was one of country music's first great promoters and bookers. Frank moved to Louisville about 1935 from Chicago, where he had worked with WLS stars and been instrumental in furthering Gene Autry's career. During his tenure in Louisville, from 1936 to 1939, he was able to persuade WHAS to offer lucrative weekly salaries to lure country music performers to the station. He was instumental in building the career of Pee Wee King (in fact, Pee Wee married his daughter), and he pioneered booking techniques in the area. After he moved to Nashville in 1939 he helped develop the careers of stars like Roy Acuff and Ernest Tubb, earning for himself the nickname "The Flo Ziegfeld of Country Music."

Throughout the 1940s two bands dominated the Louisville airwaves and dance halls, Cliff Gross's Texas Cowboys and Clayton "Pappy" McMichen's Georgia Wildcats. The two bands had much in common: each was headed by a skilled veteran fiddler who had won a reputation elsewhere before moving to Louisville; each played a peculiar amalgam of traditional string band music and swing; each utilized wind instruments as well as string instruments; and each served as a training school for later country musicians.

Clifford Gross (1898–1956) was one of the greatest, and one of the most unsung, of Kentucky fiddlers. He was born in Butler County, near Bowling Green, in the same general area that produced the Carver Boys, Tex Atchison, and Bill Monroe, and learned his trade by playing at old roadhouses along the Green River. During his apprenticeship he picked up scores of old Kentucky fiddle tunes that he later was to record: "Green River Waltz," "Sleepin' Lula," "Stony Point," "Rocky Mountain Goat," and a tune called "Houchin's Waltz" that he may well have learned from W.B. Houchens. In 1931 Cliff got a letter from a pair of distant cousins, Kermit and June Whalen, who had grown up in nearby Warren County but migrated to Texas when a sister married and moved there. The Whalens, guitarists and singers, had formed a group called the Bluegrass Trio that started playing over WBAP in Fort Worth in 1925, and within a few years they were involved in the beginning of the western swing movement. (June, in fact, was to become a charter member of Bob Wills's original Texas Playboys, and later to appear on the NBC network in the mid-1930s.) In 1931 the Whalens were playing for a band called the Hi-Flyers, and needed a fiddler; that's when they wrote Cliff. He came and began working with groups around Fort Worth, and for a time had his own group, the Kentucky Hillbillies, over KTAT in 1933. The times were not good for a new band, though, and within a few months Cliff joined one of the area's leading western swing bands, the Light Crust Doughboys. This band, headed by colorful radio personality W. Lee O'Daniel (later to become governor of Texas) and sponsored by Burris Mills Flour Company, was one of the most influential of the early western swing bands. In fact, the fiddler Cliff replaced in the band was a young man named Bob Wills, who had left to form his Texas Playboys. Cliff—by now known as "Doctor" Gross—played lead fiddle on the Doughboys' first records, made in 1933, including their famous version of "Beautiful Texas." A string of successful Doughboys records followed, including several of Cliff's fiddle originals, such as "Saturday Night Rag," "Kill 'em," and "Texas Breakdown," records which featured Cliff playing in a breakneck style that included take-off solos and dazzling bow technique. Ironically, this Kentucky boy made a considerable impact on other Texas fiddlers who heard him and picked up his tunes. In 1937 and 1938 Cliff also recorded eighteen fiddle solos with just a guitar back-up, under the names of "Cliff and Ray" (Ray DeArmond, a Texas guitarist) or "Clifford Gross and Muryel Campbell"; these included fiddle standards like "Waggoner" as well as many of Cliff's early Kentucky tunes. Issued on the Vocalion and Melotone labels, these records were for years about the only new fiddle solo records issued by commercial companies.

In 1938 Cliff organized another Texas band, the Universal Cowboys, but soon left it to return to Kentucky. He settled in Louisville in 1939, organized Cliff Gross's Texas Cowboys, and began playing over WINN. He sent for one of his fellow members of the Doughboys, James "Doc" Eastwood, to play tenor banjo and guitar in the new band, and hired Doc's wife, Linda Lou, as vocalist. "We spent a lot of time working these little water holes around here and starving to death," recalls Doc. "It's a good thing we had had some money saved up. Finally Clayton McMichen was able to get us on that job he had at the Howell Furniture Company over WAVE and we were able to really get started." The Howell Furniture Company, on Main Street in downtown Louisville, had a huge building with a stage on the second floor. For several years in the 1940s the company sponsored a live broadcast from this stage every day at noon and on Saturday night, over WAVE. "That Saturday night show was something," recalls Linda Lou. "We would merge the two bands, the Texas Cowboys and the Georgia Wildcats, and we'd have four fiddles playing together."

Personnel for the Texas Cowboys at times included Sonny Haley, a guitarist from West Memphis, Arkansas; Gabe Tucker, a trumpet player who later went on to become one of country music's most successful managers and to enjoy a close association with Elvis Presley; Sleepy Howell, an accordion player; and Oscar Sullivan, who played mandolin and drums and later became half of the comedy team of Lonzo and Oscar. Gross made no recordings of any substantial sort during these years, but was vastly popular around Louisville and hosted numerous guests who came through the area—Smiley Burnett, Roy Rogers, Minnie Pearl, and others. He "retired" to Bowling Green about 1953 and still played part time with local bands there until his death from a heart attack in 1956.

The Georgia Wildcats who shared the Howell Furniture stage with Gross had been together in various forms since 1931, when Clayton McMichen broke away from one of the most famous old-time bands of the 1920s, the Skillet Lickers. McMichen (1900–1970) was a native of north Georgia who early in his life mastered the "long bow" technique that permitted him to embellish his fiddle solos with long, graceful runs. Throughout the 1920s he was a studio musician for the Columbia Record Company in their Atlanta studio, the Nashville of the 1920s, appearing as a back-up man on dozens of records, including some by his friend Jimmie Rodgers. McMichen soon tired of playing what he referred to as "swamp opera," though, and left Atlanta to organize a western swing type of band, the Wildcats. Throughout the 1930s this band held forth at radio stations in the South and even Northeast, made a series of exciting records for Decca, and was home for a number of inventive young musicians, including Merle Travis, Carl Cotner (later music director for Gene Autry), Jack Dunigan, Slim Bryant (an innovative guitarist), and fiddler Kenny Newton. In 1940 McMichen moved to Louisville and reorganized the band, bringing in local musicians like Chick Sale (bass), Paul Sapp (guitar), Dixie Lee (piano), George Eaglelite (fiddle), and guitarist Bernie Smith. "We played country clubs, theaters, school houses, fiddlin' contests, court houses, what have you," recalls Smith. "Any place that paid money. During this time Mr. Howell, who owned the furniture company, had made a trip to St. Louis and heard a show out there on KMOX called 'The Uncle Dick Slack Show' that was performed from a furniture store. He talked to us about doing our radio show from his store, which he had moved to Main Street."

About this time Mac decided to organize a dixieland band. "There weren't many good dixieland bands around then," recalls

Smith, "and we set out to get the best local men we could find. We got Tiny Thomale on piano, Buddy Gray on sax, Clark Horn on clarinet (and doing arrangements), Jess Carmen on drums, Chick Sale on bass, and Owen Kopp and later Frank Catterton on trombone. Our first trumpet man was Johnny Reiger, later replaced by Tony Sheeler. We really had a swingin' band. Our band sounded so great that people came all the way from New Orleans to hear and see us." At one point the Howell noon show was so popular that a survey indicated that eight out of ten listeners were tuned to it. Mac (or Pappy, as he came to be known to Louisville fans) first used as his theme song the old fiddle standard "Sweet Bunch of Daisies," and then later changed it to "South." Many people today remember Bernie Smith's electric guitar (replete with modifications by Mac, who was an electrician) and the way he played fiddle tunes on it. Others remember Pappy still unable to stay away from Kentucky fiddle contests; he had been national champion over a dozen times, and as late as 1968 was able to win the Kentucky State Championship at Mayfield. Pappy retired in 1955 and ran a tavern in Louisville for several years before his death in 1970.

As McMichen's star in Louisville was falling in the late 1940s, a new one began to rise: that of a slender, good-natured young man who fronted a smart-suited band called the Golden West Cowboys and played an unlikely country instrument, the accordion. His name was Pee Wee King, and though he was not born in Kentucky he made Louisville his adopted home town during two decades that saw him write and record some of the most beloved country songs, including "Tennessee Waltz," and pioneer all kinds of innovations in the music. From the time they moved to Louisville in 1948 until the time they broke up in 1969, the Golden West Cowboys introduced thousands of country fans to such uptown elements as trumpets, drums, accordions, twin fiddles, and elaborate vocal arrangements. In one sense, they saw what McMichen was trying to do and took it a step further; indeed, when Pee Wee first came to Louisville in the 1930s he even then recognized how important McMichen was. "They were the Glenn Miller of the country music field," he said of the Georgia Wildcats. "They had a *fine* band." With the help of his father-in-law, master promoter J.L. Frank, Pee Wee promoted the new uptown country style in a way McMichen never had, and watched with satisfaction as his group was voted Top Country Band from 1951 to 1955.

Frank King (the name "Pee Wee" was given to him by Gene

Autry in 1934 because, at five-foot-seven, he was the smallest member of the band) was actually born in Abrams, Wisconsin, in rich dairy country, on February 18, 1914. Pee Wee's family name was Kuczynski, and his Polish-American father had a local polka band while young Frank was growing up. Frank got his first accordion when he was fifteen, and was soon leading his own band, playing polka and cowboy songs on local stations. One day cowboy star Gene Autry, then appearing on Chicago radio, heard the band and hired them to be his back-up group. In 1934 Autry and the band moved to WHAS Louisville, but Autry was beginning to get calls from Hollywood, and after eight months he went to the west coast to work in films. (It is interesting to speculate on the effect he might have had on country music in Louisville had he stayed.) Pee Wee then took a job with Franke Moore's Log Cabin Boys, and stayed with them through 1935 and into the first part of 1936. He was to recall years later, "None of us liked Louisville at first. No, we crossed that bridge over here, said 'The Gateway to the South,' and I said, 'Let's see what it says on the other side; if it's "Gateway to the North," let's go back!' We never realized that someday we'd be here permanently." With the Log Cabin Boys, Pee Wee became a member of the Crazy Water Barn Dance, with Bob Atcher, the Callahan Brothers, the Arizona Ranch Girls, and a "Mickey" band headed by Dave Durman.* "We took it on the road—we played Shelbyville, and Frankfort and Versailles— tobacco barns, usually, in the Kentucky area." When it became obvious that Autry was in Hollywood to stay, Pee Wee formed his own band and named them the Golden West Cowboys—a name he chose, he recalls, because he "had a crush" on the popular Chicago duet, the Girls of the Golden West. Personnel included fiddler Abner Sims, singer Texas Daisy, guitarist Curly Rhodes, and for a time the comedy team of Homer and Jethro.

In 1935 Pee Wee met a girl who was then singing with McMichen's band, Lydia Frank; her father, J.L. Frank, was the promoter who had handled Autry, as well as Fibber McGee and Molly, the Hoosier Hotshots, and others. In 1936 Pee Wee and Lydia were married, and Frank began to help promote the Golden West Cowboys, as well. One of his first acts was to introduce Pee

* A "Mickey" band was one that had one or two horns, usually clarinet and trumpet, and specialized in novelty tunes and standards that were suitable for lodge dances. Dave Durham, however, had a band hotter than average; his Dixieland Swingsters did two sessions for Bluebird in 1938–1939 and merged country string band music, western swing, and the kind of novelty items done by the Hoosier Hotshots.

Wee to Redd Stewart, a Tennessee boy who had been playing fiddle on another Louisville band called the Kentucky Wildcats; later Redd was to join Pee Wee's group. In the meantime, though, the group headed for Nashville, where, on June 1, 1937, they joined the cast of the Grand Ole Opry.

They made quite an impact on that staid and conservative program. Pee Wee was one of the first members of the cast to carry a union card (many country musicians, not being able to read music, were barred from unions), his music had a distinct cowboy flavor, and his band always dressed in style. He was one of the first to use an electric instrument on stage (his steel guitarist was former Roy Acuff sideman Clell Sumney), the first to use drums, and probably the first to use a trumpet, when his horn man sounded taps for President Roosevelt in 1945. As a member of the Camel Caravan during the early days of World War II, he toured military bases across the U.S. and even into Central America. His radio fame continued to grow, but it was not until 1946 that he made his first recording under his own name: "You Were the Cause of It All" and "That Cheap Look in Your Eye," done for Bullet, a Nashville company.

During these years, a number of excellent vocalists passed through the band: Eddy Arnold, Cowboy Copas, and Pete Pyle were only three who gained fame later on their own. One of the smoothest singers, though, was Henry Ellis (Redd) Stewart, who joined the band in the early 1940s. "Redd and I hit it off right off the bat," Pee Wee recalled. "We drove the luggage truck." The luggage truck was the quietest spot in the touring caravan, and it allowed both Redd and Pee Wee to concentrate and do a little song-writing. One Friday night in 1946, the two were listening to Bill Monroe's "Kentucky Waltz" on the radio when Redd commented that it was odd that nobody had ever written a Tennessee waltz song. "So we took an old melody that we were using as our theme—the 'No Name Waltz'—and Redd started writing the lyrics on the back of a match book cover. . . . And we kept puttin' it together." Ace songwriter Fred Rose changed one phrase and pronounced the song fit for consumption. On December 2, 1947, Pee Wee, now with a new contract from RCA Victor Records, went to Chicago to record the new song; Redd and James Boyd played twin fiddles, Pee Wee the accordion, Roy Ayers steel guitar, and Sticks MacDonald drums, and Pee Wee's first record hit was born. Over the next thirty years "The Tennessee Waltz" would be recorded over three hundred times and sell over forty million records.

At the height of this new popularity, in 1948 Pee Wee decided to move from Nashville to Louisville. "The main reason I left the Grand Ole Opry was I wanted television," he recalled. The Opry management saw no future in TV; Pee Wee did. "It happened to be that I came to Louisville at the right time, because that's when we started—we were the first thing on television in the Louisville area. Stayed on for right at . . . well, almost fifteen years." Pee Wee's act had always had a strong visual dimension, with his snappy costumes and vaudeville-like sense of pacing. Soon, in addition to his show in Louisville on Thursday nights, he had a show over WBBM Chicago on Saturdays, one from Cleveland on Mondays, and one over WLW Cincinnati on Wednesdays. This pace continued throughout the early 1950s. And in addition to the four television shows, he ran a weekly network radio show.

Incredibly, his hit records kept coming, as well, and the new songs he found time to co-author with Stewart or with other partners, such as Louisville music librarian Chilton Price. Among the 400-odd songs Pee Wee wrote or helped write were "Slowpoke" (actually his most successful hit record), "Bonaparte's Retreat" (based on an old fiddle tune and put together in the last seven minutes of a record session to fill out a side), and "You Belong to Me" (a hit by pop singer Jo Stafford). Other hits for Victor included "Silver and Gold" (1952), "Busybody" (1952), "Bimbo" (1954), and "Changing Partners" (1954). From 1947 to 1957 he was associated with WAVE in Louisville, on both radio and television, and during that time invested in a number of local enterprises, including a record store. On October 23, 1971, Kentucky Governor Louie B. Nunn issued a written proclamation announcing Pee Wee King Day in Kentucky. A huge crowd, as well as dozens of luminaries from show business, attended the festivities at Madisonville. In 1974 he was elected to the Country Music Hall of Fame.

Meanwhile the country music radio scene in Louisville, once so rich and promising, continued to dwindle away. Throughout most of the 1950s Randy Atcher's staff band at WHAS kept a spark of the old flame alive; it included Sleepy Marlin on fiddle, Shorty Chesire on guitar, Tiny Thomale on piano, George and Jane Workman on bass and guitar, and Bernie Smith. This lasted until about 1960, when WHAS got rid of all its staff musicians. The age of live radio country music in Louisville had ended, not with a bang, but a whimper.

5 Bluegrass Picking

American soldiers coming home after the end of World War II found a different world from the one they had left. It was a world of housing shortages, runaway inflation, new industries, and applied technologies that were bringing them everything from the garbage disposal to the television set. The big bands were disappearing as fast as dinosaurs, and singers were replacing instrumentalists as the kings of pop music. Fans of country music noticed that the string band at the local dance hall had a new sound, as well; the five-string banjo and the fiddle had been replaced by two new technical innovations, the steel guitar and the electric lead guitar. Country music was going uptown; no longer confined to the South, it had secure enclaves on the west coast, in Chicago, and even in New York. Everywhere the sound was becoming more modern, more sophisticated, more pop. Throughout the 1930s Kentucky musicians had done their share to help nurture this popularity, and a new generation of musicians was ready to do the same for the 1940s. Yet they were to do so not by inventing new forms for the music nor new instruments, but by injecting a new vitality into instrumental techniques, and by utilizing the most basic of all country instruments to forge a new sound that was to have a major effect on the music as a whole. During the 1940s Kentuckians set new standards for the guitar, the mandolin, and the banjo, and fitted new vocal styles to these standards. The mandolin music was redefined by Bill and Charlie Monroe, the guitar was made into a solo instrument by men like Ike Everly, Mose Rager, and Merle Travis, and the banjo was rescued from obscurity by popular singers like Grandpa Jones and Stringbean, and by technicians like Sonny Osborne. As the big western swing bands broke up and the Hollywood cowboys hung up their hats, this generation of Kentucky pickers gave the music and its fans a much-needed course in "back to the basics."

The course started with Bill Monroe's developing the brand of music that was to become one of Kentucky's most famous exports: bluegrass. The development of this style—which one folklorist has described as "folk music with overdrive"—actually dates from the 1940–1945 era, when Monroe's band was broadcasting regularly from the Grand Ole Opry, touring weekly, and commanding a huge audience across the South. Through his strong personality and stubborn dedication to his musical principles, Monroe succeeded in preserving an acoustic music in the face of a growing trend to add electric instruments, wind instruments, and even drums to the country band of the day. He did this by making his acoustic music different from any that had gone before. To the casual listener the main difference was speed: Monroe's music demanded new standards of musicianship and was taken at tempos twice or even three times as fast as normal. When the older string bands strove for an ensemble sound, usually with a fiddle lead, Monroe let instrumentalists trade leads and even tried improvised solos. He featured the mandolin, which was passé in most other country bands of the mid-1940s, and the five-string banjo, which was almost extinct in commercial music by then. Bluegrass singing was high, strong, and loud, a far cry from the crooning styles of Eddy Arnold or Jimmy Wakely so much in fashion then, and the songs tended to be cast in an older, more sentimental vein than the heart songs featured by the crooners. When Monroe finally perfected his sound, on the Grand Ole Opry stage in 1946, fans in the Ryman auditorium screamed and shouted until radio listeners couldn't hear what was happening. Bluegrass has retained this original popularity in the South, and was the first type of country music to win large numbers of fans in the northern urban areas and in colleges and universities across the country. It has been hailed as a major American art form and has been analyzed and studied as exhaustively as jazz. Yet there is no way to read the history of bluegrass without putting Bill Monroe squarely in the middle, and without seeing his vision as its principal force.

Many people tend to associate bluegrass with the five-string banjo: they think of Earl Scruggs playing the "Foggy Mountain Breakdown," or of the "Dueling Banjos" sequence from *Deliverance*, or of Roy Clark ripping off "Cripple Creek" on "Hee

Haw." Yet Monroe's prototype of bluegrass music had no banjo in it; his first recording band, the first incarnation of the Blue Grass Boys (Monroe has always spelled it as two words) in 1939–1940, had no banjo, and his first banjo player, David "Stringbean" Akeman, was used more in a back-up rhythm role than as a lead. Indeed, when talking about the instruments of bluegrass, Monroe has said: "Well, it was bound to be the mandolin, the first one, then the guitar and then we added a fiddle and a bass. A banjo was about the fifth child that was born to bluegrass, but it's helped bluegrass. It's done wonderful for bluegrass." The mandolin, popularized in the country by the turn of the century through Gibson's mandolin societies and Sears's catalogue sales, had always been more popular in Kentucky than in other southern states. Mandolins were a part of almost all the early Kentucky string bands, and early performers like Shorty Hobbs, James Roberts, the Bird family, Larry Hensley, and Karl Davis had featured the instrument on early recordings and radio. Yet the mandolin came to Bill Monroe because as a boy he was the runt of the litter and his older brothers had already appropriated the more popular instruments.

This was in Rosine, in western Kentucky, where William Smith Monroe had been born on September 13, 1911. There Buck and Malissa Monroe had a 655-acre farm which they worked with their eight sons, farming, cutting timber, and even doing some coal mining. Buck was an exacting and demanding father who instilled in his children a sense of discipline and a strong work ethic, qualities both Bill and Charlie were to display later in their music as well as their personal lives. Most of the music in the family came down through Malissa's side, the Vandivers; Malissa herself liked to sing ballads like "The Butcher's Boy" and to play the fiddle and accordion. But the primary musical influence on the boys was Malissa's brother Pendleton Vandiver, or, as Bill was to call him later, "Uncle Pen." Music meant more to young Bill Monroe than to his brothers because his very poor eyesight prevented his playing baseball or engaging in many of the normal recreations of country boys.

By the time he was twelve or thirteen, young Bill was travelling by mule with his Uncle Pen to local dances, backing him on the guitar for two or five dollars a night. After his father died, Bill moved up to Pen's cabin and lived with him, learning his vast repertoire of fiddle tunes and transferring them to the mandolin. "One thing that did stay in my mind," he recalled later, "is the fiddle numbers that Uncle Pen played. Now that really stuck to me. I can play 95 per cent of each tune he played. I must've listened awfully close when he was playing." Another influence on young Monroe's instrumental technique was a local black guitar player named Arnold Schultz; some fans of Monroe have jumped to the conclusion that since Schultz was black, he was responsible for the "blues" element in Monroe's later music. Monroe is careful to note, though, that he listened to Schultz play in a conventional black string band, featuring numbers like "Sally Goodin." (As we shall see, Kentucky was home for a strong "black hillbilly" tradition for generations.) "There's things in my music, you know, that come from Arnold Schultz—runs that I use in a lot of my music. . . . In following a fiddle piece or a breakdown, he used a pick and he could run from one chord to another the prettiest way you ever heard."

The "high lonesome" quality of Monroe's singing, so often copied and analyzed in later years, came not from local blues singers but from Monroe's own experiences. "There was a time there when my brothers, they'd all left, you know, and my father and mother had passed away, and I lived on the farm a long time, and all that I heard was the foxhound or the birds or something like that. And I would sing kindly the way I felt. I'd be out in the field, maybe, rabbit hunting or something like that, and—I always liked a touch of the blues, you know, and I put some of that into my singing." Notions of vocal harmony came from the old shape-note singing schools held every summer at the Methodist and Baptist churches, which Bill and his brothers attended.

As it turned out, two of Bill's older brothers were to be important in his music: Charlie, who was a guitarist and fine lead singer, and Birch, who played fiddle and string bass. In 1929 young Bill joined these two in Indiana, where they had gone to work in the auto industry, and for the next five years the trio played at local dances, with Birch playing fiddle, Bill chording along on the mandolin, and Charlie on guitar. In 1934 Texas Crystals, a patent medicine company, offered the group full-time radio work; Birch dropped out but Bill and Charlie decided to have a go at it. They reworked their act to concentrate on vocal music and, lacking Birch's fiddle lead, they were forced to use Bill's mandolin to play melody on instrumental passages. While their vocal duets were certainly adequate—Bill always sang tenor, developing even more his "high lonesome" sound—it was their instrumental virtuosity that began to attract attention: they took numbers at breakneck speed, with Bill playing lead and fills and "turnarounds" on the mandolin with dazzling dexterity.

The mid-1930s was the age of the vocal duet in country music, and the Monroe Brothers were only one of a number of similar duet acts on southern radio at that time: Karl and Harty, the Callahan Brothers, the Bolick Brothers (the Blue Sky Boys), Lonnie and Roy, the Delmore Brothers. In the fall of 1935 their sponsors sent the Monroes to the Carolinas, and suddenly they found their audience. In Spartanburg, in Charlotte, in Greenville, they found that their radio shows drew in sacks of mail and that they were able to book personals with surprising ease. They were so successful on radio, in fact, that when an RCA Victor talent scout asked them to record, they felt they were too busy and ignored the request. Fortunately the Victor representative, Eli Oberstein, was persistent and finally got the brothers into a temporary studio set up in a warehouse in Charlotte. "They had two mikes set up in this place where they kept the records," recalled Bill. "It wasn't nothing fancy. We sung on the same mike, I remember. But one thing—if Charlie said one word and I said it different, why, they never did correct us. I was real young, and we let a few things like that get by that should have been corrected. . . . I guess if we had to do it over, some of the songs would be pitched higher than we had 'em back in those days." In spite of all this, the first session, held on February 17, 1936, was a success, for it yielded the Monroes' first hit record, "What Will You Give in Exchange for Your Soul?," an old sacred song the boys had learned as teenagers back in Rosine. In fact, over half the tunes from this first session were gospel numbers, reflecting how much a part of their repertoire then was devoted to gospel songs. Throughout his later career, Bill was to feature such old-time gospel numbers, and for years on the Opry featured the Blue Grass Quartet doing old-time gospel quartet numbers at the end of a set.

The career of the Monroe Brothers only lasted about four years, and is today often seen as a prelude to greater things for both men. But the Monroe Brothers were important in their own right, and a substantial part of the music scene of the 1930s. The sixty recordings they made for Victor between 1936 and 1938, which included relatively few original songs, carried their native Kentucky music throughout the South and established such standards as "My Long Journey Home," "Roll in My Sweet Baby's Arms," "All the Good Times Are Passed and Gone," "He Will Set Your Fields on Fire," and "New River Train." At this time the boys were not writing much original material but depending on old traditional songs they had learned as boys, old prewar gospel songs, and the music of other Kentucky groups like the Prairie

Rambers and Karl and Harty. In spite of their close harmony, though, the personalities of Bill and Charlie were radically different: Charlie was handsome, athletic, outgoing, and friendly, always eager to please his audience. Bill was more introspective, moody, uncomfortable on stage, possessing some sort of inner drive that expressed itself mainly through his mandolin playing. It was in part this difference in the men and their approaches to music that eventually caused their split in 1938.

While Charlie formed a band that was called simply Monroe's Boys and continued to work the Carolinas, Bill took off for Arkansas, where he organized his first band, the Kentuckians. For the next couple of years he experimented with different musicians and sounds (for a time he even had a jug player) at different stations, eventually naming his band the Blue Grass Boys while playing on an Atlanta station. He auditioned in 1939 for the Grand Ole Opry on WSM Nashville with this band. "I'd already decided on using the name 'bluegrass,' because that's what they call Kentucky, the Blue Grass state. So I just used 'Bill Monroe and the Blue Grass Boys' and that let people throughout the country know I was from Kentucky, saved a lot of people from having to ask me where I was from." After playing "Mule Skinner Blues" and "John Henry" and an old fiddle tune, "Bile'em Cabbage Down," Monroe was hired by Judge Hay, the Opry's founder. "They said I had the kind of music that National Life needed—that the Grand Ole Opry needed," recalled Bill. This was in October 1939, and Bill has remained with the Opry ever since.

Actually, few members of this early band were from the Bluegrass State. Stringbean, David Akeman, who played banjo from 1942 to 1945, was a Kentuckian, but most hailed from Tennessee or the Carolinas. The first recording session by the Blue Grass Boys (held in a hotel room in Atlanta on October 7, 1940), for instance, featured North Carolinian Clyde Moody (vocal and guitar), Georgia fiddler Tommy Magness, and Tennessean Bill Wesbrook (string bass). Later Blue Grass Boys were to include Tennessean Howdy Forrester (later Roy Acuff's fiddler), North Carolinians Art Wooten and Earl Scruggs, Tennessean Lester Flatt, and Florida native Chubby Wise.

The band also brought a new caliber of technical musicianship to the Opry stage. In addition to the up-tempo, split-second timing, Monroe "pitched the music up where it would do a number some good." "We was the first ever to wear a white shirt on the Opry or wear a tie. We was the first outfit to ever play in B-flat or B-natural and E. Before that it was all C, D, and G. Fiddle men had a fit and they wouldn't hardly tackle it and they'd swear that they wanted to play straight stuff and they figured that's where I should sing. And there's where bluegrass really advanced music." The advances went into overdrive in 1945, when Lester Flatt, Earl Scruggs, and Chubby Wise all joined within a few months. Flatt added his considerable songwriting talents to the group, and a strong lead voice that had, ironically, been honed through an apprenticeship with Charlie Monroe in North Carolina. Wise added his blues-tinged fiddle to the sound, and Earl Scruggs added an electrifying three-finger banjo style that soon threatened to become the music's prime characteristic. Old-timers on the Opry didn't quite know what to make of Scruggs—Judge Hay liked to refer to him as "the boy who makes the banjo talk"—but audiences did, and they shook the Ryman with their screams and applause. The 1946 band was considered by many to be the greatest bluegrass band of all time, and it was the main trunk from which all the other branches sprang.

The band's Columbia records, some forty of them, done between 1945 and 1948, achieved wide popularity and remained in print for years—indeed, are still in print today. They include original versions of many of the bluegrass classics. "Kentucky Waltz" was a song Monroe had originally written back in 1935 but did not record until 1945, and it became so popular that Pee Wee King and Redd Stewart later wrote their follow-up to it, "The Tennessee Waltz." Other Monroe compositions were equally heavy on nostalgia and sentiment, and many focused on Kentucky as a source of this: "Blue Moon of Kentucky," later to be even more famous as one side of Elvis Presley's first recordings, or "I'm Going Back to Old Kentucky," probably based on an older minstrel tune known for years in Kentucky. One big hit, "Molly and Tenbrooks (The Race Horse Song)," was based on the well-known folk song dating from the 1880s. There were hot blues numbers—"Heavy Traffic Ahead" and "True Life Blues" and "Rocky Road Blues"—and new up-tempo love laments like "Will You Be Loving Another Man?" and "Why Did You Wander?," most written or rearranged by Monroe. About a fourth were gospel tunes, including one of Monroe's most popular original gospel songs, "Wicked Path of Sin," and others like "I'm Travellin' On and On." These songs pretty much defined the basic bluegrass repertoire for years, and were the models for dozens of later songs.

Flatt and Scruggs left Monroe in early 1948 and, along with the Stanley Brothers, began to plant new seeds of bluegrass in other states, especially the Carolinas, east Tennessee, and Virginia.

Monroe continued to work from his Opry base, consolidating his music and using his band as a training ground for dozens of other musicians who were to make their mark on the music. He began recording for Decca in 1950—one of his first popular Decca records was his famous "Uncle Pen," his tribute to Pen Vandiver—with a band that included Jimmy Martin and a very young Vassar Clements, both to become bluegrass stars in later years. For a time in the early 1950s the Nashville studio producers managed to push Bill in the direction of a more modern "country" sound: some recordings from this era featured lead electric guitar, drums, and on one or two forgettable occasions, a vibraphone.

The mid-1950s were lean years for Monroe, for bluegrass, and for any form of older country music. Elvis Presley and rock and roll were changing the face of pop music, and for a time threatened to submerge any other forms. The acoustic string band music of Monroe, regardless of how innovative it was or how skillfully it was played, seemed doomed. Monroe's first reaction was to create larger, more elaborate ensembles, and for a time he was carrying as many as three fiddlers with his group and spotlighting hot instrumental numbers like "Tall Timber," "Wheel Hoss," and "Roanoke." This was winning back some of the audience that had been lost to rock, but bluegrass began to acquire a new audience at the end of the 1950s when northern urbanites and college students discovered it. In 1959 *Esquire* magazine published a groundbreaking piece on bluegrass by Alan Lomax, and the renewed interest in folk music across the country began to make it possible for bluegrass musicians to get bookings at folk festivals. In 1963 Monroe made his first college concert appearance at the University of Chicago Folk Festival, as well as his first New York appearance; in July his band opened the Newport Folk Festival before an audience of 15,000. Bill began to realize the extent of his appeal to non-southern audiences even more when a young northern college graduate named Bill Keith learned his music and joined his band as banjoist. This began a period when "outsiders"—musicians from outside the southern tradition—began to invigorate the Blue Grass Boys: guitarist-singer Pete Rowan from Cambridge, fiddler Richard Greene from California, singer-guitarist Roland White from Maine, banjoist Vic Jordan from Washington, and fiddler Byron Berline from Oklahoma. Many of these musicians went on to form the second or even third generation of bluegrass styles, including experimental forms that were later called "newgrass."

As a way to reach this new heterogeneous and widespread bluegrass audience, promoters hit upon the idea of a bluegrass festival. The first major festival was held in Roanoke, Virginia, in 1965, and was designed as a history of bluegrass, with Monroe as the central figure. Dozens of the musicians who had served in Bill's band came back to rejoin him on stage and delight a large audience. Within ten years, the idea of the festival had caught on, and over a hundred were being scheduled each summer from Pennsylvania to California. Bill himself started one of the most successful of these festivals in the mid-1960s at a tract of land he owned at Bean Blossom, Indiana, near Bloomington; since then the Bean Blossom festival has been one of the country's most dependable sources of authentic bluegrass music. Also throughout the 1970s two other key musicians emerged from the Blue Grass Boys: Monroe's son James, who developed into an excellent guitarist, songwriter, and singer, and who eventually formed his own band; and Kenny Baker, the latest in a long line of superb Kentucky fiddlers, and the latest to add his talents to Monroe's band. A former coal miner and part-time hog farmer from Jenkins, Kentucky, who has been with Monroe from 1967 to the present, Baker is without doubt the most influential fiddler playing today. His dozen-plus solo albums show that he has command of many old Kentucky fiddle tunes that would otherwise be ignored, and that his style—a sophisticated mixture of Texas, modern country, and Kentucky styles—is adaptable to everything from western swing to polkas.

Charlie Monroe, meanwhile, had his own successful career in country music until his retirement in 1955. When Bill struck out for the Grand Ole Opry, Charlie continued to work in the Carolinas, where he organized a band that was a mix of country and bluegrass. He often used a lead electric guitar, and was more prone to include novelty acts that were successful on radio and personal appearances. By the early 1940s he was calling his band the Kentucky Partners and appearing on radio in Greenville, Raleigh, Wheeling, Greensboro, Winston-Salem, and, for a year or so, over WHAS in Louisville. Among the noted musicians who worked with Charlie over the years were Lester Flatt, Curly Seckler, Red Rector, Tex Isley, and Stringbean. Charlie made a series of influential records for Victor in the early 1940s, including a song that was to become his most requested number, "Down in the Willow Garden," a well-known American murder ballad also known as "Rose Connelly." Charlie's 1947 recording of this tune established it as a standard and in later years it even found its way onto an album by pop singer Art Garfunkel. Other successful songs, most of which Charlie wrote himself, include "Who's Calling You Sweetheart Tonight?" and "Rubber Neck Blues" (both 1946),

"I'm Coming Back But I Don't Know When" (1947), "Memory Lane" (1948), and the gospel favorite "Camping in Canaan's Land" (1948). Unlike Bill's records during this period, Charlie's never featured a five-string banjo, though in one 1948 session he utilized two mandolins. In the early 1950s Charlie joined Decca Records with the idea of reuniting with Bill; while the brothers did begin to appear on stage and in concerts together, the joint recordings did not come about. Charlie retired in 1957 to run a coal mine and coal yard near Rosine, though he often made special guest appearances in later years and was recording for various small labels almost until his death in 1975. Tributes poured in hailing him—especially his singing, songwriting, and guitar playing—as an important contributor to the foundations of bluegrass.

Though Bill Monroe built bluegrass from the raw material he found in Kentucky as a youth, he never actually played regularly on any Kentucky radio station; he defined bluegrass *per se* from the stage of the Grand Ole Opry in Nashville. Likewise, many of the first generation of musicians who followed and developed Monroe's music came not from Kentucky but from east Tennessee and the Carolinas. Three conspicuous exceptions were Harley "Red" Allen and a pair of brothers from Hyden, Kentucky, named Bobby and Sonny Osborne. Allen was one of the strictest of the traditionalists, adhering closely to the Monroe-Flatt-Scruggs style, while the Osborne Brothers finally emerged in the late 1960s as the most innovative and the most commercial of all the bluegrass bands. Oddly enough, their story begins when the three of them joined forces and walked out on the stage of the Wheeling Jamboree one evening in 1956.

Bob Osborne (born 1931) played mandolin and sang tenor, while his younger brother Sonny (born 1937) played the banjo. Coming from a family that migrated north to Ohio after World War II, both grew up listening to their music in the rough, smoky bars of the central Midwest. Both were professional musicians while still in their teens: Bob worked with the Lonesome Pine Fiddlers and Jimmy Martin, while fourteen-year-old Sonny actually did a season with Monroe on the Grand Ole Opry and had a hit recording with his version of a clever banjo piece called "Sunny Mountain Chimes" for the small Gateway label in 1952. When Bob returned from the Korean War (where he was wounded by a shell fragment), they spent some time with Jimmy Martin, recording with him a famous piece called "20-20 Vision" on RCA Victor, and then joined forces with fellow Kentuckian Red Allen to win a berth on the "Wheeling Jamboree."

Both Allen and the Osbornes were veterans of the Ohio "skull orchards," where they had learned to sing loud in order to be heard, and now the three of them found that by blending their voices into a smooth-harmony trio they could achieve a whole new sound in bluegrass. Until then most bluegrass singing had been done solo or in duets: Monroe and Flatt, or Flatt and Curly Seckler. Bobby Osborne had developed one of the strongest—and highest—tenor voices in the music, and could even out-Monroe Bill Monroe's version of classics like "Muleskinner Blues." In the new band he applied this voice to an old tune he had learned from Cousin Emmy, "Ruby"; done at a breakneck tempo, featuring twin banjos, with Bobby's voice soaring into the stratosphere at the end of the phrase "Rub—eee," the song thrilled audiences everywhere and won for the group a contract with MGM records, Hank Williams's old label. The band tried several follow-ups in the mold of "Ruby," but the Osbornes didn't find their own vocal style until 1957, when they developed a new way of singing harmony. In this new style, Bobby's tenor was given the lead, or melody line, pitched up in the tenor range, in the role Monroe had always reserved for harmony. The baritone sang the next part below the tenor lead, and the regular tenor did his part an octave below normal. This arrangement was supposedly derived from the harmonics of the pedal steel guitar in modern country music; the Osbornes themselves have said it developed because Bobby's voice was so high they were forced to do it to keep from playing in impossible keys. The first record featuring this style was a conventional country love song called "Once More," a record that was so influential that one bluegrass historian has referred to it as "possibly the most revolutionary performance in the history of bluegrass."

The Osbornes and Allen parted ways in 1958. Allen went to Washington, D.C., to become part of the active bluegrass scene there, and the Osbornes began a series of college concerts and then moved south to join the Grand Ole Opry. They continued to innovate: Sonny broke out of his Scruggs-style banjo playing. He later recalled: "I realized in 1957 that I couldn't copy Scruggs anymore because, when he was through and couldn't play anymore, that I'd still have some time left." He began to improvise solos, and to base them on horn or piano solos, and he even added a sixth string to his banjo. Yet the brothers found that, within the broader country music community, they were looked down on for being bluegrassers. Sonny said: "I can understand thoroughly the feelings of black people and Indians and any minority group now. I'm for them 100% because we're in the same boat by being bluegrass pickers. You're looked down upon by these disc jockeys, if you want to call them that. I think they are more like robots."

This all changed on Christmas Day 1967 when the brothers released a song on the Decca label called "Rocky Top." It became an instant hit, and over the years since has become one of the top four or five bluegrass favorites, and the song most frequently associated with the Osbornes. The song's popularity was not really all that surprising: it came from the pen of two of Nashville's most successful songwriters, Boudleaux and Felice Bryant. The Bryants had written hit after hit for another Kentucky duo, the Everly Brothers, in the 1950s: "Bye Bye Love," "Wake Up, Little Susie," "Devoted to You," "Bird Dog." In the late 1960s they began to repeat the process for the Osbornes, and bluegrass and the Nashville sound moved closer together in the wake of hits like "Georgia Pineywoods," "Tennessee Hound Dog," and "Muddy Bottom." In 1969 the Osbornes took the ultimate step—for a bluegrass group— and amplified their banjo and mandolin. A lot of traditionalists screamed their outrage at the prospect of electric bluegrass, but the Osbornes stuck to it, got as many bookings as any mainstream country act, and took some solace from the fact that the 1970s saw other young progressive bluegrass bands use electric instruments of one sort or another. Dozens of awards have followed, including the Country Music Association's "Vocal Group of the Year" honors. In 1976 they switched record labels, though, unplugged their instruments, and delivered a fine set of LPs that proved they could still play exciting traditional bluegrass along with the best. The career of the Osbornes is an example of what can happen—in both frustration and innovation—when strong, creative individuals encounter the highly structured, highly disciplined music of Monroe. It was a scene to be repeated in the 1970s as other young Kentuckians began to explore the bluegrass heritage handed down to them.

Many of these new groups played what was called "progressive bluegrass," or simply "newgrass," and Lexington and Louisville emerged as centers for the new music. The Newgrass Revival, based in Louisville, gained popularity in the early 1970s with their use of the chromatic banjo, electric instruments, a repertory that included everything from Monroe standards to current rock favorites, and a fondness for allowing players to take extended instrumental solos, as in jazz or rock. The Newgrass Revival was founded on the talents of Sam Bush (mandolin, fiddle), Curtis Burch (guitar, dobro), and Courtney Johnson (banjo), and had a hit in the early 1970s with their newgrass version of rock singer

Leon Russell's "Prince of Peace." (They also toured with popular performers like Russell in addition to making the more conventional bluegrass festival scene.) Many older bluegrass fans were upset at what the Revival was doing, but the Revival members argued that they were simply expanding on the changes already made by the Osbornes and others. Sam Bush told a reporter: "Bill Monroe, if he is the man who created bluegrass, must have upset all the old-timers too."

Equally impressive was a Lexington, Kentucky, band headed by banjoist J.D. Crowe and calling itself, significantly enough, the New South. Crowe's own experimental banjo style and strong baritone voice were the common denominator of the group's personnel, and in the early 1970s he was attracting a lot of attention with an eclectic repertoire, the use of drums, piano, and pedal steel, and some brilliant sidemen, including Jimmy Gaudreau, Glen Lawson, Bobby Slone, and Keith Whitley. In fact, some critics have compared Crowe's band to the so-called Outlaws (Waylon Jennings, Willie Nelson) in country music, men who aggressively and purposefully set out to change the music. Two of the Crowe alumni were Tony and Larry Rice, superb musicians who later moved directly into jazz and jazz-flavored "dawg music" developed by mandolin player David Grisman. Through a variety of personnel changes, Crowe kept his band together. One of his most popular songs, "My Home Ain't in the Hall of Fame," became an anthem, not only for Crowe but for like-minded young experimentalists who had little respect for the so-called "Nashville sound."

In 1974 Crowe hired a young mandolin player and fiddler named Ricky Skaggs, an artist who has emerged as possibly the most influential of all the younger generation. Born in 1954 in Cordell, Kentucky, Skaggs was playing mandolin in a family band on a weekly country radio show by the time he was six. A couple of years later he was a full-fledged child prodigy appearing even on the Flatt and Scruggs radio show; by the time he got out of high school his talents were so obvious that he was able to walk into jobs with leading bluegrass bands of the time, first Ralph Stanley and then the Country Gentlemen. In 1974 he joined Crowe and was stimulated by the exciting new sounds he found there, so much so that he and dobro player Jerry Douglas soon left to form their own band, a short-lived group called Boone Creek. Meanwhile, Skaggs had begun to do studio work and was especially successful at working with singer Emmylou Harris, who was on her way to becoming country and bluegrass's premier lady singer. Skaggs joined Emmylou's Hot Band in 1978 and became a featured part of her music and her albums. It was no surprise that his 1979 solo LP was voted one of the top five country LPs by *Rolling Stone*, and that his music began to transcend bluegrass in both style and popularity. "Hopefully I can really do something for bluegrass," he says. "That's . . . one of my main missions." By 1981, as one of the few tradition-based artists signed with a major record company (CBS), he seemed well on his way to fulfilling this.

Older, classic forms of bluegrass continued to flourish into the 1960s and 1970s, often rejuvenated by numerous individual performers who worked behind the scenes in others' bands. One such performer is fiddler Curly Ray Cline from Pike County, who has for years played fiddle for bluegrass legend Ralph Stanley. One of the most colorful performers on the scene, Cline has in recent years been doing a series of solo albums which show his solid if unspectacular fiddle style. Fiddler Van Kidwell, who, like Doc Roberts, learned fiddle tunes in his youth from Owen Walker in Madison County, in the 1970s teamed with a young popular string band from southern Ohio called the Hotmud Family.

While Bill Monroe was forging his western Kentucky string band heritage into a new music called bluegrass, another western Kentucky musical style was beginning to attract the attention of guitarists around the country. Aside from Charlie Monroe's early work with the Monroe Brothers, bluegrass music had not developed a solo role for the guitar—not, at least, to the extent that it had for the mandolin, the five-string banjo, or the fiddle. The guitar in Monroe's Blue Grass Boys had always been used as a rhythm instrument or restricted to brief "runs" like Lester Flatt's famous "G run" used to punctuate an instrumental passage. This was ironic, since the area just south of Monroe's birthplace in Rosine, the area in and around Muhlenberg County, was in the 1930s full of traditional guitar players who were developing a distinctive solo style for the instrument. This style, which has been called by guitar historians "western Kentucky choking style," or simply "Travis style," allowed the guitarist to create at the same time his own rhythm and melody: the thumb provided an alternating, muted-bass accompaniment, while the other finger (or fingers) picked out the melody. It was a style that came out of the western Kentucky coal fields and within the span of two decades was the dominant picking style in country music everywhere, thanks to the skill of its two most famous practitioners, Merle Travis and Chet Atkins.

Travis was born in Rosewood, Muhlenberg County, on

November 29, 1917, and grew up in Ebenezer, where he learned to play tunes on a guitar his older brother Taylor had built for him. He also began to absorb the local picking style from older musicians in the area. In 1980 Merle recalled one scene with special vividness: "Another reel in my memory shows a possible dozen people gathered around two young men in their early twenties. The two are playing guitars. One, a sandy-haired tall man seems to enjoy everything around him. He laughs constantly, even in the middle of a tune. The other fellow, sitting on a railroad tie, where they're making their music near the Drakesboro, Kentucky depot, has broad shoulders, a handsome face, and seems a little more serious. As he leans over his guitar a lock of hair falls over his forehead like Clark Gable's or Jack Lord's. His name is "Plucker" English. The sandy-haired one is Mose Rager. The bug-eyed kid watching is me."

Travis has always hastened to credit the pioneer guitarists in Muhlenberg County who were experimenting in the 1920s with what later came to be called "Travis picking." Most of these guitarists never recorded or left any tangible evidence of their music, except in the memories of those who listened to them and learned from them. They included names like Levi Foster, who played in an open tuning and experimented with sliding a knife up and down his strings to get a steel guitar effect; Jody Burton, a coal miner and ball player who was playing a curious form of thumb-style blues as early as 1924; and Amos Johnson, who adapted ragtime syncopation to the guitar. Both blacks and whites worked in the mines in the area, and partially because of this there was a free interchange of ideas between black and white musicians as well. Mose Rager, Travis's immediate teacher, recalls: "Man, we always got along in this part of the country with black people. There's some fine black people lives here in Drakesboro, and we've always got along, played music together, and, oh, have big gatherings." And black guitarists contributed to the Muhlenberg County picking style, as well; Rager especially remembers Jim Mason from Bevier, who developed a choke lick on the blues, and Mutt Smith from Bowder. The whole tradition of secular, non-blues black music, which was widespread across the South in the nineteenth century, was especially strong in the western Kentucky area, where it survived well into the twentieth century and was a major influence on much white string band music. Richard Nevins, a leading authority on the development of fiddle music, has written about the area: "Nowhere else in America did the black population take to white fiddle music so immediately, and nowhere else did an almost separate black fiddling tradition grow to such eminent stature as to then greatly influence the very tradition its roots came from." In addition to numerous fiddlers who influenced people like Doc Roberts and Dick Burnett, black guitarists and banjoists emerged as influential soloists, as well.

One center for this black non-blues string band tradition was Louisville. Like Cincinnati, Louisville had river traffic that stimulated a rich mixture of black folk music composed of part jazz, part pop, and part hillbilly. Travellers have reported accounts of black string bands in the area since the 1870s, and by the end of World War I such bands were an established musical mode in Louisville. Jug bands—groups featuring various stringed instruments and propelled by the sound of one or more members creating an artificial bass or tuba sound by blowing across the mouth of an empty jug—were active in the city as early as 1905, many of them drawn from outlying areas during Derby week. Walnut Street was Louisville's equivalent to the more famous Beale Street of Memphis, with numerous jazz and blues musicians meeting and jamming together. In the 1920s a plethora of these jug bands got onto records, many with colorful names like Whistler's Jug Band, the Old Southern Jug Band, Phillips' Louisville Jug Band, Clifford Hayes' Louisville Stompers, and Earl MacDonald's Original Louisville Jug Band. This last band, donning chef's costumes and appearing as the Ballard Chefs, did a popular series of radio programs for WHAS in the late 1920s, and travelled widely to Memphis and Nashville. A number of early white country musicians heard and liked their music, and Henry Miles, the band's creative fiddler, was a direct influence on Tex Atchison, who later became lead fiddler for the Prairie Ramblers.

One of the most gifted and influential black musicians to emerge from this rich and heady Louisville music scene was a guitarist and banjoist named Sylvester Weaver (1897–1960). For decades almost nothing was known about Weaver's personal life, but recent research has unearthed some fascinating details. Born in Louisville, he learned to play guitar and banjo as a young man; his musical training apparently included strong doses of ragtime as well as jazz and folk music, and his remarkable creativity allowed him to cross-pollinate these styles into a unique fusion: he played rags on the guitar and blues on the banjo. By 1923 he was touring the vaudeville circuit with blues singer Sara Martin, another famous Louisville native whose widespread recording fame in the 1920s was a ticket for numerous black Louisville musicians to get on records. Weaver himself gained access to Okeh Records as early as 1923, making him the first black guitarist to record (and one of the first guitar solists *per se* to record). His showpiece, which he recorded twice, in 1923 and again in 1927, was "Guitar Rag," which was later appropriated by Bob Wills's western swing band to become a country and western anthem called "Steel Guitar Rag." Weaver's recording of "Smoketown Strut," a composition which resembles the ragtime standard "Dill Pickles Rag," has much in common with the later finger picking of Mose Rager and Merle Travis, and is probably the earliest known example of this major regional style. For a few years Weaver was quite well known, touring and recording extensively; he even acted as a "talent scout" for Okeh, much as Dennis Taylor did for Gennett, auditioning performers and bringing them to recording sessions in St. Louis and New York City. Among his early discoveries were the great jazz singer Helen Humes, another Louisville native, who went on to fame with Count Basie and Harry James; Whistler's Jug Band; and the Kentucky Jubilee Four. For a time Weaver also played in an early string band headed by black fiddler E.L. Coleman. By the end of the 1920s though, he began to slip out of music, and he spent most of the rest of his life working quietly as a chauffeur in Louisville. He died in obscurity in 1960, never having told his story, never having explained where he got his guitar artistry or whom he passed it on to. Today his original recordings are rare collector's items and his remarkable guitar playing is heard only by a few scholars and enthusiasts.

Even more influential, and about as legendary, was another black instrumentalist from the area named Arnold Shultz. As folklorist Bill Lightfoot has pieced together the early development of the Travis lick, a key figure in the chronology seems to be Shultz, the same musician from whom Bill Monroe and his brothers learned so much as boys. Though he died in 1931, Shultz is still talked about by hundreds of musicians from western Kentucky who knew him, heard him play, or heard of him. Reports of his ability on the guitar and fiddle are legion. Tex Atchison, lead fiddler for the Prairie Ramblers, even credits him with teaching him to play the "long bow" style of "swing fiddle" as opposed to the short "jiggy bow" style Tex had learned from his father. Researchers have found that Shultz was born in Ohio County in 1886 near the Rough River town of Cromwell; his father was an exslave and most of the family members played in a string band while Arnold was growing up.

Friends recall that as a young man Arnold possibly played on riverboats, and that he travelled widely in the days before World

War I. No one knows what other influences he may have been exposed to during these travels, but probably by 1900 he had evolved a distinct finger-picking style that involved picking out the lead and using the thumb to generate his own rhythm. At one point he was apparently using goose quills for finger picks. He was what the local lingo called a "musicianer," a musician more noted for his instrumental abilities than his singing, and he often travelled with a man named Walter Taylor, a well-known mandolin player. This is probably the same Walter Taylor who later led a Louisville string band and recorded for Victor and Paramount under the name Taylor's Weatherbirds. Taylor's guitarist was John Byrd, a remarkable songster who recorded a version of "Old Timbrook Blues" (a "Molly and Tenbrooks" song) in 1930, suggesting that Taylor's band shared some elements of white folk music tradition. Shultz routinely played with dozens of white string bands in western Kentucky, including those headed by Bill Monroe's famous "Uncle Pen" Vandiver, teaching white and black alike new chords and new styles. Forrest Faught, a well-known white band leader from McHenry in the western coal-mining district, for a time performed with Shultz as the lead fiddler of his band. He recalls that occasionally people at dances would come up to him and say, "Hey, you got a colored fiddler. We don't want that." Faught would respond, "The reason I've got the man is because he's a good musician. The color doesn't mean anything. You don't hear color, you hear music." Faught later recalled, "Around McHenry, white people would invite Arnold Shultz into their homes. He was very welcome. Big crowds came in to listen to him. It was something unusual."

Shultz was a familiar figure throughout western and central Kentucky in the 1920s, wandering around with his guitar slung across his back by an old cord, playing a tune for a nickel at coal camps, railroad depots, courthouse lawns. For much of his life he continued to work during the days loading coal, and perhaps gathering for jam sessions under the coal tipples at night or playing in the rough roadhouses of the area for fifty or seventy-five cents a night. One of his fellow musicians remembers how Shultz looked in those days: "He always wore a big black hat and he'd hang it on the back of the old split-bottom cane chair he sat in." He would play "an old common flat-top guitar that probably didn't cost over twenty dollars. It was a large guitar and I'm sure that it had a round sound hole and the old-time pegs that hung down under it." Other people recall that Shultz's guitar was "huge," much bigger than average. He never sought to record, possibly because of an inveterate shyness (he also disliked having his photo taken), possibly because record companies were not receptive to black musicians who played "hillbilly music." By the mid-1920s, according to most accounts, Shultz was using a straight pick rather than a thumb pick, and playing in a style which some witnesses compared to that of Blind Blake, a black Florida guitarist whose records were widely heard in the 1920s. Shultz died prematurely at age forty-five in 1931, and members of his family repeat a well-known tale that he was poisoned by jealous white musicians. Others, though, tell a more probable story that he died from a stroke while getting on a bus. His death certificate indicates that he died from a "mitral lesion," an organic heart disease.

About 1920 Shultz had met and impressed a young white man from the area, Kennedy Jones. Jones was from Cleaton, just south of Central City; by 1923-1924 he was adapting some of Shultz's style to fit his own music, and was playing pop tunes of the day, like "Tuck Me to Sleep in My Old Kentucky Home" in a rhythm-and-melody style that had everyone talking. One of his pupils, Mose Rager, recalled: "He was the first guy I ever saw play with a thumbpick. And so I just went crazy about that kind of pickin'. He'd go way down on the neck, you know, and he could pick a tune out on the guitar and it'd sound like *two* guitars playin'." Kennedy also showed locals how to make more sophisticated and complicated chords. In the end, though, he decided not to pursue his music and eventually moved to Cincinnati.

By the late 1920s the rolling hills around Muhlenberg County were filled with coal miners experimenting with the new guitar styles. While other parts of Kentucky enjoyed fiddle and banjo contests as an outlet for local amateurs, Muhlenberg County was routinely staging guitar picking contests. Whereas eastern Kentucky musicians stuck to age-old fiddle tunes and ballads, the western Kentucky musicians were more interested in doing their own versions of popular songs of the day: "Yes, Sir, That's My Baby," "Five Foot Two," "Sweet and Lovely," "House of David Blues." To be sure, they did them in folk-derived finger-picking styles, but did them nonetheless. Two key men emerged from this "third generation" of choke-style pickers: Ike Everly and Mose Rager. Ike was a second-generation coal miner who lived and worked around Drakesboro and Central City; he and his brothers Charlie and Leonard formed an Everly Brothers string band that won a certain local fame. Then Ike made a fairly successful attempt to go professional: he worked with Charlie Underwood, Walter Cobb, and Melvin Bethel in Chicago in the 1930s, touring with the WLS road show. Walter Cobb recalls that Ike was playing "Cannonball Rag" by this time, and telling him, "You play the five string banjo—why can't I play it that way on the guitar?" Later Ike teamed with Red Green and performed over WJJD in Chicago, but made only a handful of recordings. By 1952 he was back in Kentucky running a local "Everly Family" radio show that helped his two sons, Phil and Don, get started on their own careers as one of the most popular rock and roll duos of the 1950s.

Mose Rager was born in 1911 near Centertown and grew up around Greenville, hearing family members pick and sing, attending travelling minstrel shows, and studying the other guitarists in and around Muhlenberg County—especially Kennedy Jones. By the time he was fifteen, Mose, like most boys in the area, was working the coal mines, but during the Depression this kind of work grew scarce. "The mines, back then, during the Depression, the mines would run, would get down to one day a week," recalls Mose. "And that's when we'd get together and get out and have parties, and have guitars, and fiddles, and mandolins, and what have you." Mose began to team up with either Ike Everly or Plucker English and to create twin-guitar duets for local dances. "There was a lot of guitar pickin' goin' on. When we first started, me and Ike, when we first got started playin', me and Plucker, everywhere we got a chance to play, we'd hunt somebody to play for 'em. . . . We'd go all over the country . . . even hitch-hike, sleep in beer gardens." By the mid-1930s, though, Mose had settled in Drakesboro, where he ran a barber shop and worked part-time in the mines. This lasted until 1943, when he quit the mines and made an attempt to enter professional music. He worked for a time with Grandpa Jones on the Grand Ole Opry in the late forties, delighting audiences with his rendition of "Tiger Rag" on the guitar. In 1947 he was working for Curly Fox, then one of the nation's most popular fiddlers, and made his very first recordings while with Curly—a series of King sides made in Cincinnati. One of these was Curley's version of "Black Mountain Rag," a record which was to become the biggest-selling country instrumental of the decade, and one to be copied by almost every fiddler in the country. As impressive as Curly's fiddling on the piece was Mose's electric guitar solos, some of the first "hot" guitar work in modern country music.

Being on the road did not appeal to Mose, though, and he returned to Drakesboro to settle into a routine of giving guitar lessons, playing in local bands, and watching the success of his one-time pupil Merle Travis. Mose and Ike passed on their style to

Travis as early as 1932. Where Kennedy Jones had added the thumbpick to the style, Mose had added to it a battery of substitute chords, choke techniques, a playfulness and love of embroidery, and these are what he passed on to Travis. In 1936 Travis took this distinctive regional style out of western Kentucky to Indianapolis, and began the process of popularizing it on a national level. For a time the progress of the style was closely linked to the progress of Travis's own musical career. For the next ten years, Merle served his apprenticeship with some of the key figures in Kentucky music: starting with Clayton McMichen's Georgia Wildcats, he moved on to the WLW band, the Drifting Pioneers, featuring fiddler Sleepy Marlin and two former members of the western Kentucky Hack Band, Walt and Bill Brown. In the early 1940s he met and played with Grandpa Jones on WLW, and he and Grandpa made their first records together for the King label. Their very first recording was issued under the name the Shepherd Brothers, and Merle played electric guitar breaks on many others issued by Grandpa himself, and even appeared on gospel quartet records as a member of the Brown's Ferry Four. Before any of these endeavors really met with success, though, Merle was called into service in World War II.

After his stint in the service—an experience he later dramatized as an actor in the film *From Here to Eternity*—Travis settled on the west coast and quickly emerged as a solo star in his own right. A new record company called Capitol Records had been formed in Hollywood, and guided by far-sighted men like Ken Nelson and Lee Gillette, was quickly establishing itself as a force in American pop music. By 1946 Merle became associated with Capitol as a singer, guitarist, and songwriter. In fact, his song about "nicotine slaves," "Smoke, Smoke, Smoke (That Cigarette)," became Capitol's first million-selling record when it was recorded by Merle's friend Tex Williams. Later songs were to become even better known. In August 1946, Capitol recorded a 78 album by Merle entitled *Folk Songs of the Hills* as an attempt to cash in on the popularity of artists like Burl Ives, Josh White, and Leadbelly. The album itself was only moderately successful, but it contained four songs that were to have a tremendous impact on bluegrass and country music: "Sixteen Tons," "Dark as a Dungeon," "I Am a Pilgrim," and "Nine Pound Hammer." "Dark as a Dungeon," quickly covered by country singers like Grandpa Jones, eventually became a favorite of folk singers and country singers alike, and has even been collected as a folk song by the Library of Congress. "I Am a Pilgrim," based on an older hymn and learned from Mose Rager, featured Travis's unique picking style in an arrangement that became as popular as the song; it was later featured by country-rock-bluegrass groups like the Byrds and Clarence and Roland White. "Nine Pound Hammer," another Travis piece based on much older songs, with its famous line, "It's a long way to Harlan, it's a long way to Hazard," has become a bluegrass standard as well as a favorite of singers like Johnny Cash and John Prine. "Sixteen Tons," though, was the most famous, especially after it was picked up and recorded by Tennessee Ernie Ford in 1955; Ford's record, done with a spare orchestral background instead of a "country" background, sold over four million copies in two years and became one of the most widely known songs in pop music. *Time* magazine reflected about the song's appeal, "We all live on credit and owe our soul to some sort of company store." Merle's song was actually based on his memories of life at the Beech Creek mines near Greenville, where his coal-mining father Uncle Rob Travis worked in the 1920s. The term "sixteen tons" itself, according to historian Archie Green, referred to the practice of initiating young miners into work there. Though most miners usually loaded between eight and ten tons a day, when a newcomer joined the crew the older ones helped him exceed this figure to make sixteen tons on his first day. It was a sign of manhood to be able to load sixteen tons.

Meanwhile, though, Travis was enjoying success in other musical areas. In fact, in 1946 Travis was best known as a country honky-tonk singer who had hits like "Divorce Me C.O.D.," one of the biggest country sellers of the postwar era. Almost as popular were pieces like "No Vacancy" (stimulated by the postwar housing shortage) in 1946, "So Round, So Firm, So Fully Packed," one of the first in a long line of country songs to be based on advertising slogans, and later efforts like "Re-Enlistment Blues" and "Sweet Temptation." At the same time, he was recording a series of guitar solos that carried the western Kentucky choking style to guitarists across the nation. Especially noteworthy here were his Capitol recordings of "Cannonball Rag" (which had come down all the way from Kennedy Jones), "Steel Guitar Rag," "Merle's Boogie Woogie," "John Henry," "Lost John Boogie," "Two Fast Past," and Travis-Rager-Everly versions of standards like "Up a Lazy River." By the 1950s Merle was comfortably settled into the west coast music scene, appearing routinely on radio and television. Meanwhile guitarists like Chet Atkins and Doc Watson, who had heard Travis throughout the years and modelled their styles on his, were popularizing the style even more. (Both Atkins and

Watson so admired Travis that each named one of his children Merle.) Travis's election to the Country Music Hall of Fame in October 1977 capped a decade of recognition in which his music was played at numerous college folk festivals, at the Smithsonian Institution, and in Carnegie Hall. A talented prose writer and cartoonist as well as instrumentalist, songwriter, and singer, Merle Travis ranks today as one of American music's most creative and wide-ranging talents.

In 1979 Merle Travis's close friend, Louis Marshall Jones— Grandpa Jones to his fans—celebrated fifty years in show business. When he started singing on the radio in Akron, Ohio, Herbert Hoover was president and Jimmie Rodgers was establishing country music as a national phenomenon; in many ways, Grandpa's career has paralleled the growth of country music and mirrored its changes and moods. It has made Grandpa a major figure in the field for years, and has given him a national reputation that was crowned in 1978 by his election to the Country Music Hall of Fame. Yet in a recent conversation Grandpa pointed out an interesting thing about his career. "Really, if you look back, I never did have any one record that really took off; some of them, like 'Old Rattler' and 'Mountain Dew' would continue to sell steadily over the years, but I never had any really smash hits."

In one sense, of course, the same could be said for Merle Travis: certainly his *Folk Songs of the Hills* had influence far beyond its commercial sales. Yet Travis was able to use his popularity as a singer of modern country songs to promote his guitar style and traditionally-derived song. Paradoxically, Grandpa Jones was able to achieve commercial success only when he turned his back on modern country songs, swapped his guitar for a banjo, and began to feature songs in older modes, songs derived from his own rich Kentucky heritage and from the repertoires of other Kentuckians like Cousin Emmy and Bradley Kincaid. Grandpa's career shows that it is possible to be a major influence on country music and never have a million seller—that it is possible to use radio, personal appearances, and songbooks as effectively as records to promote one's music. By the time Grandpa made his first record in 1944 he had been a country music professional for fifteen years and a star in his own right for half of that time.

Born into a sharecropping family in Niagra, Kentucky, in 1913, Louis Marshall Jones was playing local dances by the time he was eleven, and in 1930, when he was a student at West High School in Akron, Ohio, he won a local talent content sponsored by Wendell Hall, known nationally for his early hit recording of

"It Ain't Gonna Rain No More." This won him a local radio show over WJW in Akron, where he was billed as "The Young Singer of Old Songs," and the next year he teamed up with Joe Troyan, a native of Pleasant City, Ohio, who played harmonica and did comedy. (Troyan later called himself "Bashful Harmonica Joe," toured with Bradley Kincaid, and made a string of records with a cowboy singer named Pie Plant Pete.) They were heard by Warren Caplinger and Andy Patterson, veteran recording artists of the 1920s who were lining up talent for the popular "Lum and Abner" radio show, and for a time young Marshall and Joe Troyan became members of the house band on that show. When the "Lum and Abner" show moved from Cleveland to Chicago, Marshall and Troyan joined Bradley Kincaid, then at the peak of his career and broadcasting from WBZ in Boston. Throughout the mid-1930s young Jones (who was soon christened "Grandpa" by Kincaid because he sounded so grouchy on early morning shows) served a valuable apprenticeship with Kincaid, learning songs, stage technique, and the music business, and gaining confidence in himself as a performer. Bradley gave Marshall his famous high-topped leather boots, which he still wears today, and black-face comedian Burt Swor, then at Boston, helped him rig up his first mustache, as the show toured small towns around New England, Marshall's "Grandpa" image developed.

In 1937, when he was twenty-four, Grandpa published his first song (a follow-up to a hit, then very much a part of the music, called "An Answer to the Maple on the Hill") with the M. M. Cole Company, then one of the country's leading sheet music publishers. He also struck out on his own, getting a job at WWVA's "Wheeling Jamboree." He spent the next five years at various West Virginia stations, working by himself and with a vocal trio. Until then, Grandpa's singing had been quite different from his work today: accompanying himself on guitar instead of banjo, he specialized in sentimental songs and material learned from his mentors, Bradley Kincaid and Jimmie Rodgers. Moving from WWVA to WCHS (Charleston) to WMMN (Fairmont), he continued to perfect his style, working with artists like Hugh Cross, Buddy Starcher, and Cowboy Loye (Loye D. Pack). The earliest known recordings of Grandpa date from this period, a couple of 1940 transcriptions from the WMMN "Sagebrush Round-Up," and they are quite revealing. On one he sings "Rainbow's End," a mellow cowboy song, with a trio called the Grandsons; on another he joins a quartet to do a pre-Brown's Ferry Four version of "Turn Your Radio On"; on a third he leads the cast in the program's theme song, "Raise a Ruckus Tonight"; and on a fourth he does a sentimental number called "They Needed an Angel." Though he had recently learned—from Cousin Emmy—to frail the banjo, no banjo playing is evident on these early shows.

Moving to WLW's "Boone County Jamboree" in 1942, Grandpa began working with people who were to have a substantial impact on his later career: the Delmore Brothers, Merle Travis, Ramona Riggins (later to become his wife), and Syd Nathan, a record store owner who was to found King Records in 1944. But before much developed in Cincinnati, Grandpa found himself caught up in World War II; for a time he served in the army as an M.P., and found his way to Germany, where he organized a band called the Munich Mountaineers, which broadcast daily at 8:15 A.M. over the Armed Forces Network in Munich in 1945.

Returning to Cincinnati in 1946, Grandpa began his recording career in earnest. He had recorded a few sides before he went into the service—his very first record was a duet with Merle Travis released under the pseudonym the Shepherd Brothers on King 500, the first King release—and had garnered a fair-sized hit in "It's Raining Here This Morning." Now he continued to record, with the Delmore Brothers, Merle Travis, Ramona, and others. By 1947 he had produced his most famous numbers, "Mountain Dew" and "Old Rattler." He also became part of an old-time gospel quartet started by Alton Delmore and called the Brown's Ferry Four. Soon Grandpa's records were receiving national attention and he was asked to join the Grand Ole Opry in 1946.

Grandpa's King years include an important watershed in his career: his recording, in the spring of 1947, of a song called "Old Rattler." This session marked the first time Grandpa recorded with the banjo, and its success caused him to change the direction and style of his repertory. Before that session Grandpa had recorded thirty-eight songs for King; most of them had a common format: Grandpa playing acoustic guitar and singing solo vocal, backed by an electric lead guitar (usually his close friend Merle Travis) or an electric steel (usually Billy Strickland). The performance style was not unlike many mainstream country recordings of the day. Nor was the type of song much different. On twenty-four of the thirty-eight selections Grandpa was clearly identifiable as composer. Gone were the old sentimental songs, the traditional songs, the Jimmie Rodgers songs; in their place were modern country love laments. The only older songs in this early period were the gospel songs Grandpa did with the Brown's Ferry Four and his hit song "Mountain Dew." As Norm Cohen has shown, "Mountain Dew" was first codified in its present form in 1920 by Asheville folk song collector and singer Bascom Lamar Lunsford, and it probably is related to an even earlier Irish song, "The Real Old Mountain Dew." Two other early songs, "New Pins and Needles" and "Eight More Miles to Louisville," were derived from older models; "Eight More Miles" was inspired, Grandpa recalls, by the older Delmore Brothers song "Fifteen Miles to Birmingham." In fact, two of Grandpa's most famous songs, "Eight More Miles" and "Mountain Dew," had been recorded orginally without the banjo. Going into that 1947 session, Grandpa's best selling records were King 545 ("East Bound Freight Train" / "Get Things Ready for Me, Ma") and King 575 ("Heart Stealing Mama" / "Darling Won't You Love Me"), followed closely by King 532 ("Louisville"). These records, furthermore, were selling quite well; King 545 was already up to 41,000, an impressive figure for a couple of years' sales to a still-limited market. In short, in the spring of 1947, it was not a lack of commercial success that drove Grandpa to experiment with the five-string banjo on "Old Rattler," and to subsequently change his image and, to a lesser extent, his repertory.

Both "Old Rattler" and Grandpa's banjo playing date from his days at Wheeling. "Cousin Emmy taught me the banjo. I kept after her for several months, and finally she got mad, and said, 'Well, I'll just teach you.' And I watched her and learned it." The history of "Old Rattler" is a good deal more complex. Grandpa recalls: "I think I might have learned that at Wheeling. It was a shout tune that everybody did for a while, and then it sort of became my tune. It seems to me the guy I learned it from was from east Tennessee, but I can't remember who it was." A version of the song had been recorded as early as 1924 by an east Tennessee singer named George Reneau, but the song's first appearance in print was in Bradley Kincaid's *Favorite Old Time Songs and Mountain Ballads*, Book 2 (Chicago, 1929), where it appears under the title "Rattler." The first recording of Grandpa's version (with the refrain) was done in April 1933 by the Cumberland Ridge Runners. Another early version in print was "Here Rattler Here" in a 1934 songbook put out by Cap, Andy, and Flip, *Old Time Songs and Mountain Ballads*, probably published in Charleston, West Virginia. Grandpa had strong ties with the compilers of both songbooks and may have learned it from either—or vice versa.

Regardless of its source, the song struck a responsive chord with the 1947 country audience. Grandpa's version (recorded in Nashville with Ramona on bass, Cowboy Copas on guitar, and

Grandpa on banjo) sold almost 39,000 copies in the three months following its release in the fall of 1947, and almost 80,000 copies by the end of 1948. Its success was certainly more spectacular than anything Grandpa had done to date (most of his records had sold more modestly but steadily) and this impressed Grandpa. "It was really the thing that made me start up with these banjo tunes," he recalls.

Thus in 1947 and 1948, when Grandpa was enjoying new heights of national popularity and when full-page ads for his latest releases graced the pages of *Billboard*, he began to abandon the idea of being a country crooner and to move more to "banjo pieces"—up-tempo tunes, old-time songs, comedy songs. "I don't really have the voice to be a good ballad singer," Grandpa notes. "My voice is really too thin for that." His records and his performances began to include more numbers like "How Many Biscuits Can You Eat?," an old English lying song called "Darby's Ram," and other old Kentucky banjo tunes like "Pretty Little Pink," "Goin' Downtown," "The Bald-Headed End of the Broom," "Chicken Don't You Roost Too High," and "Uncle Eph's Got the Coon." He even began to record a few songs he had learned from his own family, such as the local murder ballad "Daisy Dean," which he acquired from his mother. He began to stress more the comedy bits in his act. as well.

An important influence on Grandpa during this time was his wife Ramona, who customarily appeared with him, playing back-up guitar, fiddle, and mandolin, and doing some singing, as well. One of the daughters of a coal miner and fiddler named Homer Riggins, Ramona was born about sixty miles north of Niagra, in Davis County, Indiana. Inspired by the radio broadcasts of Karl and Harty, she began playing mandolin and fiddle, and even before she had graduated from high school she was appearing on WHAS with Sunshine Sue and the Rock Creek Rangers, a popular local group built around Sue and George Workman. Ramona performed with this band and others through the war years, usually playing the fiddle and specializing in old tunes like "Ragtime Annie" and "Listen to the Mocking Bird." She met Grandpa at WLW in Cincinnati, and they were married soon after they moved to Nashville. Ramona had a strong devotion to traditional, older country music, and a keen awareness of its importance; this too was to affect Grandpa's commitment to that style, and his interest in rejuvenating it for the modern audience. His career continued to flourish; by the end of 1950 he had sold a cumulative total of almost a million copies for King Records and had signed with the Jolly

Joyce Theatrical Agency, a Philadelphia firm which by then had the biggest country bookings in the East.

Grandpa and Ramona stayed in Nashville until July 1950, when they (along with several other Opry members) were lured to Washington, D.C., to become part of the new television show started by entrepreneur Connie B. Gay, former conductor for "National Farm and Home Hour," one of the oldest rural programs in America. Gay's new television show was called "Town and Country Time," and it originated from WARL in Arlington, Virginia, just across the river from Washington. Just as Bradley Kincaid had years earlier introduced country music to the northeast, now Grandpa and Ramona helped introduce it to Washington. A couple of years later they moved down to Richmond, where they headlined "The Old Dominion Barn Dance." Before that, in March 1951, as the Korean War raged and as President Harry Truman fought with General MacArthur, Grandpa and Ramona took a show troupe to the Korean front, carrying their music even farther afield. Their reception was so intense that they played no less than fifteen shows their first day over there.

In 1952 Grandpa returned to Nashville, where he was to stay for the next twenty-eight years. By this time he and Ramona had a couple of children and a new contract with RCA Victor Records, the nation's leading label. For a time Grandpa went through a period of recording "topical" songs, such as "T.V. Blues," "I'm No Communist," and "That New Vitamine" (about the newly-discovered vitamin B-12), but these did not bring the popular success his producers had hoped for, and by the end of the 1950s Grandpa was returning to his traditional and tradition-based songs. In 1962 he had a big hit with his version of Jimmie Rodgers's "T for Texas"—again recalling Grandpa's earliest influence and yodelling style. Another popular smash was a recitation called "The Christmas Guest"; Grandpa recalls that "Ramona found that poem in one of these old, old books. It wasn't signed, and we had to change it around some." The poem tells of an old mountain man, Conrad, who dreams that Christ will visit his lonely cabin on Christmas day. The story itself is an old folk tale from the Appalachians which, like many songs, probably had its roots even further back in European tradition. Grandpa's hit recording brought it alive again, and sent it to radio stations all over the country, where it has become a Christmas standard.

Grandpa meanwhile became one of the established stars of the Grand Ole Opry and one of that program's strongest links with the folk music that had founded it. In the fall of 1968 Grandpa found yet another outlet for his talent as a singer and comedian: a new CBS television show called "Hee Haw." The show was a nation-wide fad for a couple of years, and then left the network for independent syndication. Today the show appears in over one hundred markets and is the nation's most successful syndicated program. Grandpa's famous routine in the kitchen ("What's for supper, Grandpa?"), and his comedy routines with Minnie Pearl, are high-lights of the show, and he was responsible for reviving the old-time country gospel quartet featured on many of the programs. All this was climaxed by what Grandpa calls "the greatest day of my life," his election to the Country Music Hall of Fame in 1978. In more recent years, two rounds of heart surgery have slowed Grandpa's pace somewhat, but his musical heritage is in good hands. A 1979 album, *The Grandpa Jones Family Album*, featured Grandpa and Ramona along with an array of second-generation Joneses who have as much talent and respect for tradition as their parents.

One of Grandpa's best friends on the Opry was the show's only other banjo-playing comedian, David "Stringbean" Akeman. Like Grandpa, Stringbean had parlayed his old-time Kentucky frailing banjo style and shout tunes into a successful career in a modern country music dominated by steel guitars and electric basses. They were a study in contrast: Grandpa, diminutive in his white mustache and spectacles and old brown knee-length boots, and Stringbean lean and lanky, with his big horn-rimmed glasses and old striped shirt that stretched down to his kneecaps, where a cinched belt held up a tiny pair of pants. Yet they were good friends, shared a love of old tunes and a love of fishing, and had farms near each other in the hills north of Nashville. Both did stints on the Opry and were featured on "Hee Haw." For years Grandpa listened to Stringbean's wry, sardonic comments on life, and one of these comments summed up String's philosophy of life as well as anything. "A man who plays the five-string banjo has got it made," he liked to say. "It never interferes with any of the pleasures in his life."

On the night of November 10, 1973, Grandpa stood in the wings of the old Ryman Auditorium to watch String do his num-bers on the Opry. Tex Ritter introduced him, and String duck-waddled on stage, tipped his old gray hat to the audience, and began singing: "I come out of old Kentucky, early in the spring / Headin' for the Grand Ole Opry, boys, to make myself a name." After the show, Grandpa and Stringbean made a date to get up early the next morning to go fishing. Both drove back up their rural farmhouses near Goodlettsville. Grandpa turned in for a peaceful night's rest, but Stringbean ran into a pair of burglars who had been waiting for him. He and his wife were shot and killed. The crime shocked and horrified Nashville, and even after the murderers had been caught, friends of String's continued to muse about what kind of cosmic injustice could cut down such a gentle and ingratiating man.

In some ways, Stringbean was even more a part of Kentucky musical heritage than was Grandpa Jones. The Akeman clan hailed from the small town of Annville, Jackson County, in the middle of eastern Kentucky, about halfway between Corbin and Richmond. The area was a veritable nest of old-time music, producing banjoists like Marion Underwood, Buell Kazee, B.F. Shelton, Dick Burnett, Lily May Ledford, and dozens of good string bands and singers. String was born there June 17, 1914,* about midway in a pack of eight kids. His father planted corn and tobacco in the daytime and played the banjo at neighborhood dances at night. Young David Akeman was suitably impressed. His brother recalls: "He used to go around before he got a banjo and he would get an old shoebox and some of my mother's sewing thread, and thump around on it, and pick up one of those legs and flop on it like he was playing the banjo, and he'd say, 'Boy, you'll hear me over the air one of these days.'" By the time he was twelve, he traded a little banty hen and a rooster for his first real banjo.

Before long, young David quit school to help his family weather the Depression. Years later he recalled those hard times, and remembered that his family was one of the first in the area to qualify for government relief. For some bureaucratic reason, all they got was a case of macaroni. "We even had it for breakfast. By God, it tasted like the best stuff there ever was." By 1935 young David had joined the Civilian Conservation Corps, planting trees and building roads, and at night practicing his old banjo. One night in 1935 String heard that radio star Asa Martin was holding a "talent contest" in nearby McKee, in Jackson County. David entered, and impressed Asa Martin, who was looking for a banjo player for his band. "He didn't actually win first place," recalled Asa years later, "but I really wanted to hire him. The next morning he showed up with his banjo, ready to go to work. I never did figure out just how he got out of that CCC camp, but I hired him." When Asa got ready to introduce his new band member on stage, he couldn't remember David's real name, but he looked over

*Though most histories give Stringbean's birth date as 1915, his brother Robert has checked the family Bible and has confirmed it was 1914.

at the long, skinny young man and announced him as "String Beans." The name stuck, and within a few weeks the new banjo player was known by this name; later, on the Grand Ole Opry stage, the name was to be changed to the singular form, "String-bean." It was an appropriate name; not only did Akeman physically resemble a specimen of *Phaseolus vulgaris*, but he dearly loved to eat string beans. His brother recalls: "Our mother used to have green beans on his birthday, and he'd always come and visit just to get there and to have some green beans. He loved 'em, them and that good old country ham."

Still, Stringbean (or String Beans) was not really doing anything except clawhammering the banjo on Asa's shows. But as he travelled with the show he began to watch the comedian, and in his spare time entertained the boys with imitations of the comedian's jokes and routines. As Doc Roberts recalls it, "One night this comedian got sick down in Hazard, when they had a big show lined up that night in Hindman. Acey insisted that Stringbean go on as the comedian—in fact, he said he'd fire him if he didn't. String had never sung in public, and he didn't think he could make people laugh, but he went backstage and got himself fixed up. When he came on stage, the crowd gave him the awfullest hand you'd ever want to see. He straightened up right then and made the best comedian Acey had ever seen. When they got into the car that night, Stringbean said, 'Well, you can fire me if you want to, but I'll never play nothing but comedian again.'"

For the next four years, String worked with several bands around the Lexington area, and was heard often over station WLAP. For a time he was with a band called Cy Rogers and His Lonesome Pine Fiddlers, during which time he picked up a lot of the tunes that were to become favorites in later years: "Pretty Polly," "Mountain Dew," "Get Along Home, Cindy," "Suicide Blues," and "Crazy War," a variation of an old Spanish-American war protest song which String later updated and performed as "Crazy Vietnam War." He continued to work with Asa Martin, and by 1939 was enough of a star to get personal billing in the ads for Asa Martin's Morning Round-Up Gang; he was billed as "String Beans and His Old Banjo."

During these years String was following another occupation that gave him as much pleasure as playing the banjo—baseball. For several years he played semi-pro ball in his spare time with various sandlot teams around central Kentucky. In fact, says Roberts, String's ballplaying ability was what first attracted Bill Monroe to him. "Bill come up here and got him when he [String] was playing on WLAP and living at Winchester; Bill went up there to get him to play baseball for his team. He first hired him as a baseball pitcher. As far as I know, Bill didn't even know he played banjo when he hired him. After he found out he could play, he went to playin' a little with Bill's band." After a stint with Charlie Monroe, String joined Bill Monroe on the Grand Ole Opry in July 1942.

"Stringbean was the first banjo picker with me," recalls Monroe. "What I wanted was the sound of the banjo, because I'd heard it back in Kentucky, and I wanted it in with the fiddle and the rest of the instruments. So Stringbean gave us the touch of the banjo and he was a good comedian." The term "touch of the banjo" aptly describes String's role in the band, for the banjo was anything but featured in the early Monroe band. By listening carefully one can hear delicate finger picking by String on the 1945 Columbia version of "Footprints in the Snow," "True Life Blues," or "Blue Grass Special," but on most of the hot numbers it is Monroe's mandolin and Chubby Wise's fiddle that take the lead. In 1945 String was replaced by Earl Scruggs, whose style was more in line with that of the new band.

After he left Monroe, String began a three-year partnership with Lew Childre, working on the Opry and doing tent shows. "Doctor Lew" was an old veteran minstrel man who was as fast-talking as String was laconic, but who shared with String a love for old songs and comedy numbers. He also shared with String a passionate love for fishing—one of his featured numbers was "Fishing Blues" ("Everybody's Fishing, I'm a Goin' Fishing Too"), which String himself later featured. The team was an immediate success on the Opry, so successful that WSB in Atlanta tried to hire them away from WSM, but they elected to stay. By this time Stringbean had devised his famous "short pants" costume, and was making it his trademark. Kirk McGee says, "String once told me that he borrowed that idea from an old comedian somewhere up north, I don't remember his name, who had worn a costume like that and String had seen him. When he retired and didn't use it any more, that's when String started working with it." John Lair has said that String copied part of his costume from that worn by Slim Miller at Renfro Valley.

During this time String also came under the influence of the Opry's premier banjoist-songster, Uncle Dave Macon. When String met him in 1942, Uncle Dave was 72 years old and was still going strong in a career that had begun in 1923 in vaudeville shows and primitive recording studios. He was still a headliner for the Opry, and the show's most beloved comedian; he came from an age when banjo-picking and comedy were not separated, and utilized a bag of jokes, tricks, bits of poetry, and other baggage he had preserved from the nineteenth-century stage. String became fascinated with Macon's stage style. He later remarked, "Uncle Dave was the greatest entertainer I've ever known. He would play to an audience 45 minutes and then go back for seven or eight encores. It takes a hoss to do that." Gradually, Uncle Dave accepted String as a pupil and began to help him by showing him licks and teaching him songs that he had made his own: "You Can't Do Wrong and Get By," "Eleven Cent Cotton and Forty Cent Meat," "Mountain Dew," and "Chewing Gum," and in time these became Stringbean favorites, as well. One story is true: when he died in 1952, Uncle Dave did will String one of his banjos, and String used it on later records; it was an old Gibson that Uncle Dave himself had used in the 1940s.

By 1950 String was getting national recognition as a banjoist and singer. He became a regular on the Red Foley portion of the Opry that was broadcast nationwide over NBC, and was on many of the Opry's AFRS (Armed Forces radio network) shows that were recorded and sent around the world to military bases. On these programs he shared the stage with Red Foley, Hank Williams, the Old Hickory Singers, and comedians Rod Brasfield and Minnie Pearl; he seldom did any comedy routines himself but would specialize in old banjo songs like "Going Down the Coun-try," "Lonesome Road Blues," and "Mountain Dew." A listener would hear Williams or Foley finish a number, hear applause, and then suddenly String's driving clawhammer banjo would start up, vamping while Foley would introduce him to the crowd. It wasn't until about 1960, after some twenty-five years in show business, that Stringbean began to make any serious solo recordings. His first album, done about 1960 for Starday, was "Old Time Banjo Pickin' & Singin'," and it was pitched to the popular folk revival market then thriving. The liner notes stressed the songs String had learned from his folks back in Kentucky, some of which dated "back to the 16th century." Included were some of his favorite stage pieces like "Barnyard Banjo Pickin'," his own version of "Hot Corn, Cold Corn," an old Kentucky moonshine piece, the autobiographical "Stringbean and His Banjo," and a handful of Macon songs.

In the summer of 1968 Stringbean became a charter member of a new CBS television show called "Hee Haw." Along with Archie Campbell, Junior Samples, and Grandpa Jones, String brought generations of country comedy tradition into living rooms across the nation. String's droll, laconic wit and Chaplinesque figure added ballast to the barrage of one-liners that punctuated the show. His "cornfield crow" quickly became a favorite part of the show, along with his great one-liners, the most famous being, of course, "Lord, I feel so unnecessary."

Even before "Hee Haw," String was achieving national popularity. Bob Hope once quipped that when he landed in Nashville he was surrounded by fans wanting his autograph because they mistook him for a big country star—Stringbean. He played Las Vegas, was on big talk shows and dozens of syndicated country shows, and toured with Ernest Tubb and Hank Williams, Jr. But he always came back home to the country. He bought a 134-acre farm up near Goodlettsville, north of Nashville—"After all," he told a reporter, "a fireplace man needs a lot of wood"—and spent his spare time doing what he liked best, hunting and fishing. Most mornings, after several cups of coffee and several pipes, he and his wife Estelle would lift their boat into the station wagon and head for a nearby lake. It was a good, sane life, and when he died it was as if a long Kentucky summer had ended.

6 Queens and Ramblers

It was a warm Saturday evening in April 1946. In downtown Nashville the street lights were going on and a line of country music fans stretched down Fifth Street and around the corner onto Lower Broadway waiting to get into the Ryman Auditorium to see the Grand Ole Opry. Juke boxes in nearby bars were playing the big country hits of the day—western swing like Spade Cooley's "Shame on You" and cowboy songs like Dick Thomas's "Sioux City Sue"—and the talk was about the new baseball season and whether batting star Stan Musial, back from the navy, would be able to help the St. Louis Cardinals win another pennant. For many of the 3,200 people crowding into the old tabernacle, it was their first trip to the Opry since being discharged from the service, and they were curious to see how much the music had changed while they had been away.

Backstage, though, things were tense. Roy Acuff, one of the show's leading and most traditional singers, had left weeks before in a contractual dispute. While the entire Opry was broadcast by WSM and heard throughout the mid-South, only thirty minutes of it, the Prince Albert show, were carried by national network radio. That had been Acuff's segment. To fill the gap, the sponsor, R.J. Reynolds Tobacco Company, and its advertising agency had put pressure on the Opry staff to bring in Red Foley, long-time star of the "National Barn Dance" in Chicago. Many Opry people resented this interference in Opry affairs by New York sharpies, and were suspicious of Foley. Though he had been born in the South—in Blue Lick, Kentucky, to be precise—and though he had been in country music since 1931, Foley's smooth baritone and easy-going "modern" style were a distinct contrast to the raw-edged mountain tenor of Acuff. Old-timers snorted that they had heard Foley had even taken voice lessons, and they joked about his 1945 hit records done with pop bandleader Lawrence Welk, famed for his "Champagne Music." They watched him rehearse with the band he had imported from Chicago, and wrinkled their brows over the fancy new licks being played by Foley's lead guitar player, a skinny young man named Chet Atkins. Others, though, came to Foley's defense. He had done some good country singing in his time, and no one could quarrel with the effect of his 1944 hit, "Smoke on the Water," with its patriotic message about carrying the war to Japan. In 1945 he had made the first modern country records in Nashville, recording for Decca in a temporary studio and helping to set the stage for Nashville's role as music city.*

As the crowd filed in, the musicians began to gather backstage and to work out their schedules of who played when. Young Chet Atkins, nervously waiting to go on with Foley, recalled: "There must have been 200 people backstage—musicians and songwriters and managers. Everybody was running around, tuning up and talking and drinking Coke. There were wires strung all over the floor and ropes hanging from the ceiling, supporting old canvas flaps and backdrops. . . . It reminded me of the pictures I had seen of Times Square on New Year's eve." Finally it was time for Foley to go on. "Ladies and gentlemen, Red Foley," the announcer said, and the crowd began to cheer and whistle. "There were even rebel yells," recalled Atkins. "The tension was broken." Foley did a song that had become his trademark, "Old Shep," his famous account of a boy and his dog, written back in 1933; as a child in Kentucky, Red had had a German shepherd named Hoover who had been poisoned by a neighbor. In 1941 he had made a hit recording of the song, and it was becoming a country music standard. By the time it was over, recalled Atkins, Foley had made his point. "It was clear to everyone just how popular he was." Before the first commercial Foley introduced Atkins, who played "Maggie," using a style he had adapted from Merle Travis. Thus, on an evening that marked one of those curious watersheds of

---

*This historic session took place on January 17, 1945, when Foley recorded four selections: "I'll Never Let You Worry My Mind," "One Little Lie Too Many," "Open the Door," and "A Pillow of Sighs and Tears." No classic hits emerged from the session, though "I'll Never Let You Worry My Mind" made it onto the *Billboard* charts for one week. One side, "One Little Lie Too Many," was never even issued.

history, a singer from eastern Kentucky and a guitar player using a style developed in western Kentucky helped usher in the modern era of country music history.

To even a casual observer, the difference between the country music of the 1950s and that of the 1930s was all too obvious. To begin with, the very sound was different. The banjo and, to a lesser extent, the fiddle—the two basic standbys of Kentucky folk music—were replaced in country bands by the electric guitar and the pedal steel guitar; the piano became a fixture, and often drums were used. Technology also added the portable sound system and new microphones, and the country bands were much louder than the older bands. Songs were different, too. Sentimental songs about death, heaven, and children were replaced with honky-tonk songs about drinking and lost love. Tributes to mother, home, and sweethearts were replaced with songs about broken marriages, truck driving, and "slippin' around." The lone singer playing his own guitar accompaniment was replaced by the country star with his own five-piece band. As radio began to decline, records became much more important and received national distribution. The setting for playing records changed: the prime market was now no longer the home Victrola but the juke box in the local cafe, tavern, or roadhouse, and records were designed to appeal in these new settings, to become "operator's specials." Beer-drinking and lost love songs were in; sentimental and moralistic songs were out.

As country music became "nationalized" and as it followed more and more the pattern of pop music, the importance of geography began to be less obvious. Professional song publishers like Hill and Range or Acuff-Rose began to have more influence on the repertoires of singers, and the new breed of professional songwriter began to create songs that had fewer pronounced regional characteristics. Regional culture was still an influence on young musicians growing up in the area, who continued to learn much from first-hand experience with area musicians, but even the youngest aspiring picker or singer was by 1950 bombarded with "outside" songs on the radio or records or television. Geography was still to be meaningful in modern country music, but in an indirect way; and Kentucky musicians were still to seek their fortunes away from Kentucky.

A few performing styles remained constant, though, linking the older prewar styles with the new. Event songs continued to have a regional appeal. In 1949 a singer from Winchester, Kentucky, Jimmy Osborne (1923–1957), had a hit recording with "The Death of Little Kathy Fiscus," a song about a little California girl who fell into an abandoned well. And in 1957 the wreck of a school bus in Floyd County, Kentucky, yielded several songs that had regional popularity, including "No School Bus in Heaven" by Hobo Jack Adkins, an orphan from the hill country who had a successful radio and songwriting career. Another Kentucky songwriter, Harlan Howard, born in Lexington in 1929, penned several successful "story songs" like "The Blizzard" (1961), a fictional account of a western storm, and "Streets of Baltimore" (1966), an influential song about a rural couple selling the farm to get to the bright lights of the city. By the 1950s, with the proliferation of recording studios and record manufacturers, it had become much easier to make records, and to make records designed only for regional appeal. Many later event songs and story songs keyed to specific local events were issued on these labels, or even various "vanity press" labels. A number of independent record companies started up in Kentucky, and these allowed other outlets for preserving the regional styles and musics, especially bluegrass and gospel music. Such companies included Acme, Kentucky (actually based in Cincinnati), Arrow (Columbia, Kentucky), London, Laurel, Lemco, King Bluegrass, Pine Mountain (run by A.L. Phipps of Barbourville), Country Life (the McLain Family), and more recently June Appal (Whitesburg). Dozens of other companies emerged during these years, pressing records in lots as small as 500, distributing by hand, and in general establishing a strong grassroots counterpart to the increasingly slick and commercial sounds of Nashville country.

Even while they fully commercialized and nationalized their music, many Kentucky artists throughout the 1950s, 1960s, and 1970s continued to maintain surprisingly strong ties to the past. The Everly Brothers, for instance, in the midst of their rock and roll success in the late 1950s, found time to record a hauntingly beautiful album called *Songs Our Daddy Taught Us*, full of songs by Karl and Harty, Gene Autry, and others, and a tribute to the music of the generation of their father, Ike Everly. Indeed, many of the modern country stars from Kentucky could be seen as transitional figures, linking the older music with the new.

In fact, one could make a strong case for Red Foley being a transitional figure. As we have seen, he began in the days of the local talent scouts, auditioning for Dennis Taylor as a young man. In 1927, when he was seventeen, he also won an Atwater-Kent talent contest (they were common events of the late 1920s) and left his first semester at Georgetown College in Kentucky to follow the other east Kentucky balladeers to Chicago. There he became associated with John Lair and the Cumberland Ridge Runners, and made his name in radio and on records as Ramblin' Red Foley. He later helped Lair establish Renfro Valley, but soon left that show to join comedian Red Skelton in 1939 on a radio show called "Avalon Time." This NBC network show was heard coast to coast, making Foley one of the first country stars to have a regular national network show of his own, and to be closely associated with a popular "mainstream" artists. He later worked on the Mutual Network's "Plantation Party," where he gained fame as a singing announcer and an easy-going emcee. Years of working in the North helped erase his Kentucky accent, and his singing style, which had never really reflected the "high, lonesome" sound of many Kentucky country and bluegrass singers, began to take on more of the lilt of a Bing Crosby. In doing this, Foley was setting the stage for a later generation of country crooners like Eddy Arnold, Jim Reeves, and Don Williams. When he returned to the NBC network segment of the "National Barn Dance" in the early 1940s, he was being billed as "The Sweet Singer of Songs of the Hills and Plains" and his ads showed him in a cowboy suit astride his favorite horse. At the 1944 Chicago Rodeo, Red attracted 210,000 people to Soldier's Field in two days.

Thus Red Foley had participated in nearly all facets of the commercialization of Kentucky music, from the early talent scout days to the success on radio and at Renfro Valley. Like many other Kentuckians, Red left the state to find a base for his musical career. But unlike the earlier musicians who went this route, Red carried it further—beyond regional and then seminational radio stations like WLS to the full-fledged national network, even to films. His first national hit recordings for Decca in the 1940s were in a western mode: Bob Wills favorites like "Hang Your Head in Shame" and "Smoke on the Water," and other pop items like "Pals of the Saddle," "Montana Moon," and "Ridin' Home." He rejected the efforts of some of his producers to start recording with big orchestras; he told a reporter that he had no intention of leaving the field of "folk music." "I was born and raised on it," he said. "It's a music that comes straight from the heart, the kind that expresses our real emotions."

Still, by the time he joined the Opry as its main star in 1946, there was little in Red's repertoire from his Kentucky folk heritage except his favorite "Old Shep." His repertoire soon began to change, though, once he was back in the South. He did not suddenly begin to sing old Kentucky ballads, but his songs took on a distinctly southern flavor, and came from mainstream country music rather than Hollywood songwriters. His 1947 hits included a blues-like piece from the Delmore Brothers, "Freight Train Boogie," a Cajun-flavored piece called "New Jolie Blon," and a song by sister-in-law Jenny Lou Carson called "Never Trust a Woman." Later favorites deliberately romanticized southern life: "Sunday Down in Tennessee" (1949), "Tennessee Border" (1949), "Birmingham Bounce" (1950), "M-I-S-S-I-S-S-I-P-P-I" (1950), and "Alabama Jubilee" (1951). And on the radio Red delighted listeners by including in his shows old recitations, many of them dating back years and known to thousands of southerners from rural schoolhouse "exhibitions" and gas-lit stage declamations. This was another aspect of his rural Kentucky heritage that he made use of on the national media. While some of these old poems were simply favorite pieces by popular poets like Whittier, Longfellow, and Guest, others had more in common with folk songs: they had been passed on through several generations, their author long forgotten. Invariably sentimental, occasionally humorous, frequently inspirational, these poems were the stuff from which "Old Shep" had been made, and Red's budding abilities as an announcer and even actor made them a favorite part of his Opry programs. Soon people were even sending him poems they remembered as recitations, and in 1948 Red issued these in a little book. Though country entertainers had been making recitations a part of their acts since the 1930s, none did them as well or made them as popular as Red Foley.

Foley's greatest debt to tradition, though, was his use of gospel songs and spirituals. Like most country singers, Foley had always used sacred numbers to end shows, and had been familiar with such pieces as a child. In fact, he had won his Atwater-Kent audition in Louisville in 1927 by stumbling through "Hold Thou My Hand, Dear Lord." (Three times he forgot the words, calmly stopped, walked over and asked the lady accompanying him on the piano for the words, and finally got through the song.) In later years, Foley had worked occasionally with the Brown's Ferry Four, the country's most popular country gospel group, headed by the Delmore Brothers and Grandpa Jones. But in 1950 and 1951 Red began to find that sacred songs had unheard-of commercial potential. In fact, three songs recorded during those years—"Steal Away," "Just a Closer Walk with Thee," and "Peace in the Valley"—actually became million-selling records for him, his only ones except for "Chattanoogie Shoe Shine Boy." Even as late as 1950 it was rare for a country singer to have one gold (million-selling) record, let alone three; recent research has dispelled the notion that early country giants like the Carter Family and Jimmie Rodgers and Bradley Kincaid had strings of "million-sellers." Foley's accomplishment is therefore all the more impressive; in fact, in a 1949 *Billboard* poll based on radio appeal, personal appearance attendance, and record sales, Foley handsomely outpointed the legendary Hank Williams. To be sure, some of Red's success with sacred material was due to a nationwide fad for that kind of song in the early 1950s, but its impact was undeniable. "Peace in the Valley" became forever associated with him; it was a gospel song written in 1939 by the famous black gospel composer Thomas A. Dorsey, and Red's version made it a standard with country singers. It was even recorded in later years by Elvis Presley.

Personal problems beset Red Foley in the early 1950s, including the death in 1952 of his wife Eva, as well as a bout with the Internal Revenue Service and an unsuccessful early attempt to take a country show into New York City to play on the Hotel Astor roof. The hit records continued, and Red's back-up band, the Cumberland Valley Boys, featuring the fiddle of Tommy Jackson, the guitar of Louis Innis, and the steel guitar of Jerry Byrd, had the distinction of being the first real Nashville session men. In the late 1940s, this group began to back Red on his Nashville records, and they became so good at working together that record companies began to use them for other singers, as well. Soon they were backing everybody from Grandpa Jones to Hank Williams, and when they decided to leave Red and go to Cincinnati in 1951, the record companies even tried to follow them to stage sessions there. The band finally returned to Nashville in 1952, and the idea of the studio band was established. One of the Boys, Zeke Turner, was a Virginian who specialized in crafting exciting and influential electric guitar leads.

In 1954, Red left Nashville to move to Springfield, Missouri, where he headed up KWTO's "Ozark Jubilee," an Opry-like show that made national network television in the mid-1950s. In 1955 Red had one of his last big hits in "A Satisfied Mind," which he did as a duet with his daughter Betty. Another daughter, Shirley, married singer Pat Boone, part of the new rock and roll style that was swamping country music in the mid-1950s. By the early 1960s, Red was moving more into acting and had a role in an ABC-TV series (with Fess Parker, of "Davy Crockett" fame) called "Mr. Smith Goes to Washington." Red died on September 19, 1968, in Indiana, after a personal appearance on a Grand Ole Opry tour.

Bob Atcher also filled several complex roles as a transitional figure during this time. He began as a highly self-conscious promoter of Kentucky folk songs, but achieved his greatest fame as a singer of popular cowboy ballads. He ended his career as a respected civil servant in Illinois, but achieved his first wide fame with an outrageously comic record parody. He spent several years making Hollywood potboiler cowboy films, but in recent years has turned to gospel music and has organized his family into a new gospel group.

Born on May 11, 1914, in Hardin County, where his father had a large tobacco farm, his early life was similar to that of many other Kentucky musicians: having a father who was a noted squaredance fiddler, playing the guitar at a young age (in this case four), listening to his grandparents sing their ballads and love laments. But one change occurred when Bob was a young boy—in 1918 the government bought his parents' farm to add it to the Fort Knox reservation, and as displaced persons the family moved to the Red River Valley in North Dakota. There Bob was exposed to genuine cowboy life and developed a love of cowboy songs that was to stay with him throughout his life. In 1926, when Bob was twelve, the family moved back to Kentucky. As early as 1928 young Bob, along with a friend named Forrest Curl, began performing on WHAS. By 1931 the precocious youth was enrolled in the pre-medical program at the University of Kentucky, where he met Elmer Sulzer, head of the university's radio division and an ardent student and collector of folk songs. Through Sulzer's help, Bob began doing an educational radio show called "Early American Songs," heard over both WHAS and WLAP. By this time Bob could identify and present a repertoire of some 500 songs—folk, country, and sacred—and give some history on most of them. His program was soon heard throughout several states, and he became known as "The Kentucky Mountain Minstrel," probably because Bradley Kincaid, "The Kentucky Mountain Boy," was enjoying such success on WLS in Chicago.

By late 1931 Bob's fame had spread far enough that he got an offer to go to Chicago and appear on station WBBM. He left college and began an odyssey that was to take him to various radio stations in Chicago, as well as Atlanta and Charleston. His popularity grew to rival that of Kincaid. For one stretch of time, he had simultaneous programs on three different Chicago stations—three daily programs on WIND, three on WJJD, and one on WBBM—and two on the CBS network. He had an unusual WBBM program on which he would take human interest stories out of the newspaper and set them to music on the spot—a sort of "singing news." This led to some less than memorable lyrics, as when he once sang, after a fire at the old Congress Hotel, "The Con-ger-ess, it's now two floors less." By the end of the 1930s he had become a popular fixture in Chicago, was touring and playing show dates, and was making his first records. Off and on throughout his career he appeared with a succession of girl singers known as Bonnie Blue Eyes,* and often with his younger brother Randy.

In 1939 Columbia Records released Atcher's version of the old 1929 Carter Family chestnut, "I'm Thinking Tonight of My Blue Eyes," a song that had become a standard with all sorts of radio singers. On the label of Bob's record, though, appeared the note: "Sobbing with guitar acc." Though he did not tinker with the words at all, Bob created a deathless parody by acting as if he were overcome by the emotion of the song, and he began sobbing and bawling and weeping halfway through the tune. Years later Bob was to recall how this unusual style came about. "I could always do a great sharp scream like a panther, and one night on the radio, after another singer had finished, I added my panther yell to the applause after the number. But I was the next performer to go on, and before I knew it, I had reached for a high note and this scream came out. Well, stacks of mail came in next week, asking me to do that song with the cry in it again. I couldn't break into a scream from a low note—I had to have a high note to start from—so I took the old A.P. Carter song 'I'm Thinking Tonight of My Blue Eyes' and rewrote the melody so that each four bars started with a high note. Later on, Roy Acuff used my melody on the song, and Kitty Wells used it for 'It Wasn't God Who Made Honky Tonk Angels,' but it originated there with me." The result was a runaway best-seller and a hit record that was ranked in the year's top five.

Throughout the early 1940s Bob continued to have hit records, including important early versions of such cowboy standards as Bob Nolan's "Cool Water" and Paul Rice's "You Are My Sunshine." After his hitch in the army he continued his recording and established himself in films, on network radio, as a fixture on the WLS "National Barn Dance," and as a pioneering television star. He emphasized his cowboy material more and more. He was one of the first stage cowboys to use the services of California tailor Nudie, who designed for him custom hand-crafted topcoats with elaborate lacing and piping, and he often appeared

*The most important "Bonnie Blue Eyes," and the one who did most of the recording with Bob in the Columbia years, was Leota Applegate, a Kentucky singer who has since died.

on a palomino stallion named Golden Storm—quite a feat on programs that often originated in downtown Chicago. Still, in the early 1950s he did an album for Columbia called "Early American Folk Songs," a popular and influential album that paid tribute to Atcher's Kentucky roots and offered a rare modern recording of the classic "Hunters of Kentucky."

In 1959, while still an active performer, Atcher was elected mayor of the northern Chicago suburb of Schaumburg, and for the next sixteen years he devoted himself to politics and to successfully running a growing city. In 1975 he came out of "retirement" and began to make appearances with his grown family, creating a full-blown show somewhat like the King Family show, to play state fairs, conventions, and suburban nightclubs.

Another key transitional figure in modern Kentucky country music had a shorter, more spectacular, and in some ways more symbolic career than Bob Atcher. She was Molly O'Day, a remarkable stylist who, in the four years she was in the national spotlight (1946–1950), made a strong bid to become the first "Queen of Country Music." Though she dissipated much of her talent and energy by radio station-hopping in the 1940s, though she never really had a big hit record on the *Billboard* charts, and though she voluntarily cut short her career because of ill health, many veteran record executives of the time agreed with the judgment of Art Satherly, Columbia Records' ace producer, that Molly O'Day was the greatest female country singer ever. The scant three dozen recordings she made for Columbia betwen late 1946 and 1952 have exerted an influence on music far beyond their initial success. The strong, heartfelt emotions with which she delivered her best songs—sentimental "tear jerkers" or fervent country gospel pieces—were unique in an age when girl singers were either doing "cute" up-tempo pieces of trivia or "safe" cowgirl songs in the mode of the then-reigning queen, Patsy Montana. Molly O'Day performed a service to country music similar to that of Hank Williams: she entered the scene at a time when the music was seeing its identity threatened by increasingly slick, pop-oriented performances, and gave it a strong refresher course in its southern roots. "She and Hank both came along about the same time," one of Molly's musicians remarked, "and they both made a good stab at putting the country back in the music."

In one sense, "Molly O'Day" was born in 1942, when a young girl singer named LaVerne Williamson Davis decided to start using it as a permanent stage name. Born in 1923 at McVeigh, Kentucky, in remote Pike County just a few miles from the West Virginia border, Lois LaVerne Williamson grew up playing in a string band with her brothers Skeets (fiddle) and Duke (banjo); as she grew up, she took as role models the handful of professional women musicians she heard on the radio and on records: Patsy Montana, Lily May Ledford (of the Coon Creek Girls), and Lulu Belle Wiseman (of WLS). She was especially interested in and influenced by Lily May's banjo playing, and soon learned how to frail in eastern Kentucky style. But gradually she gravitated toward western songs and aspired to be another "singing cowgirl," an image that was more acceptable to the morality of the 1930s, which somehow held that "western" music was cleaner and more acceptable for lady performers than was purer "country" music. After starting out on West Virginia radio, LaVerne joined a band headed by Lynn Davis in 1940, a band featuring the smooth cowboy sound popularized by the Sons of the Pioneers. There was no way, though, that LaVerne's strong, accented Kentucky voice could fit into this style, and the band gradually began to adapt to their new vocalist. So did the leader, Lynn Davis; he and LaVerne were soon married and began a series of jobs at southeastern radio stations that ran throughout World War II. For a time (1943-1944) they played at WHAS Louisville and on the Renfro Valley Barn Dance, but most of their radio work was outside Molly's home state.

One summer evening in 1945 Molly sang a solo of a then-popular gospel song called "Tramp on the Street" over WNOX in Knoxville; the song had been written by Grady and Hazel Cole, north Georgia gospel singers, and was based on a much earlier nineteenth-century song about a dying tramp. The Coles had recorded the song for Victor's Bluebird label in 1939, but their delivery was stiff and rushed, and the record was not successful. Molly slowed up the tempo and delivered the lyrics in a strong, expressive voice full of quivers, glides, and hitches ("feathering"). On a vacation in the nearby Smoky Mountains, Nashville songwriter and publisher Fred Rose heard the broadcast and at once contacted Molly and Lynn Davis about working with him. Rose then contacted Art Satherly at Columbia Records and arranged for a recording session for Molly in Chicago on December 16, 1946. At the time, Rose was just starting his famous song-publishing company, and had just bought several songs from a young Alabama singer named Hank Williams. He gave two of these to Molly and Lynn to record, and Molly had the distinction of being the first to record two Hank Williams classics, "Six More Miles to the Graveyard" and "When God Comes and Gathers His

Jewels." This first session also yielded two other influential re-cordings, Molly's version of "Tramp on the Street" and one called "Black Sheep Returned to the Fold."

The circuit of radio stations continued, and more Columbia recordings followed, many of them newer songs but written, like Williams's, in a traditional country mode. Her recording of "Matthew Twenty-Four" was widely imitated and won for that song a secure place in gospel music repertoires, and her version of the old Kentucky murder ballad "Poor Ellen Smith" merged her old-time banjo frailing with a strong, soulful vocal and became a model for later bluegrass versions of the song. Several songs, including "The Drunken Driver" and "Don't Sell Daddy Anymore Whiskey," were strong temperance songs which reflected both Molly's and Lynn's growing concern with church work. In fact, by the fall of 1949 they were playing in Versailles, Kentucky, and seriously wondering if they wanted to make the compromises necessary to make the country music "big time." They joined the Church of God and began to do evangelical work; after 1950 Molly refused to record any more secular material for Columbia, and in 1952 a bout with tuberculosis forced her into a premature retirement. She recovered, but both she and her husband felt their mission now was to devote their lives to their work in the church. This they did, moving to Huntington, West Virginia, and retiring from country music except for an occasional gospel album or benefit show. "She could have been the greatest woman singer in country music history," recalls Wesley Rose, Fred Rose's son and Nashville's leading publisher. "But when she got religion, she just wouldn't record the songs we picked out for her." Molly's old records continue to be popular today, and in 1975 the John Edwards Memorial Foundation issued a "bio-discography" of Molly's work compiled by John Morris and Ivan Tribe—the first such scholarly treatment accorded a woman country singer.

In addition to Bob Atcher and Molly O'Day, other Kentucky musicians provided less important but equally distinctive links between the older music of the 1930s and the newer styles of the 1950s and 1960s. The York Brothers, George and Leslie, had the misfortune to see their career peak during the confused years of World War II, obscuring their considerable fame on WSM's "Grand Ole Opry" and at other stations in Detroit and Ohio. Born in 1910 (George) and 1917 (Leslie) in Louisa, Kentucky, the Yorks anticipated by several years the popular mix of nostalgia, modern heart songs, and traditional echoes that won later success for Red Foley. Their first record, "Hamtramck Mama," was released on the Universal label in 1939. Later sides, including many of Leslie's originals, followed for Decca, for the Mellow label, and finally for the King label, where the Yorks created an interesting southeastern honky-tonk sound by featuring a piano. The York repertoire ranged all the way from the older sound of "Kentucky" and "Mississippi River Blues" to country versions of the early rhythm-and-blues standard "Sixty Minute Man."

Another Kentucky duo that had more enduring success was the comedy team of Lonzo and Oscar, in reality two brothers named John (Lonzo) and Rollin (Oscar) Sullivan, born in 1917 and 1919 in Edmonton in southern Kentucky. Of the two, Rollin was more interested in show business, working in various bands around Louisville during the early 1940s and eventually teaming with Ken Marvin, the first "Lonzo." This duo had a spectacular hit recording for RCA Victor in 1948 with a wild song called "I'm My Own Grandpa," a popular Tin Pan Alley song based on a Mark Twain story about marriage paradoxes. John Sullivan soon became Lonzo, and the team held forth on the Grand Ole Opry for almost twenty years, from 1947 until 1967, when John died. They were for years the show's leading comedy act, specializing in bizarre songs like "You Blacked My Blue Eyes Too Often," "Take Them Cold Feet Out of My Back," "Did You Have to Bring That Up While I Was Eating?" and parodies of hits like "I'm Movin' On." After John's death, Oscar rebuilt the act with a new partner and continued on the Opry. Other performers who featured comedy in their music included James "Goober" Buchanan, from Simpson County, who did rube comedy work with everyone from Jamup and Honey to Bill Monroe, and who popularized "When It's Tooth Pickin' Time in False Teeth Valley"; and Lazy Jim Day, a Short Creek native who for years held forth over WLW in Cincinnati and originated the idea of "the singing news."

Other women singers followed the lead of Molly O'Day in the 1950s and 1960s and brought the high lonesome sound of the Kentucky hills into the national limelight, no longer feeling the need to disguise their music with cowgirl trappings or "cute" little-girl songs which distorted their own experience with life. June Stearns, from Albany, appeared with Roy Acuff and on the Grand Ole Opry, and had a hit record with "River of Regret" in 1967. And Connie Hall, from Walden, had a string of interesting Mercury releases in the late 1950s, including "We've got Things in Common" (1958). Most successful, though, was Skeeter Davis, a remarkable woman whose career was full of tragedy, odd turns, and controversy.

Born Mary Frances Pennick on December 30, 1931, at Dry Ridge, a few miles south of Cincinnati, Skeeter began working with a high school friend named Betty Jack Davis from the music-rich town of Corbin, singing duets as the Davis Sisters over station WLEX in Lexington. After a few years of paying their dues (which included occasionally appearing with bluegrassers Flatt and Scruggs on "The Kentucky Barn Dance" over WVLK in Lexington), they made a record for RCA Victor that established them as a major act; the song was called "I Forgot More Than You'll Ever Know," and it spent six months on the chart, actually becoming a Number 1 hit in 1953. All the more remarkable was the song's theme: it was a hands-down account of a woman rebounding from a bad affair with grace, style, and even humor. The Davis Sisters seemed on their way to fame, but while the record was still on the charts, the Davises were involved in a serious automobile accident on their way to Cincinnati. Betty Jack was killed and Skeeter was seriously injured. Physical recovery took months, but it took even longer for Skeeter to recover emotionally from what seemed a cruel act of fate. For a time she gave up singing, but friends in Nashville knew her potential and continued to encourage her. Ernest Tubb finally persuaded her to begin touring with his show in the late 1950s, and RCA's key producer, Steve Sholes, who had signed Elvis Presley, finally talked her into recording as a solo act. Her recording of "Set Him Free" was a hit in 1959, and in 1962 "The End of the World" won her a gold record and a reputation that extended overseas.

The early 1960s saw Skeeter established in Nashville, a member of the Opry, and married to WSM radio-TV personality Ralph Emery. Her records continued to be hits, and included "I'm Gonna Get Along Without You Now" (1964) and "I'm a Lover, Not a Fighter" (1969). Surprisingly, her records began to show up on the pop charts as well as the country charts, and for a time in the mid-1960s she seemed on the verge of becoming a full-fledged middle-of-the-road star. She was almost a regular on Dick Clark's television show, she appeared with jazz great Duke Ellington on television, and made a special guest appearance on the Rolling Stones' special. In Nashville, she became a rebel of sorts. After her marriage to Ralph Emery collapsed, she moved into a large house that had enough room for her twelve dogs, her ocelot, her Siamese cats, and her dove in a gilded cage, and a front room decorated with floor-to-ceiling graffiti like "Give to mental health or I'll kill you." She began refusing to perform in places that sold liquor, and gave up raising tobacco on her farm because, she says, "as a Christian, I think it's harmful to my body." In 1973 she was suspended by the Grand Ole Opry when she criticized the Nashville police department for "harassing" some young "street Christians" who were soliciting in a Nashville shopping center. Later reinstated, she often appears now to sing gospel or religious songs, and has involved herself in a campaign to save the old Ryman Auditorium, the original home of the Opry, now deserted. In the 1980s Skeeter Davis seems at times a walking contradiction, blessed with a singing style and personality suited to the most modern of Nashville music, and at the same time gifted with a strong sensitivity toward the past, toward tradition, and toward the values she learned as a child in Dry Ridge.

Skeeter Davis was not the only modern country singer to be haunted—and inspired—by the Kentucky heritage. Others reflected this ambivalence more directly in their music. One such artist is the man who has been called "the Mark Twain of country music," Tom T. Hall. Tom Hall (he didn't add the "T" until he began performing his songs himself in 1967) was born in 1936 in the northeastern Kentucky town of Olive Hill in Carter County. He was the son of a preacher, and by the time he was into his teens he had his own local bluegrass band, was working with his Uncle Curt, who toured rural towns running old cowboy movies, and was playing and announcing on radio station WMOR in Morehead. Hall played bass for his band, called the Kentucky Travellers, and managed to get them to Nashville to make a few records for the Starday label. The group finally broke up, though, and Hall began to work full time as a disc jockey. Enlisting in the army in 1957, he used the opportunity to expand his horizons and, like another country musician named Johnny Cash, began to write songs in the army. When he returned to civilian life he considered himself more of a songwriter than anything else, and produced rather typical country songs like "D.J. for a Day," which became a hit for Jimmy C. Newman in 1963.

Like many writers, Hall was not able to put his personal hometown experiences into artistic perspective until he had escaped from that environment. In his case, the move was to Nashville; he drove into Music City in a rose-colored Cadillac on January 1, 1964, and went to work as a full-time songwriter for Newkeys Music. Where other Kentucky singers and songwriters had been inspired by specific artists from their home regions, Tom T. Hall was inspired by the people themselves, by their lives, by the details of their small triumphs and frustrations. These began to emerge in a string of sparkling song-stories that Hall crafted while living in an old Nashville apartment and making the rounds of the seedy bars along Broadway. He made friends with some of the new Nashville songwriters who were congregating in the city in the early 1960s, much as an earlier generation of young American writers and poets had gathered in Paris in the 1920s: Kris Kristofferson, Chris Gantry, Willie Nelson, and fellow Kentuckian Harlan Howard, a Lexington native who wrote such hits as "Heartaches by the Number," "Pick Me Up on Your Way Down," and "I Fall to Pieces." Though he was a "young Turk" and a Nashville rebel after a fashion, Tom T. Hall still clung to his traditional political views; in the early 1960s he even had two hit patriotic war songs about Vietnam, "Hello, Viet Nam" (recorded by Johnny Wright) and "What We're Fighting For" (recorded by Dave Dudley).

The first of the really memorable songs was "Harper Valley P.T.A.," written in 1965; a country singer had asked Hall to write her a song in the vein of "Ode to Billy Joe," a cryptic soap opera of a song then enjoying spectacular success. Hall respected "Billy Joe" and felt that both it and "Harper Valley" were "musical versions of Erskine Caldwell's writings." He based "Harper Valley" on an incident from his small-town Kentucky childhood. "You see, when I was a small boy, there was a lady in town who had taken on the entire PTA for their indiscretions. I was always amazed that one very unimportant lady could be so brazen as to take on the aristocracy of the community. The idea stuck with me for years." Hall hung onto the song for three years, resisting offers to record it if lines would be changed; finally in 1968 an unknown singer named Jeannie C. Riley recorded it, and Hall found himself author of a million-selling song.

Other songs about his Kentucky childhood followed. In 1967 he wrote a song for bluegrass stars Flatt and Scruggs called "I Washed My Face in the Morning Dew." "It was inspired by an old folk medicine tale: If you wash your face in the morning dew, it will help remove blemishes from your skin. I changed it around to mean that the morning dew would purify your soul." Flatt and Scruggs found it a bit heady for their brand of bluegrass, but the song also became a hit when Tom T. made his own recording of it in 1967. "A Week in a Country Jail" (1969) stemmed from an early personal experience when Tom T. was arrested in Paintsville, Kentucky, for not having a driver's license and not having tags on his car; the judge's grandmother died that night, and what should have been an overnight stay turned into a week when the judge went to the funeral. "The Ballad of Forty Dollars" (1969), which Hall describes as "a very bitter and hard look at the old-time funerals that took place in my home town when I was a child," also reflects some of the bitterness Hall felt about his mother's painful death from cancer, made more graphic by the family's poverty and inability to buy treatments and medicine for her. But the most requested of all Tom T. Hall's songs to date, and his own personal favorite, is "The Year that Clayton Delaney Died" (1971). Delaney was a real person, a guitar picker who inspired the young Tom Hall to go on with music and songwriting, and he was a legendary tragic hero to people in eastern Kentucky. He symbolized the long tradition of Kentucky guitar picking, of musicianship, and of creativity—as well as the confused and tangled personal life so typical of country musicians.

To renew his inspiration and to keep in touch with the common people of rural Kentucky who figured so prominently in his music, Tom T. began to make periodic visits back to rural Kentucky. He would set out in a car, often travelling with a photographer friend, and drive around the back roads, observing people and life, visiting, taking notes. Though he seldom wrote songs on these trips, he often drew upon the subject matter later, after ideas and images had lingered in his mind. In one sense, he was doing the same kind of thing Bradley Kincaid had done in the 1930s, when he used his vacations from WLS to scour the hills in search of old ballads he could use. Only Hall was not looking for folk ballads so much as for the raw material for new songs. But both Hall and Kincaid were transmuting their Kentucky heritage into their own highly successful art forms. Hall extended his concept to include entire LP albums based on this idea: his first "song-hunting" trip yielded *In Search of a Song* (1971), and later ones yielded *Songs of Fox Hollow*, an album of bluegrass tribute entitled *The Magnificent Music Machine*, and in 1982 an album with Earl Scruggs.

In his 1979 autobiography (*The Storyteller's Nashville*), Hall tried to put his finger on the role that geography or the sense of place has for the modern country songwriter. "The thing that fascinated me most during my childhood were the people that I grew up with. I saw the whole environment of my early days as a large stage with parts being played by real people in real life. I watched some grow old and die; I saw some born and grow to be more of the same characters playing the same role—survival. I heard the grammatical mistakes passed from father to son; I saw the values and the prejudices passed from generation to generation. The diet, the religion, the farm—and so on, the entire culture—protected by some unwritten law. I was awed by these people, and I admired them and feared them. I was also one of them."

Earlier songwriters, from Will S. Hays to Bill Monroe to Karl Davis, had rhapsodized Kentucky in vague, glowing generalities. Tom T. Hall and the younger writers of his generation turned away from these generalities and stereotypes, and etched in their song lyrics sharply detailed portraits of specific individuals whose lives in Kentucky were seen as representative of thousands of lives elsewhere. Hall wrote in one of his songs, "I suppose that death is just as real in Olive Hill as it is in some big city by a mill." This, of course, was the lesson Kentucky's poets and novelists had learned years ago, and a lesson earlier Kentucky songsmiths had known but had been unwilling or unable to express. But with the new freedom of country music in the 1970s and 1980s, and with the new emphasis on more mature, more complex lyrics, Hall was in the vanguard in expressing himself for his generation.

As we have seen, most of the singers who gained fame in country music also maintained a strong interest in gospel music. While Kentucky did not play as large a role as Georgia or Tennessee in the development of commercial gospel music, the impulses that drove the Great Awakening of the nineteenth century continued to be visible in both grassroots and commercial music of the state. Through the 1950s to the present day, hundreds of amateur and semiprofessional family singing groups and quartets across the state have routinely packed up their instruments and made the circuit of local churches, playing for love offerings or "gas money." In spite of the romance of bluegrass music, old-time fiddling, and ballad singing, for the last twenty-five years gospel singing has without question been the most popular music of the folk—even though much of it has been learned from books, records, or radio. Between 1971 and 1977, the number of gospel radio stations in Kentucky doubled in number, to over forty. Rural communities across the state still hold monthly "singing conventions," where the best singers of a county gather to sing from shaped-note songsters and hear more modern gospel quartet music. A typical one is the Cumberland County convention, held the fourth Sunday of every month since 1946 at various churches in the county. Even more venerable is the annual "big singing" (featuring a shaped-note book from 1835 called *Southern Harmony*) at Benton, Kentucky, an event dating back well over one hundred years and described in detail in George Pullen Jackson's *White Spirituals in the Southern Upland*.

In recent years two singing families from the same town, Madisonville, have made international reputations by parlaying this tradition into the commercial world of modern Nashville gospel music. The first of these was the Happy Goodman Family, originally from Evansville, Indiana, who soon settled in Madisonville and made that their base of operations. The Happy Goodman Family eventually became a large group that spanned three generations of Goodmans and featured a variety of vocal and instrumental styles. Formed originally around Howard and Gussie Mae Goodman, the group soon added other family members and began to win fame in the 1950s, touring the South and often appearing at Wally Fowler's "All-Night Singings." One of their recorded hits, "I Wouldn't Take Nothing for My Journey Now," became a gospel standard, and by the end of the 1970s the group had won a Grammy award, had branched out into television and recording businesses, and had recorded some twenty LP albums for various gospel recording companies.

Genuine natives of Madisonville, however, were the Rambos, one of the most successful country-gospel groups in the nation and the source of some of the most sensitive and effective gospel songs of our times. Buck Rambo was born in Dawson Springs in 1931; his wife, Dottie Lutrell, in Madisonville in 1935. A precocious singer and songwriter, Dottie began composing songs by a creek near her home when she was eleven, taking as her inspiration the classic nineteenth-century hymns of Fanny Crosby. As a teenager she was touring Kentucky, singing at revival meetings, and even doing some preaching. After she met and married Buck, they formed a group called the Gospel Echoes in 1956, and recorded a couple of albums in Nashville. In 1951 their daughter Reba was born, and as soon as she was old enough she joined the family group. By the mid-1960s they were calling themselves the Rambos and had signed a recording contract with an arm of the venerable John Benson Publishing Company called Heartwarming Records. Their singing was effective, but equally important were the original songs produced by Dottie; unlike many gospel songs, full of vague sentiment and stereotyped images, Dottie's songs sparkled with crisp, clear, concrete images drawn from her rural background and from southern life. In one of her most popular songs, "I've Never Felt This Homesick Before," she borrows from country music the imagery of the rural homecoming, yet manages to suggest that this is only a metaphor for a more profound religious experience. Such subtlety and indirection have won the group numerous awards, including a Grammy. Dottie herself, with over 600 songs to her credit, has been called one of the music's most important women composers. Rambo songs often appear in the repertoires of mainstream country singers and bluegrass bands; and even in the concerts of black soul and gospel singers. Some of Dottie's best-known numbers include "One More Valley," "Build My Mansion (Next Door to Jesus)," "Tears Will Never Stain the Streets of That City," "New Shoes," and, one of her most remarkable mergings of country and religious imagery, "The Holy Hills of Heaven Call Me." In recent years the Rambos have restricted their touring and spent more time composing and working with their own music publishing company; Reba has developed into a successful solo artist, inheriting her mother's songwriting talent and a similar eclectic interest in different musical styles.

While many professional country and gospel singers from Kentucky were winning national reputations in the 1950s and 1960s, a new interest in Kentucky folk music was developing. This was stimulated by the so-called "folk revival" of the late 1950s, the nationwide fad for folk music generated by pop acts like the Kingston Trio and the Limelighters. This fad eventually began to attract attention to genuine folk artists, and one of these was a remarkable woman from eastern Kentucky named Jean Ritchie.

In many ways Jean Ritchie's highly successful career as a folksinger can be seen as a culmination of a family tradition stretching back generations. In her autobiographical *Singing Family of the Cumberlands*, Jean recounts how certain old songs and ballads had been associated with particular family members or family events: "A Gentleman Came to Our House" was known as "Aunt Sal's Song" and was associated exclusively with her, while "The Devil and the Farmer's Wife" recalls one afternoon when the family lost a corn hoeing contest because they got so involved in singing a song and laughing about it. Songs functioned for the Ritchies the way Polaroid snapshots do for a modern family—they were the keys to memories, capsules of family history. And some of the songs went back further than any photograph could: "Nottamun Town" went back to Crockett Ritchie, born about the time of the American Revolution and the real patriarch of most of the Ritchie clan in Kentucky.

The family was proud of its song heritage and was eager to share it with others; their songs, in fact, appeared in the earliest attempts to collect and study Kentucky folk songs. Before World War I, Jean's grandfather Solomon Everidge encouraged and promoted the development of the Hindman Settlement School, with its attendant interest in preserving and collecting the old ballads. It was through these settlement schools, in turn, that Cecil Sharp met members of the Ritchie family on his famous song-collecting trip through the Appalachians in 1917. In his *English Folk Songs from the Southern Appalachians* (1932), Sharp printed one song, "Farewell Dear Rosanna," that he collected from Austin Ritchie, Jean's grandfather, at Hindman on September 21, 1917. He also collected songs from two of Jean's older sisters, Una and May, at about the same time, and printed these as well. Jean's own father, Balis Ritchie, was so interested in old songs that he printed up on his own printing press a little songbook called *Lover's Melodies*, full of songs he had collected himself, using his own particular aesthetic: "I'd hear a part of a song, and if I liked it, I'd learn all that feller knew of it, then I'd travel around amongst the people in the country here and learn one part from one and another from another until I had the whole song." By the time Jean was born, in 1922, her family had already developed a certain self-consciousness about their old songs and a sense of their cultural importance.

None of this prevented young Jean from absorbing the songs first-hand, in their natural settings, with all their emotional and imaginative impact. Sitting next to her mother on the old porch swing in the warm summer twilight, listening to her family sing, a young girl could take to heart the old romantic ballads. Jean later recalled:

> My mind began to wander all around, and the people in the ballads would pass before me out there in the sparking dusk. The song itself seemed unreal and far, far away, telling dreamily of Fair Ellender and Lord Thomas and courts and processions, love and death, but the people my half-closed eyes saw were alive and beautiful. Fair Ellender rode slowly by on her snow-white horse, her hair like long strands of silver and her face like milk in the moonlight. . . . There was Lord Thomas, tall and brave with his sword shining in his hand, there the wedding folk around the long table. Then, in some easy manner that never had to be explained, *I* became Fair Ellender, and the movement of the swing I sat in became the slow, graceful walking of the white horse.

Some of the older singers in Knott and Perry counties also accompanied their singing with the dulcimer, and Jean became interested in this, as well. In the 1960s, Jean was to play a major role in reviving interest in the dulcimer among younger singers, so much so that the instrument became a favorite of northern folksingers and was transplanted to nearly all parts of the country. In fact, the dulcimer was never so widespread or popular in folk tradition as the banjo or fiddle, and there were many parts of the South where it was not known at all, but pockets of genuine dulcimer tradition did exist in Jean's part of eastern Kentucky and in southwestern Virginia. A three- or four-stringed instrument of uncertain origin, the little mountain dulcimer (as distinguished from the European multi-stringed hammered dulcimer) is simple to play and easy to tune. Balis Ritchie, "the finest dulcimer player I have ever known," according to Jean, recalled that dulcimers had been a part of life in Perry and Knott counties since he could remember, and that they were so popular that at least one legendary craftsman, Edward Thomas (1850–1933), made a living by making them. Thomas would push his cart full of brightly painted dulcimers up the creek roads in the summertime, Balis recalled. "He had a kind of little frame made and he hung his instruments around that frame. He'd go along, meet someone in the road, say howdy and invite the person to sit on the roadside and enjoy a little tune. Yes, he kept an old canebottom chair hooked to the cyart [*sic*], and he'd take that chair down and sit on it and draw the dulcimere cross his knees and he'd make the mountains purely *ring* with that music."

By the time she graduated from Viper High School on the eve of World War II, Jean Ritchie had developed a love of old songs and dulcimer playing, and at the same time an awareness of how modern times were threatening to change these forms of music. Her generation had seen the first train come to the valley, the first loads of coal taken from the new mines, the formation of local schools and colleges, the first record player, the first radio. "I guess if it hadn't been for the radio it's no telling how long it would have taken us to find out that we were hillbillies, or what kind of songs we were supposed to sing," she wrote later. "It got to be that if you asked any young person to sing 'Barbry Ellen,' whoever it was would look at you and laugh and look ashamed of you. 'That old-fashioned thing? Why, I don't even remember how that goes, it's been so long.' And he'd begin to twang away on a steel guitar and start out on one of the radio songs, singing 'through his nose' like the hillbillies on the programs did." Gradually, though, as we have seen in earlier chapters, the newer commercial country music and the older ballads became so intertwined and mingled that folklorists found themselves recording songs that were currently available in sheet music form, and record producers were trying to find copyright owners for "Black Jack Davy." The effect on any young singer from Kentucky was bound to be unsettling. "And so in my mind," Jean wrote, "the songs all got mixed and tangled until I came to think on the hillbilly songs as the same kind of thing, got ashamed to be caught singing either kind, got to liking the slick city music on the radio the best, and I guess most everybody else did likewise."

It took more education, and more distance, for Jean to get the perspective on her culture that would allow her to solve this dilemma. The education came at the University of Kentucky, where she graduated with honors and a Phi Beta Kappa key in the mid-1940s, and where she impressed her instructors with her knowledge of folk music and her skill in making it. The distance came when she took her degree in social work and went to the lower east side of Manhattan to gain practical experience at the Henry Street Settlement. Here she found both students and friends interested in her dulcimer and mountain ballads, and she began to learn about professional folklorists and the academic study and collection of old songs. Jean was recorded in 1946 for the Library of Congress by Artus Moser (ironically, at Renfro Valley, that bastion of "commercial" country music), and later she met and recorded for famed folksong collector Alan Lomax. Her early recordings often featured her singing *a cappella* such classics as "Father Grumble" and "The Two Sisters," singing in a high, perfectly pitched voice, clean, clear, with only a touch of vibrato. In New York she began to give recitals and concerts, and by 1952 her credentials were impressive enough to win her a Fulbright scholarship so she could travel around the British Isles to trace the roots of her family's songs. In 1956 she wrote the first of several books, *Singing Family of the Cumberlands*, an affectionate tribute to her family and a memoir of her girlhood, and by the time the urban "folksong revival" developed in the late 1950s, she had become a major figure on the national scene. She performed and lectured at the country's biggest folk festivals, at universities like Harvard and Columbia, and on national radio and television. She did over a dozen albums in five or six years (including two volumes of *Child Ballads in the Southern Mountains*), and became an inspiration to thousands of girls who were taken with her simple singing style with dulcimer accompaniment. She popularized dozens of old songs and wrote or arranged several distinctive songs of her own, including "A Tree in the Valley-O" and "Let the Sun Shine Down on Me." Best of all, she attracted attention to her family and its singing tradition, and through her efforts several family members were also recorded.

Her own creativity surfaced in a variety of ways, from her published collections of material she herself recorded in England and

Ireland, to the impressionistic evocations of song contexts found in *Jean Ritchie's Swapping Song Book* (1964), which also featured memorable photographs by her husband George Pickow. Most of Jean's earlier recorded material was faithful to the traditional modes, but in the 1970s she began to experiment with a more eclectic, more commercial sound that contained elements of pop and even country music. *None But One* (1977) is a slick New York studio product that includes electric guitars, drums, pedal steel guitar, and a variety of stringed instruments, as well as back-up vocals by veterans of the urban folk revival like Mary Travers (of Peter, Paul and Mary), Janis Ian, and Oscar Brand. Though many of the songs, such as "Wondrous Love," "The Riddle Song," and "The Orphan's Lament," are old favorites, some of the newer songs, like "See That Rainbow Shine," sound like any Top 40 country hit. The mixture of country and traditional in Jean Ritchie's career had come full circle.

The folk revival that Jean was so much a part of also attracted national attention to several other Kentucky traditional musicians at the very moment that modern country music seemed to be turning its back on its past. In 1959 a young Yale student, photographer, and folk song enthusiast named John Cohen was impressed enough with Jean's music to borrow a portable hand-cranked tape recorder and go down to the hills around Hazard looking for more music. Jean provided him with introductions to her own family, and he soon was in touch with dozens of interesting musicians. Cohen was later to write: "The mountain people are sensitive to and aware of the stereotype applied to them by the national press—and they resent it. At the same time, they are made to feel inadequate before the sophisticated luxuries which bombard them in national advertisements and they are losing pride in their local traditions." Cohen found that many of the musicians had played or sung very little in recent years, cowed by the radio and jukeboxes blaring bluegrass and rock and roll. He did record "Banjo" Bill Cornett, of Hindman, a sixty-eight-year-old sometime state representative who had sung his "Old Age Pension Blues" on the floor of the Kentucky legislature, and singer-guitarist Corbett Grigsby, a school principal and farmer. But most important, he found Roscoe Holcomb, of Daisy, Kentucky, who was in the next fifteen years to become Kentucky's most celebrated folk musician, and who was to be heralded in 1963 as "the finest performer of Southern mountain music on records today."

In some ways it is ironic that fame came to Holcomb (1912–1981) only at the end of a hard, bruising life of coal mining, construction work, and road crew drudgery, and that his music which was formed in the late 1920s should not reach beyond his home county until the 1960s. Yet these circumstances are precisely what made Holcomb's music so unique, so intensely personal, and so impervious to the music around him, which kept changing through the years. He had never seriously considered trying to make a living with his music, in part because of the economic situation in his home area, but also in part because he seemed unable to detach himself from his music, to see it as a mere commodity to be bought and sold, to be put on and taken off. Unlike modern country singers, whose very survival depends on their ability to "use" songs and engage in theatrics, Roscoe Holcomb felt intensely about the words of a song and what they meant: he experienced songs. Black fiddler Howard Armstrong once told Cohen that Roscoe's music was "pure"—that all other musicians, from Beethoven to jazzmen, had tricks or devices to help them communicate with their audiences, but that Roscoe was singing music without tricks or devices, that his singing presented the real unadorned core or spirit of the music. On some occasions Roscoe would become so moved by the words to an old song that he would choke up, unable to continue; on others, he moved his audience to tears.

When Cohen returned from his first trip to Hazard, he collected the best of his field recordings on a Folkways album called *Mountain Music of Kentucky* (1960), an influential sampler which has remained in print for over twenty years. Of the thirty-three selections, six were by Holcomb, and they give a fair notion of his repertoire: there was Balis Ritchie's favorite, "East Virginia Blues," which Roscoe sang with guitar; there was "Wayfaring Stranger," sung with banjo, which Roscoe knew from the local Holiness church and from an old Baptist songbook he carried around; there was an original song, "Across the Rocky Mountain," destined to become Roscoe's most famous composition; there was an old-time east Kentucky down-picking banjo tune, "Black-Eyed Susie," and an old blues song, "Stingy Woman Blues," which had last been recorded by the Memphis Jug Band, a famous black blues band, in 1927. Roscoe sang all of these at the very top of his vocal range, his voice high and tense, much in the manner of other old singers from around Hazard. People hearing him for the first time were stunned and moved, and more than one commented that they now knew where bluegrass singing came from. The term "high, lonesome sound," often used today to describe the music of Bill Monroe, was in fact originally coined to describe the singing of Roscoe Holcomb in the early 1960s. It was a far cry indeed from the polite clarity of Jean Ritchie, even though she grew up only a few miles from where Roscoe did.

Starting in 1961, Roscoe was invited to places like the University of Chicago and New York City to appear at various folk festivals. Here he attracted more attention, and people began to ask him about the sources of his music. Though he had been exposed to all manner of rural music when he was growing up in the 1920s, he was also exposed to the hard work and violence of the Hazard region. (He once said that neighboring Leslie County was "the worst place I ever seen for guns. I been over there, I can see how to walk by the light of pistols.") He never really got serious about playing the banjo until 1932, the year he turned twenty. "The year I started learning to play the banjo I learned 400 tunes and could sing practically every one of them, but before I got into playing music I was always skinny. I was never sick or nothing, just lean. . . . Pretty hard times, there wasn't hardly no way for a man to get work so I asked God to give me something that I could do—that I could make a little money, so whenever I got hold of this old banjo. . . ." He spent a year playing at local square dances with an area fiddler, and listening to the music around him. He heard and learned from Dock Boggs, and he was especially interested in the blues records he heard, those by Blind Lemon Jefferson, the Memphis Jug Band, and Barbeque Bob—sounds not normally heard in eastern Kentucky. His active repertoire contained relatively few of the old Child ballads so beloved by the Ritchie clan; he replaced them with blues, sentimental songs, dance tunes, native American folk lyrics, original compositions, and church songs.

Roscoe also had a complex off-on relationship with his Regular Baptist church. When he first met Roscoe, John Cohen noted that "at present he sings very seldom and few people appreciate his abilities. Like some other local musicians, he is about to give up music completely and turn to the church." Though he had learned much of his unaccompanied singing style in the church as a boy, he went through a period of his life—about ten years—when he gave up playing music on instruments and singing. He recalled: "We had nothing but the old regular Baptist up in this country then, and they don't believe in music in churches [i.e., instrumental music]. They seemed to think it was wrong—made me think it was wrong and then I found out different. . . . You know, music, it's spiritual." At many festivals Roscoe would bring his old tattered Baptist songbook to sing from, to use as a source for favorites like "Little Bessie," "Motherless Children," and perhaps his most effective, "Village Churchyard":

> In a dear old village churchyard,
> I can see a mossy mound,
> That is where my mother's sleeping,
> In that cold and silent ground.
>
> Gently weeps the weeping willow,
> Sweet little birds to sing at dawn,
> I have no one left to love me,
> Since my mother's dead and gone.

In 1962 John Cohen made a thirty-minute documentary film about Roscoe and his country, called *The High Lonesome Sound.* It was one of the first sensitive attempts to document a traditional singer in his natural environment, and over the years it has become recognized as perhaps the finest film made about an American folk musician. It gained even more recognition for Roscoe, and throughout the 1960s he continued to attend festivals at UCLA, in Berkeley, in Chicago, at the Guthrie Theater in Minneapolis, at Cornell, in Cambridge, and at various clubs from California to New York. Doubtless some of Roscoe's audiences at colleges and festivals looked upon him as a quaint and curious antique, and patronized his sentimentality and archaic banjo playing. But many more did not, and he found that his strong, powerful music had an appeal that reached far beyond Perry County. Roscoe had a favorite story he liked to tell about one evening when he sang "Motherless Children" on a stage in New York; he had prefaced it by saying how much it meant to him and how tough a time the kids in the mountains and coal camps had while growing up. When he came off the stage, a man from the audience, tears streaming down his face, came up to Roscoe and said he didn't like that song at all. Sensing a fight, Roscoe snapped, "Buddy, I didn't sing it for you." "Don't get me wrong," the man said. "Nothing the matter with you, it's just that the song is too close to home."

Roscoe's life really changed very little through all this; he still sought odd jobs in the area, even when his health would have qualified him for disability. "All my life I've worked hard—I don't know what to do when I'm not working." He produced three more record albums for Folkways (*Roscoe Holcomb and Wade Ward* [1962], *The High Lonesome Sound* [1965], and *Close to Home* [1975]), none of which attained any real commercial success but all of which helped preserve his unique music. For the famous photo on the cover of *Mountain Music of Kentucky*, Roscoe posed in front of his old unpainted shed, causing some of his country friends and neighbors to complain. Roscoe took it in stride: "You see, we live in these old mountains here and we've been raised up pretty rough and a lot of them [mountain people] does the best they can do, and they take it as if you take the worst you can find to make a picture to take back to New York to show the people. . . . Course, it don't matter with me." This shame about old things and about traditional life styles, common not only to Perry County but to much of the South, was a constant challenge to the musicians who continued to cling to older songs and forms of music throughout the 1970s. Only the strongest individuals, the fiercest champions of the music, could withstand it. Roscoe Holcomb was one of these, and with his death at a rest home in 1981, Kentucky lost one of its last genuine folk artists.

The urban folk revival also attracted attention to other veteran traditional musicians of Kentucky, though in some cases it was too late for the musicians to gain any real benefit from it. A case in point is that of Aunt Molly Jackson (1880-1960), a balladeer, union organizer, and social activist whose work had won national recognition since the 1920s. Born Mary Magdalene Garland in Clay County, Aunt Molly struggled through an incredible series of misfortunes in her early life: when she was six she saw her mother die of starvation; when she was ten she was in jail for her family's unionizing efforts among the miners; later her husband and son were killed in the mines and her father and brother were blinded there. She was a nurse in 1931, when many miners were blacklisted for union activities. She later wrote: "So I had to nurse all the little children til the last breath left them, and all the light I had was a string on a can lid with a little bacon grease on it. Kerosene was five cents a quart, and I could not get five cents. Thirty-seven babies died in my arms in the last three months of 1931. Their little stomachs busted open; they was mortified inside." With such experiences, it is not hard to see where Aunt Molly's conviction and dedication to improving working conditions came from. Having learned a good many of the traditional ballads of the area, Aunt Molly appropriated the tunes and forms and even words of some of these older songs for her own topical protest songs, such as "Miners' Hungry Ragged Blues," which she recorded for Columbia records in 1932 as "Kentucky Miner's Wife," or "Poor Miner's Farewell," which appeared in a Marxist songbook published in New York.

As an organizer in the 1930s, Molly was so successful that she was forced to leave Kentucky and move to New York. There she continued her union activities and met various intellectuals, historians, and folklorists who began to record her songs and document her career. Starting in 1939 she recorded many of her songs for the Library of Congress, but few of these were really available to the general public. By the late 1950s the folk revival movement had called more widespread attention to her work, but by the time Folkways Records was ready to let her make her first commercial LP, her health was so poor she could no longer really sing. Her young friend John Greenway then agreed to sing her songs on the album and to have her briefly introduce each song. Everything was set up, the songs chosen, the rehearsals begun, but a week before the first taping session Aunt Molly passed away at the age of eighty. Greenway went ahead with the album, and *The Songs and Stories of Aunt Molly Jackson*, featuring only Greenway, was released in late 1961. Interest in her songs continued to rise until in 1971 a group of young college students from Boston, who had formed a record company called Rounder, reissued her 1939 Library of Congress recordings on a commercial album. At long last Aunt Molly's best songs, recorded in her prime, were really accessible to the public: "Hard Times in Coleman's Mines," "I Love Coal Miners, I Do," "Christmas Eve on the East Side," and other more traditional ballads.

Though Aunt Molly was unable to reap any rewards from the folk revival, interest in her life did lead enthusiasts to her half-sister, Sarah Ogan Gunning, who had gone through many of the same kinds of experiences as Aunt Molly, and who had an equally interesting repertoire of old songs. In 1963 folklorists Archie Green and Ellen Steckert found Sarah living quietly in Detroit, like so many others who had fled the rigors of Appalachian life. Sarah had been born in Knox County, at Ely Branch, in 1910, and had grown up in the coal mining towns, raising her family and teaching them her old songs. After her first husband died in 1938 she moved to New York and married a metal polisher named Joseph Gunning. By this time she was becoming well known as a singer—she was more a singer than Aunt Molly, who often looked on songs as means to an end--and had recorded for the Library of Congress in New York in 1937. (One of her recordings was a personalized version of the old Dick Burnett song "Man of Constant Sorrow," which she called "I Am a Girl of Constant Sorrow.") Though Burl Ives, Woody Guthrie, and Hudie Ledbetter admired her songs, Sarah gradually dropped out of music until her visitors in 1963 persuaded her to start singing again. Soon she was appearing at concerts, at labor meetings, and even at the Newport Folk Festival. A newly-recorded album, *Girl of Constant Sorrow*, was issued a few years later, solidifying Mrs. Gunning's reputation as a premier performer of Appalachian songs and ballads.

The national fad for folk music began to subside in the mid-1960s, engulfed by a rock and roll rejuvenated by the Beatles and polarized by the agony of Vietnam. But it had had its effect. It had shown the nation that, in spite of the changes modern technology was wreaking on the Kentucky hills, powerful traditional voices could still be found and appreciated. Against all odds the older music survived, and through the 1970s more and more attempts were made to collect it, to study it, to preserve it, and to present it to an audience. Not all of Kentucky's newly discovered folk musicians were older musicians like Roscoe Holcomb or Sarah Ogan Gunning, nor classic ballad singers like Jean Ritchie. Some, like George and Mary Williamson, were Kentuckians who had moved north but preserved the music they remembered from childhood. The Williamsons, from their vantage point in Detroit, recorded and appeared as the Old Kentucky String Band and won a wide following. Leon Bibb, a singer-guitarist born and raised in Louisville, studied music formally and appeared in several Broadway musicals before he turned to folk music in the late 1950s, recording a half dozen albums, touring widely, and having modest hit records with "Sinner Man" and "Cherries and Plums." Closer to their roots were a number of excellent instrumentalists who had remained in Kentucky. Buddy Thomas, a fiddler who came from Emerson in northeastern Kentucky, possessed an entire repertoire from a region scarcely documented on phonograph records, but died suddenly after releasing a single album on Rounder in 1976. J.P. and Annadeene Fraley, of Rush, in Boyd County, took their fiddle-guitar music to numerous area festivals and made several LPs. W.L. Gregory emerged from south-central Kentucky to demonstrate his mastery of the fiddle and banjo styles of Dick Burnett and Leonard Rutherford, and show off his "slide banjo" technique (done with a veterinary syringe) and unorthodox tunings at a small number of festivals and on two record albums. His sometime partner Clyde Davenport, from the same area, displayed an even more archaic fiddle style on his solo records. Farther west, Rupert Francis from Hopkinsville managed to preserve a densely complex family fiddle tradition for partisans at area fiddle contests, but as yet for no record listeners.

The Ritchie family was not the only Kentucky family to gain fame as traditional musicians. Some, like the extended family of

Sammie Walker in Barren and Monroe counties, have quietly made their music for generations of local residents and a handful of folklorists who have recorded and studied their unusual fiddle and banjo tunes and old-time singing. Others have been more aggressive and self-conscious about promoting their music. The A.L. Phipps Family, from Barbourville, have kept alive the singing style of the old Carter Family and even performed some with A.P. Carter before his death. The Phippses are also champions of the old unaccompanied gospel quartet style and have carried it to numerous festivals, including several staged by A.L. Phipps himself. Phipps also started a grassroots record company, Pine Mountain (recently resurrected under the name Mountain Eagle) with which he recorded a good many semiprofessional singers and instrumentalists from the southern Appalachians. The McLain Family Band, headed by Raymond McLain, a music professor at Berea College, has adapted the concept of the extended musical family to bluegrass. Originally from Hindman, McLain, the son of a professional folklorist, organized his family at first as an amateur, back-porch group; as he began to use the music more and more in his teaching, CBS television aired a news story on him, and soon famed classical composer Gian-Carlo Menotti invited the band to appear at his Spoleto Festival in Italy. Other international appearances followed, and by 1980 the McLains had sung their favorites like "Fair and Tender Ladies" in over sixty-one countries, as well as on several national television specials. To have records to sell at their appearances, the McLain Family, like the Phippses, has started its own record label, Country Life, and currently stages its own bluegrass festival featuring family bands.

By the 1960s, after watching for years as outsiders from New York and Washington and California trouped into the state to document and celebrate Kentucky traditional music, Kentuckians were beginning to take this study into their own hands. Kentucky schools and colleges began to establish archives and collections of songs, and to encourage their students to bring in songs and tunes. As early as 1953, D.K. Wilgus founded the Western Kentucky Folklore Archive at Western Kentucky State University in Bowling Green. Though Wilgus left in 1962, the collection continued to grow under the direction of Lynwood Montell and others until by 1981 it contained over 3,000 song texts and well over 3,000 hours of recorded tape, most of it classified and cross-indexed. Today, as the Western Kentucky University Folklore, Folklife, and Oral History Archives, it serves an important regional constituency, and helps support Western's graduate-level folklore program. In the eastern part of the state Berea College continues to act as a focal point for collection and study. Its Appalachian Center, though technically founded in 1970, incorporated the older Weatherford-Hammond Mountain Collection, one of the country's best collections of printed material, which had been started in the 1920s. Under the leadership of Loyal Jones in the 1970s, the Center began to amass audio and video tapes and by 1981 could boast of over 1,500 hours of audio tape. The Center also became a home for recordings done by several major independent collectors, such as Reuben Powell, whose 3,000 hours of tape include comprehensive documentation of Renfro Valley, and John Harrod, a native Kentuckian and former Rhodes scholar who collected ballads, tunes, and vital biographical data about many eastern Kentucky musicians. Bruce Green, another independent collector, amassed hundreds of recordings of fiddle tunes in the 1970s. Powell, Green, Harrod, and others have continued the tradition of individual scholarship established so well a generation or two earlier by John Lair.

No longer do Kentucky musicians have to travel out of state to gain a hearing. By 1979, more than thirty major festivals and fiddling contests were being held in the state annually, more than in almost any other southern state. This is a far cry from the days when Jean Thomas had to struggle to get local support for her American Folk Song festival. The annual Celebration of Traditional Music at Berea (in October) has gained recognition as perhaps the most authentic regional festival of music in the South, while the Kentucky State Fiddling Championship, held at the Rough River Dam State Park in July, has continued to provide a forum for serious fiddlers from the area. Bill Monroe stages annual bluegrass festivals at Pendleton and Beaver Dam, while Louisville's annual Bluegrass Music Festival of the United States and the Festival of the Bluegrass in Lexington generally book the country's leading bluegrass acts.

As the festivals and fiddling contests continued to attract huge audiences throughout the 1970s, commercial country music began to attract a new, larger, and more affluent audience, as well. During much of the 1970s, country music experienced a renaissance that was in some ways similar to the urban folk revival of the 1960s: performers who had for years appealed to regional or sectional audiences suddenly found themselves with access to national television, expensive clubs in Las Vegas and New York, and slick newspapers and magazines like *Time*, *Newsweek*, and even *Playboy*. Riding the crest of this wave of interest, and establishing herself as the nation's foremost woman country singer, was Loretta Lynn. Her "hard-core" country singing style, so similar to Molly O'Day's in many respects, sold millions of records for her, but the success of her best-selling autobiography *Coal Miner's Daughter* in 1976, and the even more successful Academy Award-winning film made from the book in 1980, attracted national attention to her Kentucky background. In 1961, the year that Roscoe Holcomb made his debut concert at the Chicago Folk Festival, the year that John Greenway completed his tribute album of the songs and stories of Aunt Molly Jackson, Loretta Lynn was making her first Decca recording—not for the Library of Congress but in a Nashville studio; not old ballads but modern copyrighted lyric laments. At a cursory inspection there would seem to be little link between Loretta's country music and the distinctive folk music of eastern Kentucky, but as her career developed links did emerge, and, ironically, as she became more nationally known, the links became more and more evident. To be sure, much of the folk tradition of the area around Butcher Hollow had been diluted before Loretta was born, but her experience growing up there and the values she learned there formed the core of her best songs. In a more direct way, she listened closely to two other Kentucky artists, Molly O'Day and Tom T. Hall, and to the way they used their backgrounds and values in their music. Like so many other Kentucky musicians, she had to find a forum for her music elsewhere, but like them, too, she was unable to escape the influence of the land and what it represented.

In Loretta Lynn's childhood the same images that have appeared so often before in Kentucky music history appear again: the company town, the coal miner father, the family string band, moonshine, the local square dance, the tinny radio linking the household to the distant country music shows of the day. Butcher Hollow is near Van Lear, a company town for the Consolidated Coal Company, in Johnson County, a few miles west of the West Virginia border and just east of Magoffin County, home of early singer Buell Kazee. Loretta's father, Melvin Webb, was a tiny 117-pound man who worked all his life as a miner and who left her a legacy of responsibility, a sense of the past, and a tendency to have high blood pressure and migraine headaches. He died when he was only fifty-one, before Loretta started singing professionally, yet she admits that "Daddy's been the most important person in my life." His memory shows through in several of Loretta's songs, and in one hit she recorded (though didn't write) called "They Don't Make 'em Like My Daddy." She has confessed also to having several strange supernatural experiences about him. In many ways he seems to have become a symbol for her past and her inability to ignore it.

Born in 1935, Loretta was in her early life sheltered even from the popular mass media; she and her brothers and sisters occasionally went into the town of Van Lear to see cowboy films, but most music was at first learned from personal contact. Her mother taught her the song "The Great Titanic," with appropriate gestures, and she remembers a song she sang in school about "Luly Barrs" "who got pregnant by this man but he wouldn't marry her. He tied a piece of railroad steel around her neck and threw her into the Ohio River, and they found her three months later."* Her grandfather was the family's old-time banjoist, playing it with his left hand when sober and with his toes when drunk. "We didn't sing too much stuff from radio when I was little because . . . we didn't have a radio until I was eleven." By 1946 Loretta was listening to her first real country music and marvelling over Molly O'Day, "the first woman singer I can remember." Bill Monroe's music from the Opry was also popular in the Webb household, often inspiring Loretta's mother to do a little hoedown dance in front of the radio—a dance Loretta still does occasionally on stage which she calls her "hillbilly hoedown." All of this had its impact on young Loretta, and she would sit in the family's rocking chair, rocking her baby sisters and brothers while singing at the top of her voice. "I can't say that I had big dreams of being a star at the Opry. It was another world to me. All I knew was Butcher Hollow—didn't have no dreams that I knew about."

Things changed with a bewildering suddenness. Before Loretta was fourteen she married Oliver "Moonshine" Lynn (or "Mooney" or "Dolittle"), who soon packed her off on a train to Bellingham, Washington, near the Canadian border and some two thousand miles from Butcher Hollow. In between having babies and managing a household, Loretta continued to sing, and her husband began to encourage her career. Some of her early appearances at local clubs and roadhouses were made with a band that included her brother Jay Lee Webb on guitar. One night while she was singing at a place called the Chicken Coop in Vancouver,

*Loretta comments that "I'll bet you there's lots of old people who still know the song about Luly Barrs," but it is really a rather localized ballad. More commonly known as "Lula Vower" or "Lula Viers," the song describes an actual murder that took place in Floyd County, Kentucky, in 1917; the murderer, one John Coyer, was captured but allowed to do Army service in World War I and never returned.

British Columbia, she was noticed by Don Grashey, then the manager for a local Vancouver record company called Zero. He signed her to a contract on February 1, 1960, and a week later took her down to Los Angeles for her first recording session. Fortunately the studio band Grashey lined up contained two of the best musicians on the west coast: steel guitar player Speedy West, who is recognized today as one of the great innovators of the steel and who had backed stars like Tennessee Ernie Ford on their big hits, and fiddler Harold Hensley, who had grown up not far from Butcher Hollow, in the White Top area of Virginia.* "And she grinned," recalled Hensley, remembering that first session. "She's got the cutest smile and she grinned all the way through that session. She was grinning and she was just as happy as a clown. This was a big thing for her." Loretta cut four sides at that first session, all original songs: "I'm a Honky Tonk Girl," "Whispering Sea," "New Rainbow," and "Heartaches Meet Mr. Blues." The first release, Zero 1007, paired "Honky Tonk Girl" with "Whispering Sea"; the former took its theme from Kitty Wells's classic "It Wasn't God Who Made Honky Tonk Angels," and reflects Loretta's early love of Kitty's style. Loretta and Dolittle's improvised publicity tour to promote the record, a comic highlight of the *Coal Miner's Daughter* film, succeeded against all odds. As Dolittle later quipped, they "drove over 80,000 miles to sell 50,000 copies of *I'm a Honky Tonk Girl*." By July 1960 the record was actually on *Billboard*'s hit charts.

That fall, October 15 to be exact, Loretta made her first guest appearance on the Grand Ole Opry and began to attract interest in Nashville. Within a year, she and Dolittle moved there, Dolittle working at a garage to support Loretta and their family, which by this time numbered four daughters. Through the efforts of the Wilburn Brothers, who were established artists, songwriters, and producers, in September 1961 Loretta signed a contract with Decca Records, then the leading country producer and home of the nation's two leading female country singers, Patsy Cline and Kitty Wells. At first Loretta sounded so much like Kitty Wells that the recording executives were nervous, but gradually she began to establish her own style and to be billed as "The Decca Doll from Kentucky." One song from her very first Decca session, on September 8, 1961, was called, symbolically enough, "Success," and became her first major hit.

*The famous scene in the movie *Coal Miner's Daughter* in which Loretta's producer senses her talent and sends out for better musicians did not happen at the first session. Speedy West recalls, though, that something like that did happen at Loretta's second Zero session in the fall of 1960.

Between the fall of 1961 and the end of 1978 Loretta released forty-six single records; of these thirty-nine became certifiable hits and reached the *Billboard* charts—an astounding batting average and one unmatched by any other Nashville star in the fickle and fast-moving world of modern country music. Many of these hit songs Loretta wrote herself, and many of them began to chronicle working-class life from the fresh perspective of women: the house-wife, the mother, the lover. Though she was not a conscious feminist, Loretta spoke to millions of women in songs like "The Pill" (one of the first country songs dealing forthrightly with birth control), "Don't Come Home A-Drinkin' with Lovin' On Your Mind," "Rated X," "Your Squaw Is on the Warpath" (a slogan borrowed from one of her father's sayings), and "Out of My Head and Back in My Bed." In songs like "Fist City," which she wrote one night as a response to a woman who was making a play for her husband, and "You Ain't Woman Enough to Take My Man," which she wrote after hearing one of her fans complain about a dumpy girl who was trying to steal her husband, she plays the proud, avenging wife. But in "One's on the Way," written by former *Playboy* cartoonist Shel Silverstein, she shows the other side of the marriage coin, describing the resignation and sense of entrapment felt by a Topeka housewife who has three small children and "one on the way." By no means was Loretta the first country singer to sing from a woman's point of view—her mentor Patsy Cline and Kitty Wells, among others, had done that—but her songs were by far the most popular, and the most successful, of them. Their success reflected an important trend in country music: the emergence of a large female audience. By 1981 demographic surveys were to show that the average country record buyer was female, thirty-two years old, divorced, and supporting one or two kids. Loretta Lynn spoke to this new constituency. She says, "There's plenty of songs about how women should stand by their men and give them plenty of loving when they walk through the door, and that's fine. But what about the man's responsibility? . . . No woman likes to be told, 'Here's the deal.'"

Loretta's other distinctive theme was her Kentucky back-ground. "Coal Miner's Daughter" (1970), her most famous song and the title of her book and movie, the song she uses to open all her shows, is full of gritty details about her life in Butcher Hollow. "It started out as a bluegrass thing," she recalls, "'cause that's the way I was raised, with the guitar and banjo following along." The original song, in fact, got out of hand and verses had to be cut out: one about her mother papering their walls with old magazines, one about how the creek in front of their house would flood, and one about hog-killing day in December. The shortened form was the recorded version, and the success, but Loretta ran into one problem she hadn't anticipated: people believed she was exaggerating the hillbilly background she described in the piece. Other songs, though, told the same story, from "Blue Kentucky Girl" (later popularized by Emmylou Harris) to "That's Where I Learned to Pray," about her church upbringing. It was no surprise that her autobiography devoted over half its pages to her youth in Kentucky; nor was it surprising that Loretta went to Hyden, Kentucky, after a 1970 mine disaster there claimed thirty-eight men, and did a benefit that raised over $90,000 for the families of the miners.

Loretta also recorded a series of successful duets with leading male country singers, including Ernest Tubb (ironically, the first singer she had ever heard on radio).

In 1972 Loretta was voted Entertainer of the Year by the Country Music Association; it was country music's equivalent of an Oscar, and it was, surprisingly, the first time a woman had won it. Ironically, though, as Loretta found herself a regular guest on "The Johnny Carson Show" and as a cover of TV Guide, she wrote less and less original material. Some of this was due to a contractual dispute with her early managers, the Wilburn Brothers, but some was due to the pressures of touring and recording. By 1981, though, she was starting to write again, and did her first television special; no one could accuse her of resting on her laurels.

By the end of the 1970s, Loretta Lynn and Jean Ritchie had each established herself as the premier performer in her genre of music: Loretta was the queen of commercial country music, Jean the queen of folk music. Jean, from her base in New York, was continuing to promote folk music, appearing at festivals and workshops, starting her own record company to help document traditional performers, and occasionally seeing one of her original songs recorded by big popular singers like Emmylou Harris. Loretta, from her base in Nashville, was still routinely climbing on her Silver Eagle tour bus and heading for one-nighters, appearing on television shows, reading palms, and working slowly and carefully with her producer Owen Bradley in Nashville's best recording studios. The life-styles of the two singers are miles apart, and the audiences of one would probably not appreciate the other. Yet both singers came from tiny hamlets in eastern Kentucky, only two counties apart, and both came from the same general musical background. Both came from large families and both had parents who liked to sing the old ballads and folk songs. Both left Kentucky as young women and thereby gained an important perspective on their music and culture. Both, in fact, later wrote autobiographical books in which they stressed their formative childhood years in Kentucky more than their later successful careers. Both later wrote songs based on their memories of Kentucky or on the early music they heard as a child. How, then, did they end up so far apart in their music? A good answer to that question goes a long way toward explaining the complex relationship between Kentucky's traditional music and its commercial country music.

Some clues appear as details in the biographies. Jean Ritchie was born in 1922, Loretta Lynn in 1935—a difference of thirteen years. Yet both were exposed to the same sort of radio and popular culture; a ten-year-old Jean Ritchie hearing the radio in 1932 would not have heard music radically different from that of ten-year-old Loretta Lynn in 1945. More significance, perhaps, lies in family attitude. Jean's father, a farmer and part-time clerk and publisher, was rather self-conscious about his musical heritage; Loretta's father, a coal miner whom Loretta did not see after she was thirteen, was more a passive listener to music, seeing it as a relaxation from a long day at the mines. (One wonders what he would have thought of Aunt Molly Jackson or Sarah Ogan Gunning's songs about coal mines.) The Ritchie family disliked modern "hillbilly" music and Jean wrote sarcastic comments about it in her books; Loretta's family totally accepted it and gathered around the radio as a family in the same way the Ritchies gathered together to sing; Loretta's mother danced jigs to Bill Monroe's music. Jean left home to go off to college, while Loretta quit school as a teenager to move to Washington with her husband. While Jean saw the ghost stories and supernatural events heard in eastern Kentucky as an interesting and charming part of her heritage, Loretta was haunted by visions of her dead father, by premonitions, by her ability to read palms. Jean, singing in a polite, well-mannered voice, was self-conscious about her music as an art form; Loretta, delivering her music in a soulful, husky mountain voice, saw her songs as products to sell in order to make a career. Jean's music was based in Kentucky's bucolic past, Loretta's in Kentucky's blue-collar present. Yet in odd ways the two musics were different sides of the same coin.

But as the 1970s became the 1980s, even Loretta Lynn's type of country music began to sound old-fashioned, as country music moved more and more toward contemporary pop music and even jazz and rock. Yet the strong traditions of folk music and "classic" country music that so characterize Kentucky do not seem to have acted as any deterrent for such contemporary singers; indeed, it seems to have enriched their music even more. Two different methods through which contemporary singers have utilized these traditions in their music can be seen in the careers of Crystal Gayle and John Conlee.

Crystal Gayle, of course, was known for years as "Loretta Lynn's kid sister," and grew up in a family where many of her brothers and sisters were actively involved with commercial country music. (Loretta's brother Jay Lee, a fiddler and guitarist, toured a lot and worked in the Nashville studios, while another sister, Peggy Sue, wrote songs and recorded under the stage name Tracey Lee.) By the time she was sixteen, Crystal was travelling with Loretta's road show, absorbing the ins and outs of the commercial country music tradition. Though she was born Brenda Webb in Paintsville in 1951, Crystal was raised in an Indiana town, with music and culture different from that of Loretta's Butcher Hollow. As Loretta says, "She don't remember the early days in Kentucky; her ways are different from mine." In spite of this, Crystal's early successes were in the shadow of Loretta's stardom; she had a hit record in 1970, when she was nineteen, on Loretta's label, Decca, with Loretta's producer: "I've Cried (the Blue Right Out of My Eyes)." It was only in the mid-1970s that Crystal began to find her own style, with pop-sounding, "easy listening" hits like "Don't It Make My Brown Eyes Blue" (1977) and "When I Dream" (1979). By 1981 she was opening shows with the old Billie Holliday-Benny Goodman jazz standard, "What a Little Moonlight Will Do," and using a heavy rock-sounding band, replete with electric organ, drums, and a rhythm-and-blues back-up vocal group.

"When I started," Crystal recalled, "Loretta didn't want me to record country songs at all, because she always told me that I could sing a lot of things. She wanted me to have a different sound from her." The struggle to achieve this different sound for a time created an odd split personality, a split reflected by Crystal's own confusion over her stage name. When Loretta first got her sister—then writing and performing as Brenda Gail Webb—a record contract, their company, Decca, already had a child prodigy Brenda Lee under contract. They suggested Brenda Gail get a professional name, and one day as Brenda and Loretta drove by one of the mid-South's ubiquitous Krystal hamburger drive-ins, the name Crystal suddenly popped into Loretta's mind. Crystal it became, and soon Brenda Gail had an alter ego. "My driver's license already said Brenda and my records were saying Crystal and it just didn't feel comfortable," she recalled. "I don't think people understood—I felt I was trying to be somebody I wasn't." Brenda Gail was Loretta Lynn's kid sister, the country singer from Kentucky; Crystal Gayle was the sexy, articulate Indiana kid who grew up listening to rock and roll in the fifties and who let her hair grow down to her hips. "Don't It Make My Brown Eyes Blue," her big 1977 hit, did better on the pop charts than on the country charts. One part of Crystal says she cannot turn her back on the kind of music she inherited from her sister; another says she must in order to develop as an artist, and to find her own personal style and her own unique image. It is by no means a unique problem with current singers.

John Conlee is another successful contemporary singer who served a lengthy apprenticeship in older forms of country music before making his mark. With John, it was not learning old songs at his parents' knees, or even touring with a big sister or a family band on the country music circuit, but rather a nine-year stint as a disc jockey. Days and days of listening to hit records, answering requests, and learning the record business gave John a pretty good sense of modern country music and its direction, and by 1978 he had put this to use by releasing his first hit record, an original song called "Rose Colored Glasses."

Born in 1947 on a large farm near Versailles, just outside Lexington, John Conlee was playing the guitar and making a pest out of himself at the local radio station before he was ten. Friends occasionally threaten to talk about his first public performance, a rendition of Elvis Presley's "Love Me Tender," done when John was in the fourth grade. Like many modern country singers, John had a comfortable childhood and turned to music for the love of it, not as a ticket out of the coal mines or cotton fields. Like many modern singers and songwriters, he also tried to fight off his love of music by choosing a more practical career: in John's case, one of the most practical and venerable of all professions, that of embalming. After several years of this, he moved to the slightly less venerable profession of disc jockey, and after moving to Nashville (as a DJ) in 1975, he began to dabble in songwriting. Within a year he landed a record contract as a singer and recorded several songs which had regional popularity; one of these, "The Backside of Thirty," was recorded about the time John turned thirty himself, and may have reflected some of his anxiety at the time. In June 1978, when his "Rose Colored Glasses" began getting airplay, John was still working at a radio station introducing records by Fleetwood Mac and Charlie Daniels. Even after two more hit singles and after becoming the first new artist to join the Grand Ole Opry in five years (in 1980), he still held on to his 1973 Plymouth, his mortician's license, and his DJ audition tapes.

In the grand tradition of Kentucky country music, Conlee is more a stylist than a performer of original material. Though he can write songs, he prefers to use material from the remarkable stable of contemporary Nashville songwriters like Ben Peters and Don Cook and Rafe Van Hoy. Though he uses strings and background vocalists, John's voice is distinctly country: it has some of the sincerity of Merle Haggard and some of the expressive quavering of honky-tonk giant Lefty Frizzell. Like Crystal Gayle, he is emerging as a romantic, good-looking singer with great appeal to the opposite sex. Unlike her, he has not consciously made inroads into pop or jazz music, and seems to have found still more ore in the well-worn mine of mainstream country music. His response to his Kentucky background has been to accept it, to work within its confines, and to carefully plan a career that incorporates a sophisticated knowledge of the music's media. It is a different approach from that of Crystal Gayle, but one which seems to be equally successful.

It may well be that Crystal Gayle's generation of singers represents the end of a period in which geography has played a significant role in the development of popular musical styles. In part this may be because modern America is losing much of its sense of place and many of the distinctive qualities that make one part of the country, or one culture, or one music, different from another. Superhighways, chain stores, national corporations, national radio and television—all contribute toward making us a nation of sameness. Growing up in Butcher Hollow, Loretta Lynn heard only the banjo and fiddle music of her family, the ballads of her school mates, the hard country music of the Grand Ole Opry. Growing up in Indiana a generation later, Crystal Gayle heard a far more "national" and heterogeneous music from the radio, television, and records that were so readily available to her. The concept of "Kentucky music" obviously meant less to her than to her older sister, and her sense of musical geography was much more diffuse—as witnessed by the title of her 1981 album, "Hollywood, Tennessee."

7 Kentucky Music, American Country

In spite of the fact that Kentucky music has produced a variety of performers and styles, it still has its own distinct identity. In spite of its diversity, common threads run through it. To begin with, Kentucky has produced an inordinate number of good and influential musicians; it has, in fact, contributed more stars to country music than any other state except Texas, a state six times its size with four times its population. Four Kentuckians—Bill Monroe, Grandpa Jones, Red Foley, and Merle Travis—have been elected to the Country Music Hall of Fame, as has adoptive son Pee Wee King; others, like Bradley Kincaid, have been nominated for the honor and seem destined to make it. As we have seen, these musicians did not come only from the eastern mountains—as the stereotyped view of "Kentucky music" would have it—but from across the state, with western Kentucky playing an especially crucial role in the development of bluegrass and guitar styles.

Music in Kentucky developed under a unique set of circumstances. The state itself, because of its geographical position, acted as a meeting ground for northern and southern cultures, and musicians were exposed to both the traditional music of the South and the popular Tin Pan Alley music of the North. This mixture was facilitated by the major rivers of the state, which acted as conduits for music and songs, and later by the number of Kentucky workers who went north for factory jobs, workers who eagerly exchanged songs with other workers. Radio listening in Kentucky was oriented primarily to the big northern stations in Pittsburgh and Chicago rather than to the traditional southern stations in Dallas, Atlanta, and Nashville.

Musicians in Kentucky have also had less access to mass media than their counterparts in Georgia, Tennessee, and Texas. Kentucky has never developed a major broadcasting and recording center to match those of Atlanta, Dallas, or Nashville. Kentucky radio stations, which were rather slow to establish themselves to start with, did not show much enthusiasm for early country music; they never developed a program to rival the "National Barn Dance" or "Wheeling Jamboree" or "Grand Ole Opry," the kind of program that singers and pickers would travel for miles to be on. When such a program did come along, with the "Renfro Valley Barn Dance" in 1939, it was the inspiration of an individual, not a radio station, and it came along when country radio culture was already well established in most other states. Recording in Kentucky was practically nonexistent: aside from a lone Louisville session by Victor and a single Ashland session by Brunswick, record companies did not set up in Kentucky. The reasons for this are obscure, but they probably had a lot to do with the state's lack of strong radio stations, since many early recording sessions in the field were held at local radio stations and utilized many of the stations' performers. Nor, with a handful of exceptions, has Kentucky seen any significant development of local recording companies in recent years. Kentucky artists then and now have had to travel out of state—often hundreds of miles—to try their hands at making records. This has meant that only the most determined musicians have gotten access to records and that hundreds of excellent musicians who lacked burning ambition or dreams of glory have never recorded at all, or have made only a few recordings.

Lack of access to radio and records may help to explain another striking fact about Kentucky country music: that an overwhelming number of key musicians have had to leave the state in order to find an audience. Bradley Kincaid went to Chicago, Merle Travis to California, Bill Monroe to Nashville, Grandpa Jones to West Virginia, Cliff Gross to Texas. Was Kentucky unable to recognize its native talent, or unwilling to support it? The nature of commercial country music makes it necessary for artists to play over a wide territory in order to make a living and not exhaust an audience. Yet other artists have been able to establish careers close to their home states: Roy Acuff in Tennessee, Bob Wills in Texas and Oklahoma, Willie Nelson in Texas. Few states have exported so much talent to so many places as Kentucky has. Perhaps the potential audience for country music in the state was simply too small in respect to the huge amount of talent the state generated.

Or perhaps Kentuckians tended to take good music for granted, a theory that has been used to explain why a contemporary star like J.D. Crowe has difficulty finding enough work in his home base of Lexington, or why it is almost impossible to find a bluegrass band working regularly in Louisville.

Kentucky country music itself—apart from the circumstances that produced it has over the years developed a distinct identity. One of its most important characteristics has been a tendency to form itself around instrumental virtuosity. This tendency embraced master fiddlers like the legendary Ed Haley, the influential Doc Roberts, and bluegrass star Kenny Baker; banjoists, from the older styles of Buell Kazee and Dick Burnett to the comedy tunes of Cousin Emmy and Grandpa Jones to the avant-garde bluegrass of the Osborne Brothers and J.D. Crowe; mandolin players, from the pioneering artistry of Elmer Bird and Roy Hobbs to the swing of Chick Hurt to the bluegrass innovations of Bill Monroe; and a lion's share of the influential country guitarists, from early finger-pickers like Sylvester Weaver and Arnold Shultz to the smoother styles of Mose Rager and Merle Travis. Few other geographical regions can boast of as many influential instrumentalists as Kentucky, and in few other states does there still exist the same kind of grassroots pride and respect for good, demanding picking.

A second prime characteristic of Kentucky country music has been a strong sense of heritage on the part of her native sons and daughters. More than many others, Kentucky musicians have had a strong sense of their roots, and have reflected this in their music and their careers. Singers as diverse as Bradley Kincaid and Tom T. Hall, well after they had achieved fame, made trips back to Kentucky to look for songs or ideas for songs, while musicians like Merle Travis and Bill Monroe constantly paid homage to the folk musicians who influenced their music. Stringbean, Grandpa Jones, Molly O'Day, and nearly all the performers at Renfro Valley have kept alive old Kentucky songs for new audiences, and have preserved older styles in the face of modern changes. The Coon Creek Girls kept alive the older string band style in age of steel guitars and western swing; Molly O'Day stuck to her soulful, forceful mountain singing style in the teeth of a national fad for smooth, lilting, "cute" singing. Still other performers celebrated their roots not by preserving styles or songs but by actually using their past as a theme in their music: Red Foley singing "Old Shep," Loretta Lynn singing "Coal Miner's Daughter," Karl and Harty singing "Kentucky."

Some of this self-consciousness certainly comes from the fact that Kentucky has always paid homage to its older folk music. From the days of the settlement schools before World War I, enthusiasts collected and published folk songs and ballads, and by the 1930s, when most other states were barely aware of their musical heritage, Kentucky was having folk festivals. Through the work of people like Jean Thomas, John Jacob Niles, and Jean Ritchie, Kentucky folk music achieved steady and almost continuous national recognition from the 1930s to the present. This recognition influenced not only artists, intellectuals, and laymen outside Kentucky, but also Kentucky's own singers and songwriters. Performers like Bradley Kincaid, John Lair, Lily May Ledford, and Jean Ritchie became experts on folk songs; others, like Grandpa Jones and Buell Kazee, maintained an active and long-standing interest in song sources and methods of transmission. Other performers were certainly more aware of their musical roots than most of their counterparts from other areas of the country.

This self-consciousness, as well as the need for Kentuckians to leave the state to find a forum for their music, generated the third characteristic of the music: its accessibility. Many of the state's best performers became skilled at taking traditional or old-time music and interpreting it for a general audience. Bradley Kincaid, for instance, sang old ballads, not in the high, lonesome, mannered style of the eastern mountain balladeers, but in the polite, cultivated, lilting voice of a radio entertainer. Grandpa Jones did wonderful old banjo tunes, but in a colorful and driving style which made up in audience appeal what it may have lost in authenticity and complexity. Red Foley's warm baritone voice and Crosby-like style opened the ears of thousands of listeners who would have been unable to accept the "purer" music of Molly O'Day or Bill Monroe. This ability to translate authentic folk and country music into more popular styles also allowed Kentucky singers to perform in settings far removed from country music's traditional southern bases. Bradley Kincaid sold his music in Boston, Grandpa Jones in Washington, D.C., Karl and Harty in Chicago. Years before Nashville tycoons began to speak of the "crossover effect" from country to pop music, Kentucky pioneers were already forging important links to pop music through their open-minded willingness to make their music available to a wider audience.

In some ways, the history of country music in Kentucky is but a microcosm of country music in general, and many of the dreams and struggles experienced by the musicians described in these pages were similar to the dreams and struggles of musicians across the South. But important as it is in other ways, the story of country music in Kentucky is a unique, self-contained chapter with its own special characteristics. One purpose of this study has been to delineate some of these characteristics and to pay homage to some of the artists who are by necessity slighted or overlooked by more general studies. "There's a lot of good music up there," Bill Monroe once said, shaking his head in wonder at the richness of his native state. Good music, indeed, and unique music, music that forms a very large and a very key piece in the complex mosaic that makes up one of America's richest grassroots cultural phenomena.

Sources and
Further Reading

Chapter 1

The account of Mrs. Anderson's discovery of the "Pearl Bryant" manuscript comes from the author's interviews with her, as well as from publication of the ballad in *Kentucky Folklore Record* 21, no. 4 (1975): 119. A full account of the "Pearl Bryan" songs is Anne B. Cohen, *Poor Pearl, Poor Girl* (Austin: Univ. of Texas Press, American Folklore Society, 1973). An excellent account of early popular music is Sigmund Spaeth, *A History of Popular Music in America* (New York: Random House, 1948); and for Foster, William W. Austin, *"Susanna," "Jeannie," and "The Old Folks at Home": The Songs of Stephen C. Foster from His Time to Ours* (New York: Macmillan, 1975). A good account of folk song collecting is D.K. Wilgus, *Anglo-American Folksong Scholarship since 1898* (New Brunswick, N. J.: Rutgers Univ. Press, 1959). A standard collection of Kentucky folk songs is Leonard Roberts, *In the Pine: Selected Kentucky Folksongs* (Pikeville, Ky.: Pikeville College Press, 1978). Josiah H. Combs's 1925 dissertation is available as *Folk-Songs of the Southern United States,* ed. D. K. Wilgus (Austin: Univ. of Texas Press, American Folklore Society, 1967). Of related interest is Harvey H. Fuson, *Ballads of the Kentucky Highlands* (London: Mitre Press, 1930). The story of Ten Broeck and Mollie is drawn from the author's research, as well as from the following articles: D.K. Wilgus, "Ten Broeck and Mollie: A Race and a Ballad," *Kentucky Folklore Record* 2, no. 3 (1956): 77–89; and Jean H. Thomason, "Ten Broeck and Mollie: New Light on a Kentucky Ballad," *Kentucky Folklore Record* 16, no. 2 (1970): 17–34. The account of Andrew Jenkins is taken from research done by Archie Green in the files of the John Edwards Memorial Foundation, UCLA.

Chapter 2

Material on Burnett and Rutherford comes from the author's interviews with Burnett throughout 1973 and 1974, some of which were published in *Old*

Time Music 9 and 10 (1973). Material on William Houchens is drawn from the research of Guthrie T. Meade and from the files of the Country Music Foundation. Early interview material with Welby Toomey and Doc Roberts, done by Norm Cohen and Archie Green, appeared in *JEMF Quarterly* 23 (1971). A discography of the Roberts-Martin-Roberts group ran in *JEMF Quarterly* through 1971-1972; material also appears in Archie Green, *Only a Miner* (Urbana: Univ. of Illinois Press, 1972). The best account of Buell Kazee's career is Loyal Jones's notes to *Buell Kazee*, June Appal 009. A good account of Asa Martin's career, in addition to Green's, is in the record album notes to *Dr. Ginger Blue: Asa Martin and the Cumberland Rangers* (Rounder). For the discussion of Harlan County and the Corbin area, I have drawn on the excellent research by Edd Ward of Bledsoe, as well as on work by Donald Lee Nelson (on Alfred Karnes, in *JEMF Quarterly* 25 [1972]), and on personal interviews with the widow of B.F. Shelton, with Sam Underwood, and with Ernest Hodges. Some of the material on Emry Arthur was provided by Tony Russell (discographical data), from the files of W.E. Myer, and from interviews with Clarence Myer. The section on western Kentucky is drawn from interviews with Seymour Penley, Walter Cobb, Ted Gossett, Uncle Bozo Carver, and Jack Jackson, as well as newspaper clippings and Country Music Foundation files. I am also grateful to Joy Heimgarner for her early research into the Hack String Band and the Madisonville String Band. Ivan Tribe's excellent research on the career of James Roberts has been invaluable, as have James's own comments and discussions. Noteworthy as an overview of fiddle bands that recorded during this time is Guthrie T. Meade's notes to the three-LP set *Old Time Fiddle Band Music of Kentucky* (Morning Star Records, 1980).

Chapter 3

The material on Joe Steen was drawn from interviews with the Steen family and from their scrapbooks. For Bradley Kincaid, the best available account is Loyal Jones, *Radio's 'Kentucky Mountain Boy' Bradley Kincaid* (Berea: Appalachian Center, 1980). Nothing good has been published on Karl and Harty, and my account is based on interviews with Karl Davis done by Doug Green for the Country Music Foundation's Oral History Program. Bob Pinson and Ronnie Pugh have also been helpful in locating material in the CMF files. For the Prairie Ramblers I have drawn on the early discographical work and interviews by Bob Healy, as well as more recent interviews with Mrs. Glen Pedigo and Mrs. Chick Hurt; Bill Lightfoot generously made available to me an unpublished interview he did with Tex Atchison, and Linnell Gentry made available earlier material on Atchison. Dave Wylie was also an invaluable aid in dealing with Chicago material. Information on Cliff Carlisle came from personal interviews, his scrapbook donated to the CMF Archives, and an early discography prepared by Eugene Earle. Much of the material on Bill Carlisle came from my personal interviews, and from CMF files, as well as from Tony Russell's *Blacks, Whites, and Blues* (New York: Stein and Day, 1972).

Chapter 4

The various books by Jean Thomas, especially *Devil's Ditties* (Chicago: Wilbur Hatfield, 1931; reprint, Detroit: Gale Press, 1976), and *The Singin' Fiddler of Lost Hope Hollow* (New York: Dutton, 1937), have been sources for the account of her work; I have also consulted the collection of Thomas papers on deposit at the University of Louisville, as well as Marshall A. Portnoy's dissertation on Thomas, also at the University of Louisville. I have also drawn on some of Thomas's early magazine writings.

Material from Renfro Valley came from John Lair, *Renfro Valley, Then and Now* (privately published, 1957), as well as the various Renfro Valley publicity booklets, press releases, and back issues of the Renfro Valley *Bugle*. Mr. Reuben Powell, the unofficial historian of Renfro Valley, has generously loaned materials from his collection and offered advice, as have Linnell Gentry and Dave Wylie. The best account of the Coon Creek Girls is Lily May Ledford's *Autobiography*, edited by Mia Boynton and published serially in *The Seattle Folklore Society Journal*, 1975; a shorter version appeared as a booklet, *Coon Creek Girl* (Berea: Appalachian Center, 1980).

The discussion of Louisville radio comes from a number of interviews, including ones with Ira Decker, Dale Warren, June Whalen, Mrs. Mary Sprouse (former Mrs. Cliff Gross), Mrs. and Mrs. James "Doc" Eastwood, Bernie Smith, and Slim Bryant. The material on Clayton McMichen was based, in part, on earlier research by Margaret Riddle, as well as interviews by Bob Pinson and Norm Cohen. Material on Pee Wee King comes from interviews and files at the Country Music Foundation. Steve Cissler of Louisville was also helpful, and especially important to my work there were Roby Cogswell of the University of Louisville, and F.W. Woolsey of the Louisville *Courier-Journal*. I have also utilized some of Mike Seeger's research on Cousin Emmy (Cynthia May Carver).

Especially helpful in dealing with Jesse Stuart has been Prof. Harold Richardson, Stuart's biographer, through whose kind permission these sonnets have been reproduced. An excellent biographical account of Ed Haley appears in the liner notes by Gus Meade and Mark Wilson for *Parkersburg Landing*, Rounder LP 1010 (1976), the collection of Haley's home recordings.

Chapter 5

Material on Bill and Charlie Monroe was drawn from personal interviews with Bill Monroe in 1975, as well as from Ralph Rinzler's account in Bill C. Malone and Judith McCullough, eds., *Stars of Country Music* (Urbana: Univ. of Illinois Press, 1975); James Rooney, *Bossmen: Bill Monroe and Muddy Waters* (New York: Dial Press, 1971); and Neil V. Rosenberg, *Bill Monroe and His Blue Grass Boys: An Illustrated Discography* (Nashville: Country Music Foundation, 1974). For the Osborne Brothers, see Bob Artis, *Bluegrass* (New York: Nordon, 1975); and their own comments on the jacket notes to *From Rocky Top to Muddy Bottom*, CMH LP 9008 (1977). The section on newgrass was based on my own research, as well as valuable comments by Neil Rosenberg. Much of the discussion of Mose Rager was based on the research of William Lightfoot ("Mose Rager of Muhlenberg County: 'Hey, c'mon bud, play me a good rag,'" *Adena* 4 [1979]: 3-41), as well as my own interviews with Rager. Material on Ike Everly is from the author's interviews with Walter Cobb of Chicago and Mrs. Ike Everly of Brentwood, Tennessee. Merle Travis has written several autobiographical chapters for the *JEMF Quarterly*, and some of the quotes here were from his notes to the LP *Merle Travis: Guitar/Standards*, CMH 9024 (1980). An excellent account of Travis's coal-mining songs is Archie Green, *Only a Miner: Studies in Recorded Coal-Mining Songs* (Urbana: Univ. of Illinois Press, 1972).

Material on Arnold Shultz comes from the author's research and from Keith Lawrence's fine article on Shultz that originally appeared in the Owensboro (Kentucky) *Messenger-Inquirer*, March 2, 1980. Good background on the Louisville jug band scene, as well as on Sylvester Weaver, comes from articles in a "Kentucky Blues" series published in *Living Blues*, nos. 51 and 52 (Summer and Fall 1981), by Paul Garon and Jim O'Neal. A more detailed history is *The Jug Bands of Louisville*, by Fred E. Cox, John Randolph, and John Harris, to be published in 1982 by Storyville Publications in England. Material on Grandpa Jones is from my extensive interviews with Grandpa and Ramona Jones; and the discussion of Stringbean is from my interviews with Robert Akeman and Kirk McGee, and the files at the Country Music Foundation Archive and Media Center.

Chapter 6

Both Loretta Lynn and Tom T. Hall have written autobiographies: Loretta Lynn and George Vecsey, *Coal Miner's Daughter* (New York: Henry Regnery, 1976); and Tom T. Hall, *The Storyteller's Nashville* (New York: Doubleday, 1971). For details about Loretta Lynn's recording career, see Laurence J. Zwisohn, *Loretta Lynn's World of Music* (Los Angeles: John Edwards Memorial Foundation, 1980), JEMF Special Series, no. 13. Useful in gaining an overview of modern country music are Bill C. Malone, *Southern Music, American Music* (Lexington: Univ. Press of Kentucky, 1979); Dorothy Horstman, ed., *Sing Your Heart Out, Country Boy* (New York: Dutton, 1975); Pat Carr et al., *The Illustrated History of Country Music* (New York: Doubleday, 1979); and Fred Dellar, Roy Thompson, and Doug Green, *The Illustrated Encyclopedia of Country Music* (New York: Harmony Books, 1977).

The description of Red Foley's first night at the Opry comes from Chet Atkins with Bill Neely, *Country Gentleman* (New York: Henry Regnery, 1975). Other material is drawn from personal research, interviews, and the files of the Country Music Foundation Archive and Media Center, Nashville, Tennessee.

Selected Discography

Recordings by Single Artists and Groups

Dick Burnett and Leonard Rutherford. *Ramblin' Reckless Hobo.* Rounder 1004. [Sixteen selections originally recorded in 1926–1931, with illustrated booklet]

Cliff Carlisle. *Cliff Carlisle.* Vols. 1 and 2. Old Timey 103, 104. [Vintage recordings from the 1930s, including most of his hits]

J.D. Crowe. *Bluegrass Holiday.* Rebel 1598. [A reissue of Crowe's 1968 debut album with Red Allen, Doyle Lawson, and Bobby Sloane]

—— and the New South. *My Home Ain't in the Hall of Fame.* Rounder 0103. [A more recent album typical of Crowe's experimental work]

Skeeter Davis. *The Best of Skeeter Davis.* RCA LSP-3374

Red Foley. *The Red Foley Story.* MCA 2-4053. [Twenty-four selections, including most hits]

Ed Haley. *Parkersburg Landing.* Rounder 1010. [Home recordings done by this legendary fiddler in the 1940s; extensive notes]

Tom T. Hall. *Greatest Hits.* Mercury SR-61369

Roscoe Holcomb. *The High Lonesome Sound.* Folkways 2368

Aunt Molly Jackson. *Aunt Molly Jackson.* Rounder 1002. [Reissues of her 1939 recordings for the Library of Congress]

Grandpa Jones. *The Grandpa Jones Story.* With Ramona Jones and the Brown's Ferry Four. CMH 9007. [A 2-LP set of Grandpa's most famous recordings, newly re-recorded in stereo]

Buell Kazee. *Buell Kazee.* June Appal JA 009. [More recent recordings by the banjoist and singer, with an illustrated booklet]

Bradley Kincaid. *Mountain Ballads and Old Time Songs.* Old Homestead OHCS 107. [Sixteen reissues of Kincaid favorites originally recorded in the 1920s and 1930s, including "Barbara Allen" and "Some Little Bug"]

Loretta Lynn. *Loretta Lynn's Greatest Hits.* MCA 1.

Asa Martin and His Cumberland Rangers. *Doctor Ginger Blue.* Rounder 0031. [A fine cross-section of Martin's band in the 1970s, with an extensive booklet of notes]

Monroe Brothers. *Feast Here Tonight*. RCA-Bluebird AXM2-5510. [Thirty-
two selections from the brothers' 1930s recordings]
Bill Monroe. *The Original Bluegrass Band*. Rounder Special Series 06. [Twelve
of Monroe's 1946-1947 Columbia recordings with Flatt and Scruggs, with
revealing jacket notes]
———. *The Best of Bill Monroe*. MCA 2-4088. [Twenty selections from Mon-
roe's later work]
New Grass Revival. *Too Late to Turn Back Now*. Flying Fish 050
Old Kentucky String Band. *Twilight Is Stealing*. Old Homestead OHS-80008.
[A good sample of the music generated by Pike Countian George
Williamson]
Osborne Brothers. *Best of the Osborne Brothers*. MCA 2-4090. [Twenty
classics]
Molly O'Day with Lynn Davis and the Cumberland Mountain Folks. *A Sacred
Collection*. Old Homestead OHSC-101. [Reissues from her most popular
older Columbia records]
The Rambos. *Silver Jubilee*. Celebrating 25 Years in Gospel Music. Heart
Warming 2R-3560. [A fine collection of their best work through the
years, with an illustrated booklet]
Ritchie Family. *The Ritchie Family of Kentucky*. Folkways 2316. [Songs
and interviews with this famous Kentucky singing family]
Jean Ritchie. *British Ballads in the Southern Mountains*. Folkways 2301.
[Jean singing Child ballads learned from her family and others]
———. *Sweet Rivers*. June Appal 037. [More modern renditions of old gospel
songs]
Ricky Skaggs. *Sweet Temptation*. Sugar Hill SH 3706.
——— and Tony Rice. *Skaggs and Rice*. Sugar Hill SH 3711. [Old-time duet
singing, featuring only guitars and mandolin, in the style of the Blue Sky
Boys, Karl and Harty, and the Monroe Brothers]
Stringbean. *Salute to Uncle Dave Macon*. Starday-Gusto SLP 215
Buddy Thomas. *Kitty Puss*. Rounder 0032. [The only album by one of the
state's finest fiddlers, with excellent notes]
Merle Travis. *The Best of Merle Travis*. Capitol SM 2662. [Re-recordings of
his greatest hits]
———. *Guitar/Standards*. CMH 9024. [A 2-LP set, with excellent notes by
Travis himself]

Recordings by Various Artists

The Duets. Time-Life Records TLCW-05. [A 3-LP set that includes several
selections by Karl and Harty, with illustrated booklet]
Gambler's Lament. Country Turtle CT 6001. [A reissue LP of 1920s material,
including Kentucky artists Green Bailey, Shortbuckle Roark, and the
Carver Boys]
Kentucky Fiddle Band Music. 3 vols. Morning Star 45003, 45004, 45005.
[Reissues from Gennett material of the 1920s and 1930s, including
pieces by Doc Roberts, Hack's Band, Asa Martin, Ted Gossett, and
others; a large booklet of notes]
Mountain Music of Kentucky. Folkways 2317. [Cohen's 1959–1960 field
recordings done around Hazard, including Holcomb's first recordings]
Old Time Ballads from the Southern Mountains. County 522. [A reissue
anthology including pieces by B. F. Shelton and Emry Arthur]

Paramount Old Time Tunes. John Edwards Memorial Foundation JEMF LP
103. [A reissue collection featuring some Kentucky artists from the
1920s]

The Women. Time-Life Records TLCW-02. [A 3-LP set including reissued
sides by the Coon Creek Girls, Cousin Emmy, Molly O'Day, and Loretta
Lynn, with a large illustrated booklet]

Note: The author has edited a special LP anthology designed to illustrate
some of the early music discussed in this book. The album is entitled *Kentucky Country* (Rounder 1037), and it includes performances by the Prairie
Ramblers, Buell Kazee, the Bird Family, Cliff Gross, Walker's Corbin
Ramblers, Hays Shepherd, Jilson Setters, Karl and Harty, the Cumberland
Ridge Runners, Doc Roberts, and others.

Sources for Records. Many of the older LPs listed above are difficult to find
in record stores. Mail order firms specializing in such records include:

County Sales, P.O. Box 191, Floyd, VA 23091
Disc Collector, P.O. Box 169, Cheswold, DE 19936
Down Home Music, Inc., 10341 San Pablo Ave., El Cerrito, CA 94530
Ernest Tubb Record Shop, P.O. Box 500, Nashville, TN 37202
Folkways Records and Service Corp., 43 W. 61st St., New York, NY
10023
Old Homestead Records, P.O. Box 100, Brighton, MI 48116
Roundup Records, P.O. Box 147, E. Cambridge, MA 02141

Most of the above firms have catalogs and sales lists available.

Index

"Tex's Dance," 57
"T for Texas," 63, 123
"That Cheap Look in Your Eye," 94
"That Great Judgement Day," 65
"That Nasty Swing," 64
"That New Vitamine," 123
"That Old Town of Mine," 58
"That Silver Haired Daddy of Mine,"
58
"That's Where I Learned to Pray,"
166
Thawl, Bill "Willie," 58
"There's a Little Box of Pine on the
7:29," 31
"There's a Man Who Comes to Our
House," 58
"They Don't Make 'em Like My
Daddy," 162
"They Needed an Angel," 120
"This Is My Day, My Happy Day,"
38
"This World Is Not My Home," 58
Thomale, Tiny, 92, 95
Thomas, Albert, 67
Thomas, Buddy, 159
Thomas, Dick, 130
Thomas, Edward, 151
Thomas, Jean, 66-70, 72, 74-75,
161, 174
Thomas, Henry, 10
Thompson, Brag, 54
Three Little Maids, 81
"Tiger Rag," 115
"Tim Brooks," 42
"Titanic," 20
Today (television show), 71
"Tom Cat Blues," 63
Toomey, Welby, 24, 28, 29
"Too Old to Cut the Mustard," 65
"Top O' the Morning" (radio show),
42, 78
"Town and Country Time" (tele-
vision show), 123
Traipsin' Woman, The (Thomas), 70
"Tramp on the Street," 140-41
Transylvania University, 6
Travers, Mary, 153
Travis, Merle, 59, 78, 91, 96, 109-
12, 115-18, 120, 131, 171-73
Travis picking style, 109-10
"Tree in the Valley-O, A," 152
Tribe, Ivan, 141
Troyan, Joe, 119
"True Life Blues," 102, 127
"True Love Divine," 36
Tubb, Ernest, 89, 129, 143, 166
Tucker, Gabe, 91

"Tuck Me to Sleep in My Old Ken-
tucky Home," 114
Tufts, Bonaparte, 70
"Tumbling Tumbleweeds," 58
Turner, Zeke, 136
"Turn Your Radio On," 119
"T.V. Blues," 123
Twain, Mark, 142
Twenty Mountain Songs (Wyman
and Brockaway), 6
"20-20 Vision," 105
"Two Fast Past," 117
two-finger style, 12
"Two Sisters, The," 48, 51, 152

"Uncle Eph's Got the Coon," 122
Uncle Henry's Original Kentucky
Mountaineers, 86
"Uncle Ned," 15
"Uncle Pen," 103
Uncle Tom's Cabin (Stowe), 15
"Unclouded Day, The," 65
Underwood, Charlie, 41, 114
Underwood, Marion, 28, 125
Universal Cowboys, 90
University of Kentucky, 33
"Up a Lazy River," 117

Vallee, Rudy, 65
"Valley of Peace," 65
Vandiver, Pendleton, 98, 103, 113
Vaughan, James D., 54
"Venezuela," 72
"Vilikins and His Dinah," 11
"Village Churchyard," 156
Vowell, G.D., 76

"Wagoner Lad, The," 34-35
Wakeley, Jimmy, 59, 97
"Wake Up, Jake," 15
"Wake Up, Little Susie," 107
Walker, Bob, 24
Walker, Frank, 22
Walker, John V., 40
Walker, Owen, 29, 109
Walker, Sammie, 160
Walker, "Singing Billy," 13
Walling, Alonzo, 3, 4
Walters, Clay, 76
"Wandering Boy," 21
Ward, Edd, 39
Warren, Grady, 86
Warren, Henry (Uncle Henry), 86
Warren, Jimmy Dale, 86
Warren County, 89
Watson, Doc, 117
WAVE, 85, 90, 95